THE VENGEFUL
DJINN

About the Authors

Rosemary Ellen Guiley is one of the leading experts in the paranormal and supernatural fields. She has written more than forty books, including nine encyclopedias, as well as hundreds of articles. Rosemary makes numerous appearances on radio and in documentaries, and is a frequent guest on the radio program *Coast to Coast AM with George Noory*. Her website is www.visionaryliving.com and her email is reguiley@gmail.com. Rosemary and Phil have a special website devoted to the djinn at www.djinnuniverse.com.

Philip J. Imbrogno has researched paranormal phenomena for more than thirty years and is recognized as an authority in the field. He has been interviewed by the *New York Times*, appeared on NBC's *Today Show* and *Oprah*, and has been featured in documentaries on the History Channel, A&E, Lifetime, and HBO. He can be contacted by email at Bel1313@yahoo.com.

THE VENGEFUL
DJINN

UNVEILING THE HIDDEN AGENDAS OF GENIES

ROSEMARY ELLEN **GUILEY**

PHILIP J. **IMBROGNO**

Llewellyn Publications
Woodbury, Minnesota

First Edition
Fifth Printing, 2017

Cover design by Kevin R. Brown
Cover images: face © iStockphoto.com/Milan Zeremski;
    smoke © iStockphoto.com/Kenneth Crawford

Llewellyn is a registered trademark of Llewellyn Worldwide Ltd.

Library of Congress Cataloging-in-Publication Data
Guiley, Rosemary.
  The vengeful djinn : unveiling the hidden agendas of genies / Rosemary
Ellen Guiley, Philip J. Imbrogno. – 1st ed.
      p. cm.
  Includes bibliographical references and index.
  ISBN 978-0-7387-2171-2
  1. Jinn. I. Imbrogno, Philip J. II. Title.
  BF1552.G855 2011
  133.4'23—dc22
                          2010045135

Llewellyn Publications
A Division of Llewellyn Worldwide Ltd.
2143 Wooddale Drive
Woodbury, MN 55125-2989
www.llewellyn.com

Printed in the United States of America

For John Keel,
who established a path into an unknown land
so we could all follow, explore, and learn

Also by Philip J. Imbrogno

Night Siege: The Hudson Valley UFO Sightings

Celtic Mysteries in New England:
Windows to Another Dimension in America's Northeast

Interdimensional Universe:
The New Science of UFOs, Paranormal Phenomena,
and Otherdimensional Beings

Files from the Edge:
A Paranormal Investigator's Explorations into High Strangeness

Ultraterrestrial Contact:
A Paranormal Investigator's Explorations into the
Hidden Abduction Epidemic

CONTENTS

OPENING WORDS

OUR RESEARCH AND EXPLORATION OF djinn not only required an in-depth study of legends from many cultures, but also quite a number of books on mysticism and magic. The correct spelling of the word *djinn* translated directly from Arabic to English is *djinn*. Western readers may be more familiar with the commonly used phonetic spelling, *jinn*. Throughout this book, we have used "djinn" as the preferred spelling in order to conform as much as possible to Arabic translations.

During our research we spent a considerable amount of time reading several English versions of the Qur'an. Although all the translations are similar, they are not exactly the same. According to Abu Dhabi in his book *Basic Principles of Islam*, the many versions of the Qur'an in English and other languages are the result of the different interpretations by the translators.[1] This is why most Islamic scholars such as Muhammad Fahd Khaarum and Muhammad Kareem Ragheh insist that all readings of the Noble Qur'an must be done in its original Arabic form. It is astonishing to discover that no other religious work in recorded history can match

---

1 The Bin Sultan Al Nahayan Foundation.

the Qur'an in that it is recited the same and has remained unchanged for the past 1,400 years.

When Muhammad died there was no singular codex of the Qur'an. No collection of his revelations in final written form existed either, because even while he was alive, new teachings were added to the earlier ones.[2] Companions who memorized his teachings passed on the information orally to students. Early Islamic teachers in the fourth Islamic century decided to write down completed versions handed down from seven authoritative "readers," which in turn created seven basic texts in Arabic. All seven versions are basically the same but with minor variations in phrasing. For the research in this book, we used the Abu Bakr "Asim" reader version of the Qur'an. This is the predominant reading used today by many Islamic African and Middle Eastern countries.

Although we were not able to read the original Asim version of the Qur'an in Arabic, its teachings and historical information in the English version still made considerable sense to us. We both found the Qur'an a wonderful book of information and spiritual teachings, and we highly recommend its reading to all persons, regardless of religious background or philosophy concerning life. The Qur'an, like many great religious books, is a guide concerning spiritual awareness and ascension to a higher plane of existence.

---

2 *The Encyclopedia of Islam: International Journal of Islamic and Arabic Studies,* Vol. V (1989).

PREFACE

THE DJINN—CALLED THE "HIDDEN ONES" in Middle Eastern lore—are aptly named. This mysterious race of beings has remained cloaked in shadows for centuries. Created out of smokeless fire, they have powers and life spans that far exceed those of humans. Their shapeshifting abilities have enabled them to hide in plain sight the world over, either as the unseen or in a host of paranormal guises. We are interacting with them, whether we know it or not. Our awareness of otherworldly realities is rapidly expanding via both paranormal experience and science, and we need to know about the djinn, who comprise a major part of the picture.

My serious interest in the djinn began some years ago during my explorations of the paranormal and occult. I had of course, come across them in childhood, when I read Middle Eastern folk tales about the wish-giving genies, such as the famous tale of Aladdin and his magical lamp in *The Book of 1001 Nights*. Within the confines of folk tales, the genies were intriguing but seemed relatively harmless—they were mischievous tricksters who had to be dealt with carefully. Aladdin used them to his favor to gain riches, but in other tales people did not fare so well, making wishes that genies granted in peculiar, distorted, and even cruel ways. The saying "be careful what you wish for" takes on a heavy importance and an entirely new meaning when dealing with the djinn.

Years later, when I was well into my career researching the paranormal, the genies cropped up again, this time as their proper name of djinn. Despite the recognition, their identity was blurry in Western interpretations. Works on angels and demons sometimes cast them in the same light as demons, beings with supernatural powers and a dark, evil nature. I sometimes found them to be completely equated with demons. Clearly they were something else in their own right, but their true nature remained hidden. I included brief descriptions of them in some of my books, most notably *The Encyclopedia of Angels*, *The Encyclopedia of Demons & Demonology*, and *The Encyclopedia of Magic and Alchemy*.

The desire to explore and reveal the hidden drives my work in the paranormal. I have never been content to focus on any narrow field or topic. My interests and curiosity have always cast a wide net. The work I do now—full-time since 1983—was sparked in childhood by a combination of a voracious reading appetite; a fascination with mythology, folklore, the supernatural, science fiction and fantasy; a sprinkling of psychic experiences; a passion for astronomy; and an intense desire to understand the big picture and write about it. All of these things seemed naturally connected to me, and as I grew up and delved into my paranormal research career, those connections became evident in new ways. The "paranormal" revealed itself as a vast and fluid field, a constantly shifting kaleidoscope of interconnections and patterns. Pick up a thread anywhere in the paranormal—angels, demons, fairies, extraterrestrials, shadow people, mysterious creatures, psychic experiences, visionary encounters, and so on—and it will lead you to everything else. Sooner or later, the paranormal transforms into the mystical, where we confront all of the big questions about the "meaning of everything" that humans have grappled with over the centuries.

Our encounters with paranormal phenomena are subjective, filtered through a looking glass of time periods in history, cultural backgrounds, religious and spiritual views, and personal beliefs. Yet if you trace the supernatural experiences of people throughout history, you find consistent patterns lying beneath the surface, hidden from plain view. It has always seemed to me, as it has to a great number of other explorers and researchers, that there is something else behind our experiences—perhaps something that can explain them all, or at least shift us into a clearer view of them.

Thus we come back to the mystery of the djinn, the hidden ones. Are they an integral part of what lies concealed beneath the paranormal? We can make a strong case that they are.

My plumbing of the dark depths of the djinn began in earnest several years ago, after I reconnected with Philip J. Imbrogno. I had first met Phil in the early 1990s, in the course of my interests in ufology while living in New York and Connecticut. About a decade went by, and we reconnected on one of Phil's guided trips to the stone chambers in New York, which he had been exploring in depth as a result of his research into the Hudson Valley UFO wave of the 1980s and beyond. Like me, Phil had been following his own threads of interconnections. His excellent presentation of the interconnections is in his book *Interdimensional Universe*.

In catching up on our respective work, it became evident that we had been pursuing both the same and parallel paths, and that, as Phil put it, we held some missing pieces to each other's research. We began some collaborative work regarding the stone chambers, paranormal hot spots, and high-tech spirit communication. Our far-ranging discussions hit upon the djinn, and this book was born.

We believe the djinn are a strong and active—but nonetheless hidden—presence in the world. They are not confined to the Middle East, the birthplace of the lore about them. They are known by many names, many guises, and many forms. Name any supernatural entity—even the ghosts of the dead—and you can fit the djinn behind them. We may think we are dealing with angels, demons, fairies, extraterrestrials, and such, but we may actually be dealing, at least some of the time, with djinn in disguise. This does not negate the existence or reality of the aforementioned entities in their own right, but simply that the opportunistic djinn may take on appearances that fool us into interacting with them in specific ways.

Are the djinn *the* answer to our paranormal encounters? We still do not know, but the evidence points to them being a significant part of our intersections with parallel dimensions and otherworldly realities that intrude into ours. The djinn are powerful and formidable, and at least some of them seem to have agendas that are not in the best interests of humans.

This book examines the djinn from a variety of perspectives. We journey into the Middle Eastern lore, which Phil experienced firsthand in his international travels, and into science and physics. We cover the Qur'an's position on djinn and the teachings of Islamic scholars, as well as Western lore and interpretations of them. We explain djinn behavior and characteristics. We give special attention to the relationship between djinn, demons, fairies, shadow people, hooded beings, elementals, and extraterrestrials, types of entities where we have found some of the strongest evidence of djinn connections.

As mentioned earlier, the djinn are everywhere, and in the course of researching this book, we discovered what we believe are some of their modern-day habitats, right here in America. What are they doing in these pockets? Pursuing covert operations? Or have they retreated to remote areas because they wish to be undisturbed? Is it possible to have any meaningful relationship with them? We present our ideas on the intentions of djinn.

Our desire in writing this book is to put the hidden ones in the light. Few in the West know much about them. It is said that knowledge is power, and knowing about the djinn stands to benefit our understanding of the truth that is out there.

Rosemary Ellen Guiley

INTRODUCTION

THERE HAS BEEN A GROWING interest in the paranormal in the past several decades. Ghosts, poltergeists, spook lights, demons, angels, fairies, shadow people, strange creatures, and UFOs have become staples of movies and prime-time television shows. Our attraction to the supernatural is more than a passing fascination—claims of encounters with paranormal entities such as those mentioned above are not restricted to believers or wide-eyed dreamers. Accounts of sometimes frightening experiences are made by people from all walks of life—credible people—who report seemingly incredible things.

I have been investigating paranormal phenomena with an emphasis on UFOs for more than thirty years. I have found myself amazed and sometimes even confused by the variety of reports I've received. I'd often ask myself, "Where do these phenomena come from and where do they go when they aren't seen?" The answer to this question can now be answered by new ideas in theoretical physics. One of these new ideas states that our universe is composed of not one, but multiple dimensions, some very close to our own and many far away in space and time. Periodically, several of these closer dimensions may interact with our world, resulting in the merging of several realities.

My investigations over the years have led me to believe that what we call "the paranormal" takes on a variety of guises, making us humans think we are witnessing multi-faceted phenomena. Actually, this may not be the case at all. In one of these other realities or dimensions close to our own is an intelligent, ancient race that has existed before humans walked the earth—beings with great power who throughout recorded history have been identified by every culture. The Native American shamans call them the "great tricksters," and to the Hindu of India they are known as "deceivers." In the West, they are called "devils" and "demons." New Age spiritualists know them as "the con men of the universe." This ancient race may be responsible for the majority of paranormal events witnessed over the centuries. We have known very little about them, for only one part of the world has historically documented them and their effect on the human race. Ancient Middle Eastern lore tell tales of a race of mysterious and highly intelligent creatures called the djinn. In the Qur'an, a surah entitled Al-djinn frequently mentions the djinn and refers to them as "God's other people." The word *djinn* is thought to be derived from the Arabic root *janna*, which means "hidden" and should not be confused with the Arabic word *jannah*, which means "paradise."

In the West, the djinn are known as the genies of fairy tales, wish-giving entities trapped in bottles, lamps, and rings. The word *genie* usually conjures up exotic but harmless images, such as the 1960s television series *I Dream of Jeannie*, in which Barbara Eden played an obliging, well-meaning, and often ditzy genie freed from a bottle by an astronaut, played by Larry Hagman. "Genie" also has comical associations, such as in the Disney movie *Aladdin*, based on the tale from Arabian lore. In these depictions, genies may have a bit of prankster in them, but they seem benign, even helpful, and we in the West laugh at them. We have little knowledge and lack fear of the real race, the djinn.

Middle Eastern cultures have a considerably different view of the djinn, however. In many Islamic households, just speaking the name of the djinn will cause the bravest to flee in terror. They consider the djinn to be quite real and a great threat to humanity, causing misfortune, illness, possession, and even death. The djinn hide in the shadows, biding their time and watching us, looking for opportunities to strike, interacting with humans only when it suits their purpose. They are powerful shapeshifters and can live for thousands of years. To cross the djinn is to invite destruction.

My introduction to the world of the djinn began in the mid-1990s while I was traveling through the Middle East researching the Knights Templar and their connection to the Holy Grail. After two weeks of what seemed to be nothing more than a wild goose chase, I began to hear stories about the djinn. At first I had no idea what they were. An old friend, who later became my guide through some very perilous country there, explained the djinn as the origin of the Western "genie." Like many westerners, I laughed, thinking of those jolly wish-granting spirits. Well, my host took the existence of the djinn very seriously—to him, they were very real. The djinn's true nature and reality became evident to me as I collected a great deal of information on them and visited some of the places where they are reputed to enter our world. I realized they represent an aspect of the paranormal that had been largely untouched by western researchers. I also realized the djinn could be the hidden source of the diversity of paranormal events everywhere.

I briefly introduced the djinn in two of my previous books, *Interdimensional Universe: The New Science of UFOs, Paranormal Phenomena, and Otherdimensional Beings* and *Files from the Edge: A Paranormal Investigator's Explorations into High Strangeness*. Although I didn't go into much detail, I found the djinn attracted a lot of curiosity and attention among readers.

Several years ago, noted paranormal investigator Rosemary Ellen Guiley and I began investigating paranormal hot spots in New
York that generate a great number of reports relating to UFOs and
other types of phenomena. We have been exploring the possibility that in many of these high strangeness locations, portals that
connect our world to an unseen world exist. When I mentioned
my research on the djinn to Rosemary, she told me she was very
interested in them due to her research into angels, demons, fairies, and shadow people. After many long discussions, things began falling into place; we could see the connections among parallel dimensions, the emergence of paranormal phenomena, and the
race of ancient beings that exist in a reality very close to our own.
During our research, we gathered evidence of the djinn in the
Western Hemisphere and applied it to paranormal and UFO phenomena. The result is an interesting and compelling picture that
raises many questions about what people are really experiencing.
Are the djinn behind our paranormal encounters and experiences?
Are they behind some of the terrifying experiences people report?
If so, what is their purpose? According to ancient lore, the djinn
once occupied this world, and they seek to reclaim it. Are they using paranormal avenues to invade our reality? Is their reality merging with ours? We should consider all of these possibilities. There
may be a dark agenda below the surface of our experiences, and we
fail to see it because we're preoccupied with the superficial characteristics of the experiences themselves. No one has the complete
solution to this cosmic puzzle yet, but I believe we are offering a
number of important pieces to solve the mystery.

This book will take you on an adventure into a world of the unseen, hidden from us in the shadows for countless centuries. We present to you the truth about the race of beings you thought only existed in your imagination—or your nightmares. If you choose to fear
anything in your life, fear the djinn. Enter their world ... if you dare!

Philip J. Imbrogno

REALITY CHECK

F YOU TAKE A WALK on a sunny day, any number of beautiful things might attract your attention: the blue sky, beautiful flowers, green leaves on trees, or the fresh smell of nature adding fragrance and oxygen to the air. This is the world we perceive with our five senses, and our conscious mind identifies it as the reality in which we live. As we age, what we see, smell, hear, and taste comprises more of the real world, as we are taught in school that things outside our physical existence and beyond the extension of science don't exist. When we touch the ground, throw a stone, or bump our elbows on furniture, it certainly feels solid. Who in their right mind would say it isn't? Most of us are shocked to learn that what we interpret as our physical reality is not what it appears to be. There is actually a great deal of space between the atoms that compose matter. Although everything we touch feels quite solid to us, it isn't. Observations made using only one's physical senses can be very deceiving. For example: during the early Renaissance, the greatest minds would have staked their reputation on the fact that earth was stationary in space; the sun, moon, and stars circled our planet, it was said. Really, who could argue this point? When people looked up at the sky, they saw celestial objects rising in the east and setting in the west, and there was no sense of motion (rotation) on terra firma. The geocentric (or "earth-centered") theory was the logical train of thought explaining this movement because it was supported by visual observations made daily and nightly.

These Renaissance-era scientists made the mistake of arriving at their conclusions about movements on the celestial sphere based only on their sense of sight, not a very good tool for judging reality. The people who supported the geocentric idea (including the astronomer Ptolemy [90 CE–160 CE]) were considered the greatest minds of their day. However, just being intelligent and well educated doesn't guarantee that one will never be wrong. For a very long time in history, anyone who contradicted the geocentric model was laughed at and called a heretic, fool, or troublemaker. The revolutionary thinkers who opposed this idea were ridiculed, jailed, or sometimes even put to death for insisting that our earth circled the sun, and not vice versa. Today, we know these "heretics" and "fools" were correct.

The question of physicality concerning matter may seem like a wild claim, but it was scientifically proven at the beginning of the twentieth century by Dr. Ernest Rutherford and two assistants. Today, it's known as the Geiger-Marsden experiment, or sometimes the Gold Foil experiment. This experiment was performed by Hans Geiger and Ernest Marsden in 1909, under the direction of Ernest Rutherford at the Physical Laboratories of the University of Manchester, England. Rutherford's team measured the deflection of alpha particles—particles that have an atomic mass of four, consisting of two protons and neutrons, carrying a +2 positive charge.[1] Using a controlled radioactive source, the scientists

---

1 An alpha particle is actually a nucleus of the element helium having two protons and two neutrons. Its mass is 4 atomic mass units and has a charge of +2.

directed the particles to strike a sheet of very thin gold foil. They observed that a very small percentage of particles were deflected through the dense gold foil, and some were even scattered back toward the source. However, most of the particles passed through the metal sheet without hitting any gold matter at all. From this observation, Rutherford concluded that the physical space between atoms was much greater than anyone had previously thought. Although the gold metal appeared solid, it was mostly empty space! Rutherford and his associates were astonished to find that only 1 in 9,000 particles were reflected by the gold sheet and the rest passed through as if nothing was there. This result was completely unpredicted, prompting Rutherford to later comment, "It was almost as incredible as if you fired a fifteen-inch shell at a piece of tissue paper, and it came back and hit you."

In 1911, Dr. Rutherford published an analysis of his by-then famous experiment, and his results shocked the physics and chemistry communities. His observations indicated that a model of the atom with a diffuse charge was incorrect; actually, a large amount of atomic charge was concentrated at a very small point, giving it a very strong electric field. He concluded that an atom is mostly empty space, and that most of an atom's mass and a large fraction of one of its two kinds of charge are concentrated in a tiny center.

To give you a clearer idea of this theory, imagine we expand the nucleus of the atom to the size of a penny. We place the penny in the middle of Giants Stadium in New York. The first level of electrons would be in the top bleachers while the next closest atom would be about 1,200 feet from the penny's center! The apparent solidity of a substance is the result of strong electrical bonds between electrons and their nuclei. Despite their distance from the nucleus, the negatively charged electrons are held strongly in place by their attraction to the protons in the atom's center. This attraction creates a great deal of structural integrity and a strong force that repels the electrons of other atoms. To explain this principle, imagine a fan that has been unplugged—its blades aren't moving. Looking at the fan, we see there are three blades, and the space between the blades is large enough for us to stick our fingers and perhaps our whole hands through, from front to back. We plug in the fan, turn the power on, and set the control to maximum speed. The fan blades now appear as one solid object. If we attempt to stick a pencil through the blades, the pencil will be deflected, as if hitting a solid wall.

We benefit from this repellent force every day. Despite the empty spaces that exist in every atom, when we lean on a tabletop, our hands cannot pass through the wood or metal in that surface because the electrical fields of the electron clouds in the table and our hands repel each other. This gives the impression, illusion, or whatever you wish to call it, that matter is very solid … in reality, it isn't.

Now that we have uncovered the fact that our perception of living in a physically solid world of matter is nothing more than the repulsion of electrical fields, the concept of other dimensions where intelligent beings other than humans exist seems easier to accept. In order to understand the djinn and their location in time and space, you must be ready to perceive the multiverse beyond the range of your physical senses—you must explore it with your mind.

The Djinn Homeland

The word *djinn* is Arabic and means "unseen or hidden." We don't know what they call themselves, but this is the name given in Middle Eastern mythology and in the Qur'an. It suits them well, for they are hidden from our view. The word *djinn* can be used to identify any nonphysical being that exists in another reality, but we believe the Middle East used the term to describe a particular type of entity that exists between the multiverse (multiple universes) of matter and energy. The djinn exist in a dimension close to our own, and they seem to have the ability to interact with certain people who live here when it suits their purpose. To some, this idea of other dimensions and parallel universes may seem like metaphysical or New Age nonsense, but the idea is quickly becoming accepted in twenty-first-century physics circles. A new theory called "string theory" supports the structure of a multidimensional universe, and simply states that the smallest units of matter are not point particles, but two-dimensional vibrating strings. The vibration of string determines if a particle will become a proton, neutron, or electron. By adding or taking energy away from a vibrating string, one particle can change into another. Thus a proton can become an electron if its "vibration" changes. The actual energy used to vibrate each string is thought to originate from a parallel universe.

Strings can be closed or open, supporting the belief that there are at least ten dimensions in our universe. An aspect of string theory, called the Membrane (or "M") theory, states that all vibrating strings are attached to a membrane or fabric that acts as a giant web, tying all the forces of the universe together. Scientists know these membranes as "branes"; the stuff that makes up space and time. The theoretical existence of branes has expanded string theory to eleven dimensions. It is theorized that entire universes are attached to branes in a multidimensional fashion. In the multiverse, there are an infinite number of branes, each with its own particles and in some, different physical laws.

Branes allow for an entirely new set of possibilities in multiverse physics because particles confined to the brane would look more or less as they would in a three-dimensional universe and could never venture beyond it. Protons, electrons, neutrons, quarks, and all sorts of fundamental particles could be stuck on the brane, like water drops on a shower curtain. However, the mechanisms that make the fundamental particles stick to the brane of our universe do not apply to gravity. Gravity, according to the theory of general relativity, must exist in the full geometry of space.

The graviton—the particle of gravity—is thought to be created by a closed vibrating string, thus also encompassing the full geometry of all the theoretical extra dimensions and parallel universes. String theory can also be used to explain why the graviton is not stuck to any brane. Open strings are like hooks attached to a curtain. The graviton is associated with the closed string, and only open strings can be anchored to a brane. The evidence for these extra dimensions and other universes is in fact shown to us in gravity's weakness. Gravity should be a very strong force in our universe, but it isn't. The waves of gravitons filtering through other dimensions and branes of parallel universes weaken the effects of gravity in our reality. The effect is much like feeling the heat from an electric heater. If you are directly in front of the heater, you feel very warm, but if you place barriers or distance between yourself and the heater, the total amount of infrared radiation reaching you is greatly diminished.

When we consider the many variations of string theory it is easier to accept the idea that djinn exist in another dimension rather than our own in the multiverse. It's here they would definitely live up to their "hidden" nature—this race of beings would be invisible to us in our spatial plane of reality. Also, many theoretical physicists from well respected institutions of advanced learning such as Carnegie Mellon University, the University of California–San Diego, and the University of Texas–Austin are open to the possibility that these other realities may be inhabited by living beings.

So far, we have used terminology like "parallel universes" and "dimensions," but there are many people in the twenty-first century who can't differentiate between the two. In addition, the multitude of scientific papers that have been published on the subject seems to indicate that some authors are unclear if the two terms mean different things or are one and the same. A dimension is a spatial coordinate. We live in the third dimension with an X, Y, and Z axis. The fourth dimension is time—often considered to be the past, present, and future—existing in the same place, but at a different frequency, so to speak. This has made our view of this dimension more nebulous than it really is. The fourth dimension is the spatial parity within our own physical universe, and is not on any other brane in the multiverse.

In our physical universe are six additional dimensions, each existing at angles we cannot turn to see or enter. It has been theorized that these extra dimensions are folded around our reality and are nothing more than tiny pockets, perhaps no larger than the nucleus of an atom. If you were djinn, this would be a good place to hide, but its hardly enough space to harbor an entire race of beings. However, we must consider the fact that according to legends, the djinn are not physical beings but are composed of smokeless fire. Such a phenomenon is a lot like plasma, the fourth state of matter. Although many schools still teach that there are only three states of matter, there are actually four. To put it simply, plasma is an ionized gas into which sufficient energy is provided, freeing electrons from atoms or molecules, and allowing charged atoms and electrons to coexist. This "strange" fourth state of matter is actually the most common in the universe—our sun is made of plasma, as is lightning.

A plasmic creature, then, would require very little physical space to exist. Many physicists are beginning to believe that these extra dimensions are actually quite large, an idea supported by the apparent weakness of the gravitational force. As mentioned earlier, gravitons may be filtered through other dimensions and parallel universes; if these other realities were small, gravity would have no effect. The gravitational force's weakness actually supports the theory that these extra dimensions comprise a considerable amount of physical space.

The eleventh dimension is thought to be the brane on which we exist. The brane of our universe is all around us and the elementary particles that make up your body are attached to it. So why can't you see it? Mainly because you are part of it and it moves when you do. It has been calculated that the brane of our universe is somewhere in the order of a several hundred trillionths, trillionths of a millimeter in proximity to you. Scientists sometimes identify the brane our universe exists on and all the other branes in the multiverse as parallel universes. Think of the brane as the eleventh dimension rather than a parallel universe, since it is the intricate web that binds our universe together. All the planets, stars, galaxies, and extra dimensions we see in our universe, in addition to all the electromagnetic energy, belong to this brane and their existence depends on it.

A parallel *universe* is another brane with galaxies, stars, and perhaps ten or more dimensions. Some of these branes may be larger than our own, and some may be smaller. Some are far from us in space and time while others are very close and could interact with our brane. When the branes have a close encounter, two things can happen theoretically:

The first possibility: If the branes pass closely and interact at a dimensional level, wormholes or tunnels could form, connecting the two parallel universes together at multiple points for an unpredictable period of time. This might allow matter from one universe to flow into the other. If there are intelligent beings that have developed a technology in at least one of these parallel universes, they might send ships or devices through the wormhole to explore the other universe.

The second possibility: The branes may smash into each other causing both universes to be disrupted, turning all matter into nothing more than vibrating strings of energy. A controversial theory in physics states that all matter, if broken apart, will retain its information.[2] This means that after a period of time, both branes and all the material contained within them might form one new, giant universe, or a number of smaller ones. Elementary particles will eventually form, then galaxies, stars, and perhaps living beings once again.

Then Where Are the Djinn?

According to many of the Arabian stories and Islamic texts, the djinn live in a place that is very close but invisible to humans. Given this information, they may exist in another dimension, perhaps somewhere between dimensions five through ten. If the dimensions are numbered according to their proximity, then the most logical candidate would be five. The ancient people of the Middle East knew the djinn coexisted with our world, but in a place no man or woman could ever visit. This is one of the reasons why djinn were said to live in desolate caves, deserts, forests, mountain tops, graveyards, and even in the deepest depths of the sea. These areas were considered the djinn's hiding places, where humans very rarely ventured. The cultures that proposed these possible hiding places did so more than a thousand years ago, when people had no idea of the concept of other dimensions. Most would have shuddered to think that djinn could be "hidden" right next to you, perhaps in your bedroom as you sleep. Some Islamic households accepted the fact that djinn could exist on one's property or home and remain invisible. It was thought that when these djinn chose to show themselves, they would appear in the form of a snake, or their favorite, a black dog or cat.

2 Stephen Hawking, *The Hawking Paradox*, Discovery Channel, 2005.

According to the thirteenth-century Muslim scholar Iman Ibn Taymeeyah, the djinn can take the form of any human or animal they choose.[3] When a djinni takes on a physical form, it is much more vulnerable, but still very hard to kill. For this reason, the djinn do not keep physical forms for very long, but will shape-shift into hideous monster-like animals to frighten people or keep them away from what they consider their own property.

Ancient Stones

Centered in New York's Hudson River Valley are a series of myste-rious stone chambers and carved standing megaliths that have per-plexed researchers of the paranormal and archaeology for decades.[4] We have studied the chambers for more than twenty years and be-lieve they are evidence that the East Coast of North America was explored by people from Europe centuries before Columbus. The ancient people who constructed these chambers may have been druids who came to the new world in search of a gateway to the world of the gods. The paranormal and UFO phenomena associ-ated with these stone chambers today suggest they may have been used as markers to the world of the djinn. During a recent field exploration of a stone chamber located in Fahnestock State Park, a black dog joined us as we trekked through the woods. The dog seemed to have appeared out of nowhere and followed us the en-tire time. Although it appeared friendly, most of the people with us on this trip commented on how strangely the dog behaved. It followed us very closely, as if keeping an eye on us. We joked

---

3 Iman Ibn Taymeeyah (1263–1328) was a famous Muslim scholar born in what is now Turkey, close to the Syrian border. Writings from the latter part of his life warned people of the djinn and how to deal with them.

4 Documented in the book *Celtic Mysteries in New England: Windows to Another Dimension in America's Northeast* by Philip J. Imbrogno and Marianne Horrigan (Cosimo Publishing, 2005).

amongst ourselves about the djinn connection. At the time, we didn't really take it seriously, but thinking back on the day, who knows for sure?

If the djinn exist in a nearby dimension, it would stand to reason that the two realities must interact from time to time, giving us a view of their world and them a view of ours. However, because humans are three-dimensional, physical beings, we may only get a partial view of the djinn world. Instead of seeing detail, we may only see shadows, two-dimensional lines, or vague orbs of light. Since the djinn live in a higher dimension—perhaps the fifth— they should be able to perceive all dimensions below them, much like we humans can interact with the three dimensions in our space.

A belief that predates Islam states that the djinn can see us, but we cannot see them. The only time we're able to catch glimpses of them is when they allow it. Many people may find this thought somewhat unsettling, but it may be true. Have you ever been outside or in a dark basement, or even in your bedroom at night, and gotten the feeling that you were not alone—that someone or something was watching you? Most people brush off the feeling and go about with their business or fall back to sleep, but your inner voice and feelings may be telling you that a djinni is watch- ing. The djinni is in the same space, perhaps alongside of you, but in a higher dimension. As a djinni presses against the membrane that divides the dimensions it may appear as a shadow image or a ghost-like apparition. It is the Islamic belief that sightings of phan- toms and reports of hauntings are the result of djinn interacting with our reality.

Although the idea of djinn closely observing us may seem ridicu- lous to the paranormal investigators who research haunted places, it must be considered nevertheless. We must also take it into account that only certain djinn may have the ability to peer into our world when near geographic locations where their reality crosses ours. We believe their restricted entry points could account for the number of locations around the world that are considered as paranormal hot spots. Some of these may include Sedona, Arizona; the Bermuda Triangle; the Hudson Valley of New York; and the Bridgewater Triangle in Massachusetts, just to name a few.

The djinn world is very complex and may also be the home of a number of other living creatures. According to Turkish mythology, the djinn (known there as the *cinn*) have a variety of pets. The pets are said to be much different than our cats and dogs and are described as horrible monsters you wouldn't want to meet in a dark alley. Perhaps the sightings of strange creatures throughout time are nothing more than a djinni's stray pet.

Since the home of the djinn is beyond the fourth dimension, time in this other reality is most likely different from ours. One thousand years in our world may be only a year there. Whether the djinn can enter the fourth dimension and travel back and forth in time is also unknown, but they are reportedly able to tell the future. On the other hand, other accounts say the djinn cannot really tell the future—they only appear to have this ability. Some of the more powerful djinn receive their "gift" of prophecy by traveling to the higher realms and eavesdropping on the angels who occasionally meet to discuss future plans for humanity on planet earth.

The concept of the djinn and all these extra dimensions and parallel universes opens up a great number of possibilities for paranormal investigators. To fully understand the hidden secrets of the multiverse and the world of the djinn, we must change our view of reality and open our minds to new possibilities. Our thinking must no longer be rigid and two-dimensional. Rather, we must take our conscious minds beyond the confines of the physical body and use our deeper inner intelligence to help us perceive and understand what our five senses cannot. When we are able to achieve this, we will learn more about not only our own reality, but also that of the djinn.

THE ORIGIN OF THE DJINN

THE DJINN ARE CALLED "GOD's other people" and the Qur'an makes it very clear that they existed on this planet long before humans, but exactly how long ago, no one knows. According to most Islamic stories, the djinn were created by Allah sometime between one and two thousand years before the first humans appeared on earth. It is hard to accept the notion that the djinn were only masters of this planet for twenty centuries, and in that time were able to create kingdoms and societies with an almost supernatural technology. The early Islamic people believed that with each passing millennium, great changes took place on earth that affected all living things. Many human cultures throughout time used the passage of a thousand years to mark the beginning of a new age. For example, in the biblical book of Revelation, the prophet John talks about a new age of man that will last for one-thousand years after which the devil will be set free and once again attempt to corrupt the human race. We must remember that before the fifteenth century a thousand years seemed like a very long span of time; no one thought of time in terms of millions. The idea of millions of years was something that these people of long ago could not fathom, since the common belief was that God created the earth only six thousand years earlier.

Though it's believed the djinn were around for a long period of time before they were exiled from the physical universe, it's possible they appeared on this planet millions of years before mankind. In fact, many of them could still be with us today. While traveling through the Middle East, Phil gathered many tales of the djinn. A considerable number of these stories were not written, but passed orally from generation to generation. After listening to the many djinn tales, he asked a question that the typical, skeptical westerners would pose: "If you have never seen djinn, how do you know they exist?" The answer he got was always the same: "They are mentioned in the Qur'an, the word of Allah, who does not lie."

The origin of the djinn is indeed mentioned in the Qur'an in more than thirty verses, such as *"He (Allah) created man from sounding clay. The angels from light and the djinn from smokeless flame of fire (Ar-Rahman 55.15)."* The origin of the djinn also appears in Al-Hijr 15.26–42, but is slightly different: *"And indeed, Allah created man from sounding clay of altered black and smooth mud. The djinn, Allah created aforetime from smokeless fire and the angels from light."* No one really knows how long ago djinn were created, or what their past and current population number could be. However, there is a great deal of information about this ancient race of beings in the mythologies of the cultures of the Far and Middle East—but not in the Western Hemisphere.

Archaeologists agree that when dealing with the ancient legends of a Middle Eastern culture, any spirit below an angel and not human can be referred to as a djinni. The idea of the djinn pre-dates Islam. The ancient Persians believed in *jainni* and *jaini*, evil spirits of both genders who lived in an invisible world and often interacted with humans in different ways. They brought pleasures like fine food and gold, but also delivered disease and death. Inscriptions from northwest Arabia dating to three thousand years ago indicate worship of djinn-like beings called *ginnaye,* the "rewarding gods," also known as the "gods of pleasure and pain." In most of these early legends, these gods could be benevolent, but then suddenly without warning or cause, turn malevolent. These beings are similar to early Western European concepts of demons, who were summoned to teach the sciences and medicine, and locate buried treasure. If the summoner didn't perform the proper ritual or exercise extreme caution, the demon could instantly change into a hideous killing monster.

Djinn and Fallen Angels

The Christian faith believes a certain angel most beloved by God was tired of serving and decided to do things his own way. This rebel angel, known as Lucifer, conspired with other powerful angels to overthrow God and become the new masters of the universe. As a result, a war among the angels broke out. In the end, Lucifer and one-third of the heavenly host were cast into hell. In another version of this story, Lucifer and the angels of heaven were forced by God to bow before man, His most perfect creation. Lucifer convinced a great number of other angels that *they* were the true first-born, and that man should bow before *them.* God sensed Lucifer's excessive pride and disobedience, and so he and his minions were thrown out of paradise. According to Roman Catholic belief, after the Fall, God made a deal with Lucifer, allowing his demonic horde to test the human race by using enticing, tempting thoughts to encourage actions that would take humankind away from the Creator's grace.

In the Islamic faith, there are no fallen angels. Muslim people believe that angels were created from pure light and have no free will. Thus, they are above sin and can only do the work of Allah (God). However, there is a similar story in the Qur'an of a powerful being who fell from God's grace and was shunned forever. This being, whose power was almost equal to an angel's, was a djinni named Iblis.[1] The story goes that God orders all the angels to bow before Adam, the first human. All the angels obeyed God's command except for Iblis, the leader of the djinn, who had access to heaven. This lone djinni was proud and arrogant, and felt that he and the other djinn were superior to the new creation:

> It is We Who created you and gave you shape; then We bade the angels prostrate to Adam, and they prostrate; not so Iblis; He refused to be of those who prostrate.
>
> (Allah) said: "What prevented thee from prostrating when I commanded thee?"
>
> (Iblis) said: "I am better than he: Thou didst create me from fire, and him from clay."
>
> (Allah) said: "Get thee down from this: it is not for thee to be arrogant here: get out, for thou art of the meanest (of creatures). Be thou among those who have respite."
>
> (Iblis) said: "Because thou hast thrown me out of the way, lo! I will lie in wait for them on thy straight way: Then I will assault them from before them and behind them, from their right and their left. Nor wilt thou find, in most of them, gratitude (for thy mercies)."
>
> (Allah) said: "Get out from this, degraced and expelled. If any of them follow thee, Hell will I fill with you all."[2]

---

1 The word *Iblis* is Arabic that translates into to English as "he who is despaired." The name was given to this djinni after he lost favor with God. His original name is unknown. However, many Muslim scholars and holy men believe his original name was Iblis, and after his fall from grace his name became "Shaitan" or "the deceiver." In some stories he is also identified as the fallen angel Azazel.

2 Al-A'Raf, 11–18

For this act, God cursed Iblis and all the djinn who followed him, and banished them to hell for eternity. They were no longer allowed to visit heaven and mingle with angels. Iblis begged for forgiveness. God relented and gave him and all the disobedient djinn until Judgment Day to mend their ways. Iblis obtained permission from God to "prove" that humankind was unworthy of His love, and was given the power to attempt to lead all men and women astray. According to one Arabian story, after Iblis was thrown out of paradise, his name was changed to *Shaitan* (meaning "adversary") similar to Satan, as he is known in the West.

Just as in the Christian story of Lucifer, Iblis was allowed by God to test the human race with the pleasures and thoughts that tempt people to turn away from God's love. After centuries passed, Iblis convinced many other djinn that God had in fact wronged them. Iblis raised an army whose sole purpose is the downfall of the human race. He and his horde of renegade djinn have recruited many humans to their cause, promising them power, wealth, and pleasures, the so-called wishes a genie grants. However, the price those who make requests of the djinn must pay is not loyalty to Iblis, but their very souls.

Iblis as an Angel

In some early Islamic accounts, Iblis was once a powerful angel named Azazel. The name "Azazel" means "God strengthens" and this angel may have originally been a Semitic god of shepherd's flocks who became demonized as Abrahamic religions flourished. Azazel is associated with the ritual of scapegoating as an expiation of sin, as described in Leviticus 16. In verse nine, God tells Moses that his brother Aaron shall take two goats and sacrifice them: one is to the Lord for sin and the second is for Azazel, to be presented live for atonement, and then sent into the wilderness supposedly to the demon. This reference to the wilderness has led to beliefs that Azazel was a demon of the desert. Coincidentally, the desert is also considered to be Iblis' home when Allah permits him to enter our world.

In the apocryphal story *The Apocalypse of Abraham*, Azazel is mentioned as the angel of disgrace, lies, evil, wrath, and trials. He is the lord of hell, confined to earth by God because he became enamored with it. In Judaic lore, Azazel figures prominently in folk tales, along with another fallen angel, Samyaza (sometimes spelled Shemihazah or Shemhazai). Azazel refuses to bow to Adam when presented to God and the heavenly hierarchies. Islamic lore also tells of Azazel refusing to bow to Adam, and God casting him out of heaven and changing him into Iblis as a result. Although the angelic origin of Iblis contradicts Islamic beliefs, it is still considered by some scholars as a possible origin for this rebellious spirit.

According to Islamic belief, the evil that exists everywhere is due to corrupt humans and djinn who have turned their backs on Allah. Demons, fairies, ghosts, demonic possession, and even sightings of extraterrestrial aliens are believed to be the work of djinn, or in some cases, spiritually corrupt humans who have joined Iblis. If we take into account the reality of the existence of djinn, we can understand the paranormal's great diversity. Rarely do djinn present their true identity to us. Instead, they enjoy taking on many disguises. Many djinn merely play a harmless game with us for their amusement, but some have a more deadly agenda.

Stories about the djinn reveal a long history of perceived injustices and indignities from their perspective, creating valid reasons (in their minds) for many of them to plot against humanity. Believing themselves to be wronged by God in favor of human beings, some djinn have carried a deep grudge for millennia. Add to that the abuses they believe they've suffered at the hands of one of the few men to ever have dictatorial control over them—King Solomon. In order for us to understand the djinn and their feelings about humans, we must study both their past and present interactions with our race.

Solomon and the Djinn

The legendary Solomon, renowned as one of the wisest and most powerful rulers of antiquity, had absolute power to command and exorcize the djinn. Solomon ruthlessly forced them into slave labor to build the first Temple of Jerusalem and the entire city of Jerusalem as well. He sent them off into war to fight against men and djinn controlled by other men, and used them to impress the Queen of Sheba—who was rumored to be half-djinn herself. The djinn were resentful to be reduced to the status of slaves, but were powerless to do anything other than Solomon's bidding as long as he wished to control them. Even Iblis was powerless before the king, and could do nothing but provide a small measure of comfort to his kind.

Solomon's ability to control the djinn was a divine gift. He was the son of David, the second ruler of the united kingdom of Israel. According to the Old Testament book of Samuel, David's reign probably corresponded to the years 1000–970 BCE. After David's death, Solomon took the throne and ruled until his own death, circa 922 BCE. Historical details about Solomon are hard to find, but he figures as one of the most important persons in Biblical accounts of Jewish history. In Islamic lore, Solomon (Sulayman) is regarded as one of the greatest of world rulers, a true apostle, and messenger of Allah, the prototype of the prophet Muhammad.

Solomon's great powers were bestowed by God, who came to him in a dream and said, "Ask what I shall give you."[3] Many men might have asked for great wealth and power, but Solomon answered that he wanted an understanding mind for governing his people, and for the ability to discern between good and evil. Pleased with the man's response, God replied, "Behold, I give you a wise and discerning

---

3 1 Kings 3:5.

mind, so that none like you has been before you and none like you shall arise after you."[4]

Solomon's construction of the first Temple of Jerusalem brought him into direct contact with djinn, the site itself has a long, sacred history. It was the place where Cain and Abel argued over division of the earth and on whose portion a temple was to be built. It was the same spot where Abraham had prepared to sacrifice his son Isaac. During David's reign, it was the place where the Angel of Death, sent by God to punish the Israelites for David's sins, stayed his executing hand.

In his gratitude, David ordered that a great temple be built on that holy ground. Although he received divine revelation about its construction, he was forbidden from undertaking the project himself because he had shed blood. David passed the building instructions to Solomon. During the fourth year of his reign, Solomon launched construction and sent out calls for labor. According to different sources, both humans and djinn were recruited, most of them as slaves. Various rulers sent human slaves, and Solomon enslaved the djinn himself by the power and authority God had granted him.

Some accounts hold that the stones for the temple were fetched from quarries by female djinn. Some rabbinical interpretations of the Bible hold that the stones cried out in loud voices and moved themselves to the temple site.[5] The djinn dug for diamonds, dove for pearls, and brought the finest marble from all over the world.

The djinn participation is not included in all accounts of the temple: Biblical versions of the construction are given in 1 Kings 6–8 and 2 Chronicles 2–4; these omit mention of both djinn and demons. The Roman Jewish historian Flavius Josephus (37–c. 100

---

4 *Ibid.*, 3:12.

5 John D. Seymour, *Tales of King Solomon* (Oxford: Oxford University Press, 1924), p. 124.

CE) also gave no mention of the djinn in his *Antiquities of the Jews,* though he did cite Solomon's ability to exorcize demons (djinn) with the help of a magical ring.

Other sources provide a different picture of how the construction of the temple was accomplished. The great Persian poet and saint Jalal al-Din Muhammad Rumi (1207–73) wrote in his epic the *Masnavi*:

> When Solomon laid the foundations of the Temple
> Men and djinn came and lent their aid to the work,
> Some of them with goodwill and others on compulsion
> Even as worshippers follow the road of devotion.[6]

The richest details are found in *The Testament of Solomon*, a pseudepigraphic text written between the first and third centuries CE and the oldest magical text attributed to the king. Its translation from Greek into English describes the djinn as demons. Solomon controlled them, as he "mastered and controlled all spirits of the air, on the Earth, and under the Earth."[7]

Solomon acquired his power over djinn through a vampiric djinni named Ornias. During the temple's construction, Ornias crept in one day at sunset in the form of burning fire and attacked the son of the master workman, a child Solomon loved as well. Ornias stole half the boy's pay and food, and sucked out his vital life force through his right thumb. The boy grew thinner and thinner. Worried, Solomon summoned him and learned about the djinni's attacks.

The king prayed intensely night and day for Ornias to be delivered into his hands. In answer, God sent the archangel Michael

---

6 F. C. Conybeare, *The Testament of Solomon.* Revised English and partial translation by Jeremy Kapp. http://www.scribd.com/doc/2228881/The-Testament-of-Solomon-Revised-English, verse 7. Accessed November 2010.

7 *Ibid.*, verse 1.

to Solomon with a ring made of copper and iron bearing an engraved seal of a pentagram, a five-pointed star. Michael instructed Solomon to wear the ring and use it to lock up all djinn, male and female, and force them to help build the temple.

The next morning, Solomon gave the ring to the boy and told him to throw it at the chest of Ornias and say, "King Solomon summons you here." The boy complied. Ornias tried to avoid the command by offering the boy all the riches in the world. The boy refused, and Ornias reluctantly appeared before Solomon, who demanded that he reveal his identity and purposes. Ornias, bound by the ring's magic, was forced to obey. He confessed he was the offspring of the archangel Uriel, and could shapeshift into the forms of a beautiful woman and a lion. In the form of a woman, he had sexual power over sleeping men.

Solomon ordered Ornias to cut stones for the temple, but the djinni was terrified of the withering power of iron tools.[8] The iron at the time was very pure, a form called magnetite. If djinn are composed of plasma, which can be affected by magnetic fields, then the magnetic energy given off by the ore might have been harmful to them.

Ornias cut a deal with Solomon to produce the prince of the djinn in exchange for his freedom. He took Solomon's ring and threw it at Beelzeboul.[9] The prince gave out a mighty roar of flame, but was forced to appear before Solomon. Beelzeboul said he was the first angel in the first heaven, and he alone was left of the angels who fell from heaven. He ruled all the souls in Tartarus, (the underworld).[10] He had a son who haunted the Red Sea, who one

---

8 Iron has the power to weaken or repel supernatural entities, especially malevolent ones, including fairies, demons, and djinn.

9 A corruption of the name of the Canaanite deity *Baal-zeboul*, "lord of the divine abode." Beelzeboul is also given as *Beelzebub*, the lord of the flies.

10 The Greeks described Tartarus as the lowest region of the earth, a gloomy pit or abyss where wayward souls were imprisoned and tortured.

day would return in triumph. He said he incited men to murder, wars, sodomy, lawlessness, heresy, and all manner of wicked deeds. "And I will destroy the world," he vowed.[11]

Solomon sentenced Beelzeboul to sawing blocks of Theban marble. The other djinn howled in protest at this degrading treatment of their prince, which surely must have strengthened their resolve to have revenge against humanity. Beelzeboul was helpless, and he agreed to summon all djinn for the king.

The Testament of Solomon gives a catalog of some of the djinn summoned to appear. Solomon forced them to tell their names, how they harmed people, and how they could be thwarted, or nullified, by angels. Some of them appeared in monstrous, half-human, half-animal forms, while others attended him as fire or wind.

The first was Onoskelis, who appeared as a half woman, half mule. She said she was born from "a voice of the echo of a black heaven, emitted in matter."[12] She lived in caves, ravines, and precipices—some of the favorite abodes of djinn. She strangled and perverted men. Solomon sentenced her to spinning hemp ropes for the temple construction.

Onoskelis' birth is an interesting statement; today, we know that much of the multiverse is composed of what scientists call "dark matter" and dark energy. It is called "dark" because we cannot see it; scientists can only observe its effect on the visible matter in our universe. Any reference to a dark heaven or universe could be interpreted today as originating from another dimension.

The second djinni forced to appear was the powerful Asmodeus (Asmodai), who was enraged at being subjected to such humiliation. He said he was born of an angel and a mortal woman, and his

---

11 Conybeare, *op.cit.*, verse 27.

12 *Ibid.*, verse 18.

star burned bright in the heavens.[13] Asmodeus angrily informed the king not to ask many questions because his kingdom and glory would soon end. The djinni then gave a chilling prediction of the battle cry still believed today to be held by many djinn resentful of humanity: "And your tyranny will be short over us; and then we will again have free range over mankind, so as that they will regard us as if we were gods, not knowing, men that they are, the names of the angels set over us."[14]

Angry, Solomon had Asmodeus bound more tightly and flogged with ox hide thongs. The djinni was forced to describe how he ruined marriages and love relationships, drove men to insanity, and caused them to commit murderous deeds. Asmodeus confessed how the archangel Raphael had taught men to exorcize him with the smoke of burned fish gall and livers.[15] He also revealed the secret of his knowledge of the future: he could fly up into heaven and eavesdrop on angels.

Solomon sentenced Asmodeus to be weakened by iron, to carry ten water jugs, and to make clay by treading it with his feet. This was a great humiliation, for as you recall from page 18, Iblis told God that as a being of fire he would not bow before Adam, an inferior creature of mere clay. Asmodeus groaned terribly at his enslavement, but was forced to comply.

Solomon summoned other djinn. Some gave names that described their functions, such as Power, Strife, Deception, Jealousy, Error, and Battle. In addition to creating chaos and mayhem, they confessed to causing specific diseases and illnesses.

---

13 Genesis 6:1–4 and the book of Enoch tell of the Watchers or Sons of Gods, angels who broke the rules by descending from heaven to take human wives and birth monstrous offspring called the Nephilim. Here Asmodeus makes no claim to this particular origin despite his hybrid nature.

14 Conybeare, *op.cit.,* verse 21.

15 Told in detail in the apochryphal book of Tobit, probably written c. the 2nd century BCE.

Lore tells us that the proud djinn were angry and embittered at the harsh treatment Solomon had given them. The only djinni not subjected to the slave labor was Iblis. A story goes that one day Iblis visited the temple site to comfort his djinn.

"How do ye fare?" he asked them.

"We have no rest in our condition," they answered.

"Do ye draw stones from the quarry, and then return empty thither?"

"Yes!" they replied.

"Then ye have some ease!" Iblis said.

Solomon overheard the djinn talking on the wind, and he punished them by ordering them to carry loads to and from the quarry.

When Iblis came again to comfort the djinn, they complained about the increase in their burdens. He said, "Do ye sleep at night?" When they said yes, he replied, "Then ye have some ease!" Solomon retaliated by ordering the djinn to work day and night.

Again Iblis came to comfort the djinn, and they complained. Iblis responded that when situations seem to be the worst, conditions improve. According to one version of the story, Solomon died before the temple was completed.[16]

According to *The Testament*, however, Solomon completed the temple, installed the Ark of the Covenant within it, and rested in glory. He had another significant djinn encounter when Adares, the king of Arabia, appealed to him to use his power to banish an evil spirit, a powerful wind djinni who was killing people and animals. Solomon gave a servant a wine flask and his magic ring, and told him how to capture and seal the djinni in the flask to imprison it. The servant did so. When presented to Solomon, the djinni stood up inside the flask and made it walk around. Solomon tricked this djinni, Ephippas, and another djinni from the Red Sea, Abezithibod

---

16 Seymour, *op. cit.*, pp. 133–134.

(Abbadon), to raise a very large and heavy pillar into the air. He froze them in the air, as they held the pillar aloft.

Solomon would have lived out his days in peace and grandeur, according to *The Testament*, had he not fallen madly in love with a Jebusite woman. The priests of Moloch promised him the woman if he would bow to the gods Moloch and Remphan. He did, and the blessing of God left him for the rest of his days.

According to Rumi's *Masnavi*, God tested Solomon after the temple was finished. Solomon's magical ring was stolen by a djinni named Sakhar, who assumed the king's shape and impersonated him for forty days. Solomon was forced to wander about the land and beg for bread. After forty days, God restored Solomon to his rightful place, and the king began his worship inside the temple.

The stories about Solomon reinforce central themes in djinn history: outcast, abused and shamed, unable to exert their full powers in the world they coveted, their repressed resentment increased. Some djinn shrugged off the indignities and went about their lives and affairs, avoiding human contact. Others vowed revenge, biding their time over the centuries for the perfect opportunity to strike back.

It's clear that at one time humans enjoyed a more direct contact with the djinn, the latter of whom were unhappy with their situation. Knowing this, Solomon imprisoned an unknown number of djinn in brass bottles laced with iron, and sealed them with lead and a magical talisman. Some of the djinn were also held captive in magic rings made of rubies and fire opals. Many powerful but innocent djinn were also imprisoned at the time because Solomon feared that in the future, they may cause trouble for mankind.

Djinn Classifications

Before we continue presenting our research of the djinn, it's important that we clarify a few things. Djinn who choose to live next to humans or interact with them are known as *aamar*. Young djinn are called *arwaah*. Djinn who have evil intentions are called *shayteen*, and the more powerful djinn leaders are known as *afrit*. This identification of djinn is a very broad one, much like describing a person as only listening to one kind of music, or only enjoying one kind of food to the exclusion of all others. We shall see in the chapters to follow that djinn social structure is quite complex.

UNVEILING AN
ANCIENT RACE

THE FOLLOWING ACCOUNT FEATURES PHIL'S djinn experiences during a trip to Saudi Arabia in December of 1995. On his trip to the Middle East, he was able to make a number of important connections and contacts. The purpose of this trip originally had nothing to do with the djinn, but as Phil traveled from country to country he heard more of this ancient race and decided to make learning about them a priority.

Phil's Uncertain Journey

During my tenure in the United States military, I served with a number of individuals who today are in influential positions not only in the American government, but also in two foreign countries, one of which is Saudi Arabia. On a trip to the Middle East in the 1990s, I discovered that a fellow soldier I knew from our service in the Vietnam War was now a high-ranking member of the security force of the royal Saudi family. At the time I was in Israel, and sent him a telegram explaining that I would like to visit him and asking if he could arrange entrance through customs without a hassle. Within twenty-four hours, I received an invitation to join him at his home, not far from the royal palace, and one of the only luxurious places in the country. I can only refer to this person as "Jack," becaues he's an American in service to a foreign power and his position requires a great deal of anonymity. I have not heard from him in more than ten years, and as of the writing of this book, have no idea of his current situation.

I arrived at the King Khalid International Airport in Riyadh and went through customs. The officer there looked at my passport, paused for a very long time, looked at me again, and turned to his computer screen. I got a little worried and the people behind me in line began to step back as though they knew something was wrong. The customs officer then got on the phone and spoke in Arabic, a language I don't understand. He called over two nearby soldiers and had them escort me to a security room. I grew more worried. You see, King Fahd bin Abdul Aziz Al Saud, the ruling monarch at that time, had recently suffered a stroke and was unable to perform his duties as king. Many feared that dissidents would use this opportunity to seize control of the government. Perhaps my friend had already left the country, or was jailed by whoever was in control. You can understand my growing concern, thinking I might also be jailed because of my past military association with Jack.

A half hour later, a soldier walked into the small room. Speaking almost perfect English, he identified himself as Captain Yarramish and told me a car was waiting outside to take me to my destination.[1] I tried to ask him where I was being taken, but he insisted that I not ask any questions. We walked out the security area

---

1 A phonetic pronunciation.

of the customs building. My mind flashed to an incident Jack and I had in Bangkok back in 1970. I said to myself, "Surely he must have forgotten about that by now!"

Outside was a white stretch limousine. The captain got in with me and we began our journey to our destination. I thought, "Well, they sure aren't going to take me to a prison in a limo, but then again, Jack always had a strange sense of humor." As we drove through the city, I was shocked at the living conditions: people were still living as they had lived in the eighteenth century. We must have passed forty gas stations on our trip and the price was no more than ten cents a liter!

Soon, we found ourselves in the upper-class part of the city. Here, the homes were fantastically large with very expensive cars in the driveways. The difference between this area and the poor section and outer fringes of the city was like day and night. The wealthy Saudi people lived much better than Americans, and the neighborhood I was now riding through would put Beverly Hills to shame. It was clear that there were two financial classes in this country: the extremely wealthy and the poor.

We stopped at a gate with two guards who waved us in. The car pulled into a long circular driveway. As I got out of the limo, Jack appeared, and greeted me with a smile and a hug. We went into a small villa they had prepared for me and we sat down to have a drink. Jack told me he had the rank of colonel in the Saudi security force, a position he had been in for the past five years. He asked me about my life since we last met. I told him that for the past thirteen years, I had been teaching science and had written a number of books on various topics. He looked at me, laughed, and said, "Yes, but that's the cover story. What are you *really* doing?" I couldn't get Jack to believe that I was nothing more than a science teacher—he was certain I was in the Middle East doing some type of reconnaissance for an intelligence agency. Jack said we were invited to a dinner party that evening with a member of the royal family. He then excused himself to attend to his duties, and recommended I get some rest.

A Strange Dinner Party

As soon as Jack left, I fell into a deep sleep. Not too much later, I was awakened by a knock on the door. It was a secretary from the royal family asking me if I was ready for dinner. What seemed only like a few minutes of sleep was actually several hours! I must have been very tired, since it is not normal for me to sleep so deeply, especially in a strange place. I let the gentleman in and apologized for not being ready. He seemed quite upset and insisted that I hurry because Prince Khalid bin Fahd was attending the dinner party and it is a custom and show of respect that the guests arrive first and wait for royalty to make their entrance.

As I hurried to get ready, dressing in the tuxedo already cleaned and pressed for me, the gentleman identifying himself as my "advisor" gave me brief instructions on behavior and social protocol in the Arab world, especially in the presence of royalty. The instructions for proper behavior made me feel like I was back in medieval times. In a strict serious voice, he told me, "We must arrive before His Highness. When he enters the room, if you are sitting, you must stand. If you are talking, be silent. If you have a drink in your hand, set it down. If you have a cigarette, put it out at once. Most importantly, do not walk up and introduce yourself. You must wait for His Highness to come to you."

Those were just the instructions for the cocktail party—there were more concerning the dinner: "Do not walk over to the table until the servant asks all present to do so. Stand by your chair and wait for His Highness to sit first. Do not look at His Highness unless he is addressing you, and under no circumstances talk to the prince. His Highness will make a toast, so be sure you stand and hold the wine glass with your right hand and look at His Highness when he gives the toast. After the toast, you may say 'Thank you,' 'Very nice,' or 'Hear, hear.' Make sure you take one long drink and that Prince Khalid lowers his glass before you do."

After he had finished, I jokingly replied, "Is that all?" My advisor looked confused when I said, "Do you think after the toast I can give him the Vulcan salute and say 'Live long and prosper?'" Of course, I was just kidding around, but my advisor didn't see the humor in it. As we drove to the palace, I was reminded that I was not in America—disrespect in even the slightest form was taken as an insult.

At the palace, I entered the hall and started to mingle. I must have looked quite sharp in my black tie tuxedo—many foreign dignitaries whose names I couldn't remember thought I was an ambassador for some western country!

One of the servants called us into the main dining room. All the guests, including myself, stood around a large table. My position was second from the right of the head of table and I was quite excited to think I was going to sit next to the prince. At that moment, another servant walked in and said that Prince Khalid had been called away on urgent business, and he apologized to all his guests. However, the prince's cousin was to take his place and would settle all business in His Highness's name after dinner. The cousin entered the room with two large bodyguards, and everyone bowed. He sat in his chair and everyone did the same. I was thankful there was no toast and that dinner was served promptly.

The royal cousin looked to be about thirty-five years old. The other guests addressed him as "Excellency" so I assumed he was a minister in the Saudi government. My friend Jack was sitting next to me on the left and he whispered that it would all right to ask a question. Before I could open my mouth, his Excellency looked at me and asked if I was an American, and why I was visiting his country. I replied that I was interested in learning more about the djinn. When His Excellency heard the word *djinn*, his expression changed from neutral to one of concern and excitement. He seemed surprised to hear the word *djinn* come from a westerner, and it seemed to catch his interest! "The djinn!" He said the word so loudly, the entire table went silent and everyone looked in his direction. "I will tell you about them. They are very real and live in my country." The story he proceeded to tell me is unverified, but His Excellency seemed very serious; I believe it is the truth. I will relate the story to the best of my memory.

To Catch a Djinn

His Excellency said that a special unit in the United States military had been trying to capture a djinni for many years. His government would allow military and scientific missions into certain parts of the desert where djinn are known to enter our world. He said that the United States was after a technological device that allowed djinn to pass through solid walls and through dimensional windows. When I asked if they ever caught one, he replied that he wasn't sure because that kind of information would be classified at the highest level. I found this an interesting comment, and related it to a similar incident of a few years earlier in Pine Bush, New York, where numerous residents had reported a considerable amount of military activity in that area. The military's official explanation was that they were doing "training exercises," but a past associate of mine who is now in intelligence informed me of a different purpose. According to my associate, the military was supporting an operation being undertaken by a special unit to capture an "interdimensional alien" using a portal in that area of the country to enter and leave our world. The main objective of this operation was capturing its technology.[2]

---

2 Years later, Rosemary was told by a source who encountered two reptilian creatures in New Mexico wearing belts that, when touched, enabled them to pass through walls. Were these belts related to the technology the military was seeking in Saudi Arabia?

I asked His Excellency for a source of more information about the djinn and he instructed me to read the Qur'an. He turned to Jack, said something in Arabic, and then looked at me once again, and said, "This conversation is over." His Excellency then spoke with a number of his other guests. Jack knew I wanted to ask more and before I opened my mouth he elbowed me in the ribs quite hard. This I took as a very strong hint to keep my mouth shut— my conversation time with His Excellency was over.

After dinner I asked Jack what the prince's cousin had said to him. Jack told me he was instructed to take me to a mosque at the edge of the city to meet a holy man who knew everything about the djinn. I was thrilled and asked when we could go. Jack responded that the trip could be made in the morning, but he would not be going and would send his assistant, the captain who picked me up at the airport. A car then pulled up and took me back to the villa.

Visit with the Holy Man

Morning came too soon, and I was again awakened with a knock on my door. It was the captain. He said that we must leave immediately and asked me to dress in the more traditional clothes of the Saudi people in order to attract less attention. He told me that the area of the city we would be visiting was not safe for westerners. I dressed as he instructed and found the clothing quite comfortable, made of the finest Egyptian cotton. I looked like someone who had just stepped out of *Lawrence of Arabia*.

It took us about a half hour to reach our destination: a run-down part of the city inhabited by people who were quite poor. We pulled up in front of a building the captain said was more than three hundred years old and a former worship center of some sort. We were greeted at the door and taken into a room where a very old man was sitting smoking a water pipe. The captain bowed and started speaking in Arabic. He turned to me and said, "Please sit down. I will translate. You may ask any questions about the djinn but nothing more. Also, you will only get one response to each question. Do not get into a discussion with him." I was taken aback. I regretted not preparing a list of questions since my knowledge of the djinn at that time was limited only to what most westerners knew. I had no tape recorder, but it didn't matter, anyway, because tape recording was not allowed. I did take notes. Even though the meeting was more than fifteen years ago, I still remember everything the man said word for word.

A DARK STORY

According to the holy man, Allah created three intelligent races in the multiverse: Angels, djinn, and physical beings that include humans and all other "alien" races in the universe. Angels were created first, then djinn, who were placed on earth as stewards and masters. They were most loved by God. The djinn are made of fire, and have long life spans and great power. They are able to manipulate matter and change form. As a djinni becomes older, it acquires more knowledge and power. No one knows how long they live, but like all things, they eventually die and are answerable to Allah at the Day of Judgment.

In their time in the physical universe, the djinn built great cities ruled by powerful kings. The number of djinn who existed during their time on earth is unknown, but it could have been in the billions. Each group of djinn belonged to clans rather than states or countries, neither of which they had. According to the holy man, the clans frequently fought, often going to war over trivial matters. The wars lasted for thousands of years and polluted the environment. Before the djinn wars, earth was a paradise but their conflicts were turning it into a wasteland.

The djinn grew more powerful, using great and terrible weapons, eventually reaching the point of irreversibly damaging the physical universe. Allah knew that unless the wars were stopped, the djinn were also in danger of destroying themselves. Allah ordered an army of angels to stop them, but the djinn gathered their armies and engaged the angels in a war that lasted a thousand years. As the war drew to an end, the older and more powerful djinn finally fell. The djinn were cast into a parallel world close to our own. It is said that most went willingly, but some did not. They remain in this parallel dimension today.

Some of the djinn were allowed to stay in the physical universe to help repair the damage done by their race so that Allah's new creation, Adam, could populate the earth. These remaining djinn were ordered to help humans in their early years, teaching them language, the sciences, and the will of Allah. These groups of djinn were known as *amir* to the human race and interacted with men and women quite frequently. As time passed, many of the djinn who were allowed to remain behind began to isolate themselves from humans and became resentful. After many centuries, their resentment turned into hate and instead of helping humankind, they set out to destroy us. The holy man said that these djinn were influenced by Iblis, an evil djinni who made it his mission to destroy all the beings in the physical universe who were not djinn. The amir were then quarantined (by angels) into certain geographic locations, where they remain today. These areas became their home, and is the reason why many places on the planet are thought to be haunted. These places are actually occupied by djinn who can shapeshift into almost any form they please. The amir djinn's main purpose is to keep humans out by terrifying them and preying upon their impressionable nature.

WHAT ABOUT THE ROLE OF IBLIS?

I asked the holy man how Iblis fit into the story he had just told me. The holy man replied, "Iblis was the most powerful of the djinn; he was ascended and even associated with the angels. After the djinn wars, Iblis took the side of his race and refused to help prepare the world for humankind. When he refused, Iblis was cast out of heaven and could no longer associate with angels or other ascended beings."

The holy man said the majority of djinn have never seen Iblis and often debate whether he exists or not. Some of the djinn actually worship Iblis and look upon him as a savior who will help them reclaim the world they were forced to leave. To humans, Iblis is the greatest threat humanity will ever face, but to many djinn, he is considered a hero and a Christ-like figure.

The old man said that Iblis, still fearing the wrath of the angels, often takes a human form to conceal himself and lead the armies of man against each other in the hope of making them destroy themselves, thus leaving him and other djinn blameless. In one example, prior to a great battle, Allah saw that the leader of the evil army of men was really Iblis. Allah then sent the angel Jibril against Iblis.[3] When Iblis saw the powerful angel descending from the sky, he yelled out, "I have nothing to do with this! I am not part of this army and this war is of no fault of mine!" He praised Allah and fled. The great battle was stopped, and thousands of human lives were saved.

Iblis' ability to take on human form and become a great leader parallels the Christian prophecy of the coming of the Antichrist, a powerful being who is the devil incarnate that will lead the human race to a great war known as Armageddon. The holy man continued to talk of the djinn for several hours, after which he be-

---

3 Jibril is Gabriel in Judaic and Christian lore.

came tired and asked us to leave. He mentioned a cave near Oman which the djinn use to enter our world.

The holy man also said there were a number of towns and small villages in Oman, Iraq, and Syria in which the djinn have established strongholds. To me, this behavior seems to indicate they were creating beachheads to mount an invasion on the human race. When I heard about a place in Oman where these beings could enter our world, I had to see it for myself. I was already in the area, and knew that unless I took advantage of my proximity to visit the cave, I might never get another chance to explore it.

Majlis al Djinn

The djinn enter our world through some kind of interdimensional portal. We have many cases in our files where wormhole-like openings have appeared, and strange creatures or beings have emerged. These dimensional travelers would be regarded as djinn in the Middle East, but here in the Western Hemisphere, they are called "aliens." Some Muslims believe there are locations on the planet in which a djinni or a djinn family exist and share our world. One of these locations is located in Oman on the Selma Plateau in a very remote area known as *Majlis al Djinn*—"the meeting place of the djinn." Although many citizens of Oman, especially in the nearby villages, believe the cave is the home of djinn, the name was actually given by twentieth-century explorers who were fascinated with the locals' beliefs. The original Omani name of the cave was *Khoshilat Maqandeli,* which means "the place to harbor goats."

Majlis al Djinn is the eighth largest cave in the world and has the fifteenth largest chamber. The cave's main chamber is so huge, it could fit the Great Pyramid of Giza inside it and still have room. The cave was formed by water that slowly ate away at carbonate rocks in the Tertiary period.[4] The cave was not fully explored until 1983, but local residents knew of its existence for centuries and kept their distance because they believed a djinni had made its home there.

There are no visible lower exits or passages leading from the chamber to the ground above—only several openings in the ground leading straight down into the main chamber. Water entering the cave collects along the lowest part of the floor, then slowly infiltrates into the fine-grained, mud-cracked sediment. The entrances receive surface runoff from a small drainage area, so water never reaches most parts of the cave. While surface temperatures can exceed ninety degrees, air temperatures inside the chamber hover around sixty degrees. Access to the cavern is available only through a free descent of one of three vertical entrances in the ceiling, a drop of about 320 feet.

A Trip to Oman

While still in Saudi Arabia, I asked my friend Jack if he could arrange passage into Oman for me to see this cave firsthand. Fortunately, the weather was still quite cool, and the trip would not be that taxing for a person like me who was more used to the temperate climate of New England. Jack arranged for his right-hand man, Captain Yarramish, to go with me. I was delighted, as I had come to trust and know this man and his family quite well. He didn't even seem to mind me mispronouncing his last name. His first name was so long that he agreed to let me call him "Yarr." He seemed to find it amusing, and told me, "This is something only an American could say and get away with."

Saudi Arabia borders Oman, and our trip that day was short, thanks to the small passenger jet Jack had arranged for us. After about

---

4 The Tertiary period began about 65 million years ago and ended approximately 1.8 million years ago.

a one-hour flight, we landed at Seeb International Airport (now called Muscat International Airport). Yarr told me a vehicle would be waiting for us and we would drive to a small town called Fins, close to the Gulf of Oman in a region called the Eastern Hajar Mountains. In Fins, we would meet a person who would show us to the cave.

The trip in the four-wheeled drive vehicle was quite beautiful. We drove south on a major road; the view of the vivid blue gulf on our left was breathtaking, as were the mountains to the right. What impressed me the most was that everything looked very clean—there was not one piece of garbage or one sign of human irresponsibility. Oman was indeed a beautiful country, and I understood why so many statesmen in the Arab world fought as hard as they did to preserve their culture and home.

Yarr and I arrived in Fins early in the afternoon. Since we planned to make the trip the next morning, we spent the rest of the day enjoying meals, drinks, and a little sightseeing; I was even allowed to visit a mosque, a rarity in the Arabic-speaking world. Later, with Yarr as my translator, I asked some locals about the djinn. To my surprise, they were quite willing to talk to me, and I was able to gather a number of interesting legends. I was told over and over again that I should not study the djinn, as my curiosity would invite their attention and they would definitely investigate my intentions. The townspeople seemed convinced that the djinn were returning to our world and one day, if appropriate action was not taken, the djinn might rule human beings. However, it was the hope of all that the djinn would return and peaceably co-exist with us as they did a very long time ago.

I spoke with one person, a teacher, who said he always thought tales about the djinn were nothing but legends—until he had an encounter with one in the mountains, close to a town called Al Jaylah. Although the teacher refused to elaborate, he said that governments of Oman and the United States know about the djinn and are trying to deal with them. When I asked how he knew this, he replied that after his djinn encounter he ran into American, Saudi, and Omani "soldiers" who said they had been tracking a djinni for two days. He went with them to a base in the mountains where he was "interrogated" for several hours. According to the teacher, the "soldiers" told him not to give details about what he saw. He seemed more fearful of the soldiers then he was of the djinn. Despite my efforts at persuasion, he would not elaborate on his encounter.

I was eager to go to the area where the djinn have been seen and could hardly wait until morning came. We stayed at a small inn and I could not fall asleep that night—I was too excited about our trip into the mountains.

The Meeting Place of the Djinn

The next morning, we got up early, had a quick breakfast, and met our guide at the four-wheel drive vehicle. I looked in the back and saw not only climbing gear, but two 9mm pistols. I asked about the gear and was told that in order to get into the cave, one had to rappel down about a hundred meters (three hundred feet). This was all right with me—I had a great deal of experience climbing mountains and exploring caves and mines. Yarr said he brought the pistols because the area is desolate and we might encounter bandits. He and the guide expected no trouble, but they wanted to be prepared. "Better to have the guns and not need them than to need them and not have them," he said. Our guide said the cave was about ten miles to the south and we would arrive in about forty minutes. There was only one path leading to the entrance, and the going would have to be slow, as it was very rocky.

A half hour later, we stopped and got out. Our guide said that we would have to walk about one kilometer to reach the entrance. It was a sunny day and the temperature was about seventy degrees, perfect for a hike in the desert mountains. We reached the top of a hill and I saw what appeared to be a large hole with a diameter of about ten feet. I leaned over, looked into the "hole," and was quite surprised—I had heard the cave's main chamber was large, but the sight was unbelievable. I was to discover later that this was one of three cave entrances. I shined a light into the opening and the beam didn't illuminate the cave floor. Only as the sun rose higher in the sky were we able to see the illuminated ground below. I looked in once again and saw a green mist I assumed must have been coming from the cave's water. The air coming out of the cave was very cold. From my past experience in exploring deep caves and mines, I knew this meant the cave was considerably deep.

Our guide then spoke his first words of English to me, "Are you ready, my friend? You must go alone. We (referring to himself and Yarr) do not go in." I knew Yarr wasn't going to go, but I hadn't expected our guide to decline as well. In retrospect, it was probably a sign that something truly sinister was down in that cave.

We anchored several clamps in the rock and hooked the rope on the rapelling harness. I began my slow descent into the cave. The only illumination was the light of the sun projecting almost straight down into the hole from above. As I was midway down, a mist began to rise up. I thought I heard echoes coming from the darkness of the cave. They sounded like a human voice speaking Arabic. I stopped my descent and the mist appeared to take on a large form just below me. I found this strange because this part of the mist was not illuminated by the sun, yet it glowed with a greenish hue. I heard the voice again, but this time it spoke English. Although there was quite a bit of echo, I was absolutely sure it was saying, "*Leave. My place.*"

My two companions must have also witnessed the same thing because they spoke rapidly with each other and seemed quite agitated. Although I couldn't understand what they were saying, one word was clear—*djinn*. They ran away from the cave opening, leaving me hanging about seventy-five feet in the air. Fearing that they

were going to leave altogether, I climbed out and saw them running toward the vehicle. I got out of my climbing gear and yelled
for them not to leave. Yarr yelled back, "Hurry, my friend! It is
the djinn!" I scrambled to catch up with them at the car. Breath-
lessly, I asked them both, "What the hell is going on?!" Yarr replied,
"Didn't you see it?! It was a djinni taking form and telling us to get
out of this place at once!" Although I thought I heard a voice and
saw a vague, cylindrical-shaped mist, both men insisted they saw
the shape of a djinni and clearly heard a voice ordering us to leave.

Yarr and the guide refused to go back to the cave, insisting we
leave the area immediately. I wasn't going to hang around in the
mountains by myself, so I had no choice but to get in the car. On
our way back to the village, both my companions said prayers to
Allah in Arabic. Our guide refused to talk about the incident, but
Yarr kept repeating, "I had heard they were real, but didn't think
too much about it. They *are* real!"

The next day when I tried to get more information, Yarr informed me that some constable of the town had asked us to leave.
Yarr said it would be a good idea to take his advice and leave as
soon as possible. It was disappointing to be so close, yet so far from
learning more about the djinn. Apparently, the people in the town
thought I had awakened a nasty old djinni and they were afraid
of reprisals. Yarr and I made our way back on to the road and to
the airport to return to Saudi Arabia. Soon after, I spent a short
amount of time in Syria to gather more information, and not too
long after that, I returned to the United States.

Not long after my visit to Majlis al Djinn, the Omani government opened the cave to the public, and by 2007, it had seen more
than a hundred thousand visitors. It became so famous that even a
number of American and European commercials were filmed there.
For some unknown reason, the Omani Ministry of Tourism closed
the cave to all people in 2008 and now, no one is allowed to en-

ter. Their given reason was "safety concerns," but perhaps the djinn proved stubborn and unwilling to give up their "meeting place." I heard rumors from people in Oman, Syria, and Iraq that djinn have already infiltrated into our world and wield a great influence in a number of villages and cities in those countries. I will never forget the final warning I received from our guide when Yarr and I left Fins: "Watch closely, my friend—the djinn have returned to our world!"

DJINN IN THE QUR'AN,
SAHIH AL-BUKHARI,
AND THE BIBLE

THE HUMAN RACE HAS BEEN entrusted with the care, upkeep, and overall balance of our planet. This stewardship is a delicate relationship; even small mistakes can have devastating long-term results on the environment. The Qur'an makes it clear that the djinn failed in this responsibility and were replaced by human beings. If the human race takes the time to study the mistakes the djinn made when they were stewards of this planet, then perhaps we can avoid the major environmental catastrophes that might take place in the near future.

The djinn are a beautiful creation of God, made from fire or a special smokeless flame. In modern terminology, it can be said that they are beings of plasma in its most energetic state. Just like humans, they have free will and the ability to choose between good and evil. Their exercising it means the djinn have (or had) the ability to take action and better the state of their environment, or upset its balance for selfish or misguided reasons. Iblis, the ascended djinni who earned the right to live among the angels, exercised his free will when God ordered him and the other djinn to bow down in honor of man. In defiance, he yelled out, "No! I am superior to he!" As the result of this, Iblis was thrown out of the company of angels, becoming the adversary of the human race forever.

The Qur'an makes it clear that not all djinn are evil: some walk the path to God and follow the teaching of not only the Prophet Muhammad, but also Jesus Christ, whose teachings were meant for all sentient beings, not just humanity. The Qur'an devotes an entire chapter to the djinn race, enabling us to learn and understand more about our predecessors, hopefully learning from their accomplishments and mistakes.

Did the Djinn Affect Human History?

The djinn were created before mankind and were entrusted with great knowledge and power. That knowledge gave the djinn the ability to manipulate the physical world around them. Many civilizations of ancient history attribute their growth and development to one or a group of mysterious benefactors who descended from the sky and glowed or burned like fire. Were they actually djinn?

When Moses received the Ten Commandments, he saw God as a burning bush. The flame that engulfed the bush didn't consume it, and it didn't give off any smoke. When the Israelites left Egypt, Pharaoh's soldiers were held at bay by a "pillar of fire." Both the burning bush and the pillar of fire resemble the Qur'an's description of the djinn. If they were perceived as gods from the sky, they may have steered humanity in unique directions. They may have even shaped humanity's ancient religious beliefs and been responsible for the multiple gods and goddesses worshipped in ancient cultures around the world.

A Lesson to Be Learned

The djinn failed in the trust God had given them, and as a result, lost dominion over the earth. Responsibility was passed to the human race and we are now entrusted with that same knowledge and control. However, God states in the Qur'an that if humanity fails in what has been entrusted to us, God will raise up another to take our place, just as we were created to take the djinn's place. Is it possible that we may soon see drastic changes on our planet?

The Djinn and the Qur'an

Al-Djinn ("The Djinn") is the surah (chapter or book within the Qur'an) dedicated to them and what makes this chapter especially interesting is that the djinn seem to be speaking in first-person. Since translations of the Qur'an into English differ slightly from scholar to scholar, we have consulted three different versions in our research, but primarily used the *Asim* reader version. We also have included our comments at the end of a number of chapters. Please note that Qur'an references to a "him," "his," or "he" usually mean Allah (God).

The djinn are also mentioned in a number of Islamic writings, and one must read passages carefully to fully understand their meaning. We have included passages from the Qur'an and a few passages from *hadith* (one of the most well known being the *Sahih al-Bukhari),* which are texts concerning the words and actions of the Prophet, considered as important to Islamic life as the Qur'an itself.

THE QUR'AN—AL-DJINN (THE DJINN) 72.1–28

[72.1] Say: It has been revealed to me that hundreds of djinn listened (to the Qur'an) and said, 'We have really heard a wonderful recital!

[72.2] 'It gives guidance to the right path, and we have believed therein: we shall not join (in worship) any (gods) but our Lord Allah.

[72.3] 'And Exalted is the Majesty of our Lord: He has taken neither a wife nor a son.

[72.4] 'There were some foolish ones among us, who used to utter extravagant lies against Allah;

[72.5] 'But we do think that no man or djinn should say aught that untrue against Allah.

[72.6] 'True, there were persons among mankind who took shelter with persons among the djinn, but they increased them in folly.

[72.7] 'And djinn and men came to think as ye thought, that Allah would not raise up anyone (to Judgment).

[72.8] 'And we sought to reach into the secrets of heaven; but we found it filled with stern guards and flaming fires.

[72.9] 'We used, indeed, to sit there in (hidden) stations, to (steal) a hearing; but any who listen now will find a flaming fire watching him in ambush.

[72.10] 'And we understand not whether ill is intended to those on earth, or whether their Lord (really) intends to guide them to right conduct.

[72.11] 'There are among us some that are righteous, and some the contrary: we follow divergent paths. Many of us djinn worship Allah in their own way.

[72.12] 'But we think that we can by no means frustrate Allah throughout the earth, nor can we frustrate him by flight.

[72.13]. 'And as for us, since we have listened to the Guidance, we have accepted it: and any who believes in his Lord has no fear, either of a short (account) or of any injustice.

[72.14] 'Amongst us are some that submit their wills (to Allah), and some that swerve from justice. Now those who submit their wills—they have sought out the path of right conduct:

[72.15] 'But those who swerve, they are (but) fuel for Hell-fire.'—

[72.16] (And Allah's Message is): "If the non-believers had only remained on the (right) Way, we should certainly have bestowed on them Rain in abundance.

[72.17] "That we might try them by that (means). But if any turns away from the remembrance of his Lord, he will cause him to undergo a severe Penalty.

[72.18] "And the places of worship are for Allah (alone) so invoke not any one along with Allah;

[72.19] "Yet when the devotee of Allah stands forth to invoke him, they just make round him a dense crowd."

[72.20] Say: "I do no more than invoke my Lord, and I join not with him any false god."

[72.21] Say: "It is not in my power to cause you harm, or to bring you to right conduct."

[72.22] Say: "No one can deliver me from Allah (If I were to disobey Him), nor should I find refuge except in Him,

[72.23] "Unless I proclaim what I receive from Allah and his Messages: for any that disobey Allah and his messenger, for them is Hell: they shall dwell therein for ever."

[72.24] At length, when they see (with their own eyes) that which they are promised, then will they know who it is that is weakest in (his) helper and least important in point of numbers.

[72.25] Say: "I know not whether the (Punishment) which ye are promised is near, or whether my Lord will appoint for it a distant term.

[72.26] "He (alone) knows the Unseen, nor does he make any one acquainted with His Mysteries,—

[72.27] "Except a messenger whom He has chosen: and then He makes a band of watchers march before and behind him,

[72.28] "That He may know that they have (truly) brought and delivered the Messages of their Lord: and He surrounds (all the mysteries) that are with them, and takes account of every single thing."

Comments: This is a remarkable chapter, for the djinn seem to be the ones speaking. They make it clear that only the followers of Iblis are evil and there are many djinn who are Islamic, Christian, and followers of other religions. They also indicate that they have the ability to fly and in the past have often gone up to heaven to eavesdrop on the angels, but then were blocked by "fire" or some type of energy barrier. In the Bible and other Judeo-Christian literature, angels are depicted as being, or being surrounded by, pillars of fire. The cherubim, a high order of angel, wield swords of fire to guard access to the Trees of Life and and Knowledge, and the gates of Eden—in other words, the secrets of heaven.

The Qur'an—Al-Hijr (Stone Land, Rock City) 15.26–40

[15.26] And indeed, we created man from sounding clay of altered black smooth mud.

[15.27] And the djinn race, we created aforetime from the smokeless flame of fire.

[15.28] And remember when your Lord said to the angels: "I am going to create a man (Adam) from sounding clay from mud moulded into shape;

[15.29] So, when I have fashioned him completely and breathed into him the soul which I created for him, then fall down prostrating yourselves unto him."

[15.30] So, the angels prostrated themselves, all of them together. Except Iblis (Satan),—he refused to be among the prostrators.

[15.31] Allah said: "O Iblis! What is your reason for not being among the prostrators?

[15.32] Iblis said: I am not the one to prostrate myself to a human being, whom you created from sounding clay of altered black smooth mud.

[15.33] Allah said: Then, get out from here, for verily, you are *rajim*.[1]

[15.34] And verily, the curse shall be upon you till the Day of Resurrection.

---

1 Outcast or cursed one.

[15.35] Iblis said: O my Lord! Give me then respite till the day the dead will be resurrected.

[15.36] Allah said: Then, verily, you are of those reprieved, Till the Day of the time appointed.

[15.37] Iblis (Satan) said: O my Lord! because you misled me, I shall indeed adorn the path of error for mankind on the earth, and I shall mislead them all.

[15.38] Accept you are chosen among them.

[15.39] Allah said: This is the Way which will lead straight to me.

[15.40] Certainly, you shall have no authority over my chosen ones, except those who follow you of the *ghawin*.[2]

Additional References to Djinn in the Qur'an

THE QUR'AN—AL-ANAAM (CATTLE AND LIVESTOCK) 6.100, 112, 128, 130

[6.100] And they make the djinn associates with Allah, while He created them, and they falsely attribute to Him sons and daughters without knowledge; glory be to Him, and highly exalted is He above what they ascribe.

[6.112] And thus did we make for every prophet an enemy, the *shaitans*[3] from among men and djinn, some of them suggesting to others varnished falsehood to deceive, and had your Lord pleased they would not have done it, therefore leave them and that which they forge.

[6.128] And on the day when he shall gather them all together: O assembly of djinn! You took away a great part of mankind. And their friends from among the men shall say: Our Lord! Some of us profited by others and we have reached our appointed term which Thou didst appoint for us. He shall say:

---

2 Criminals or people who do evil deeds.

3 Devils or evil djinn and men.

The fire is your abode, to abide in it, except as Allah is pleased; surely your Lord is wise, knowing.

[6.130] "O ye assembly of Jinns and men! came there not unto you messengers from amongst you, setting forth unto you My signs, and warning you of the meeting of this Day of yours?" They will say: "We bear witness against ourselves." It was the life of this world that deceived them. So against themselves will they bear witness that they rejected Faith."

Yet, they join the djinn as partners in worship with Allah, though He has created them (the djinn), and they attribute falsely without knowledge sons and daughters to Him. Be He glorified and exalted above all that they attribute to him. He is the originator of the heavens and the earth. How can he have children when He has no wife? He created all things and he is the all-knower of everything. Such is Allah, your Lord! So worship Him Alone, and he is the *wakil*[4] over all things.

Comments: This chapter centers on the fall of Iblis from the grace of God. He is allowed to influence men who have strayed away from the right path, but not allowed to touch those who are chosen. Here we see that some djinn did not teach the worship of God to their children, and that some djinn have corrupted human beings. The evil djinn have assigned devils, evil men, or djinn to attack the prophets.

THE QUR'AN—AL-ARAF (THE HEIGHTS) 7.38, 179

[7.38] He will say: Enter into fire among the nations that have passed away before you from among djinn and men; whenever a nation shall enter, it shall curse its sister, until when they have all come up with one another into it; the last of them shall say with regard to the foremost of them: Our Lord! These led us

---

4 Trustee of affairs.

astray therefore give them a double chastisement of the fire. He will say: Every one shall have double but you do not know.

[7.179] And surely, we have created many of the djinn and mankind for Hell. They have hearts wherewith they understand not, they have eyes wherewith they see not, and they have ears wherewith they hear not the truth. They are like cattle, nay even more astray; those! They are the heedless ones. Some people asked Allah's Apostle about the foretellers [fortune tellers]. He said, "They are nothing." They said, "O Allah's Apostle! Sometimes they tell us of a thing which turns out to be true." Allah's Apostle said, "A djinn snatches that true word and pours it into the ear of his friend the foreteller as one puts something into a bottle. The foreteller then mixes with that word one hundred lies. And if an evil whisper comes to you from Shaitan (Satan) then seek refuge with Allah. Verily, he is all-hearer, all-knower. And they have invented a kinship between Him and the djinn, but the djinn know well that they have indeed to appear before. And on the Day when He will gather them together and say: O you assembly of djinn! Many did you mislead of men O you assembly of djinn and mankind! Did not there come to you Messengers from amongst you, reciting unto you my verses and warning you of the meeting of this day of yours? They will say: "We bear witness against ourselves. It was the life of this world that deceived them. And they will bear witness against themselves that they were disbelievers.

Comments: The Qur'an is against fortune-telling and the readings of today's psychics and mediums. Christianity also takes a similar stance on this topic.

The Qur'an—Hud (The Holy Prophet) 11.119

Except him on whom your Lord has bestowed his mercy and for that did he create them. And the Word of your Lord has been fulfilled. Surely, I shall fill Hell with djinn and men all together. This is because your Lord would not destroy the populations of towns for their wrongdoing while their people were unaware.

The Qur'an—Ibrahim (Abraham) 14.22

And Shaitan (Iblis/Satan) will say when the matter has been decided: Verily, Allah promised you a promise of truth. And I too promised you, but I betrayed you. I had no authority over you except that I called you, so you responded to me. So blame me not, but blame yourselves. I cannot help you, nor can you help me. I deny your former act in associating me (Satan) as a partner with Allah. Verily, there is a painful torment for those who do not believe or worship other gods.

The Qur'an—Al-Isra (Isra, The Night Journey, Children of Israel) 17.61–64, 88

[17.61] And when we said to the angels: "Prostrate unto Adam." They prostrated except Iblis. He said: "Shall I prostrate to one whom you created from clay?"

[17.62] Iblis said: "See? This one whom You have honored above me, if You give me respite and keep me alive to the Day of Resurrection, I will surely seize and mislead his offspring, all but a few!"

[17.63] (Allah) said: "Go thy way; if any of them follow thee, verily Hell will be the recompense of you (all)—an ample recompense."

[17.64] "Lead to destruction those whom thou canst among them, with thy (seductive) voice; make assaults on them with thy cavalry and thy infantry; mutually share with them wealth and children; and make promises to them." But Satan promises them nothing but deceit.

[17.88] Say: "If the whole of mankind and djinn were to gather together to produce the like of this Qur'an, they could not produce the like thereof, even if they backed up each other with help and support."

THE QUR'AN—AL-KAHF (THE CAVE) 18.50

And when We said to the angels: make obeisance to Adam; they made obeisance, but Iblis did it not. He was of the djinn, so he transgressed the commandment of his Lord. What! would you then take him and his offspring for friends rather than me, and they are your enemies? Evil is change for the unjust.

THE QUR'AN—AN-NAML (THE ANT) 27.17, 39

[27.17] And his hosts of the djinn and the men and the birds were gathered to him, and they were formed into groups.

[27.39] One audacious among the djinn said: I will bring it to you before you rise up from your place.

Comment: The above passages indicate the djinn formed groups or clans.

THE QUR'AN—AS-SAJDA (THE ADORATION) 32.13

And if We had pleased we would certainly have given to every soul its guidance, but the word from me was just: I will certainly fill hell with the djinn and men together.

Comment: This is another reference that Hell was not made for only evil human beings, but for the djinn as well.

The Qur'an—Saba (Sheba) 34.12, 14, 41

[34.12] And we (the djinn) made the wind subservient to Sulayman (Solomon), which made a month's journey in the morning and a month's journey in the evening, and we made a fountain of molten copper to flow out for him, and of the djinn there were those who worked before him by the command of his Lord; and whoever turned aside from Our command from among them, We made him taste of the punishment of burning.

[34.14] But when We decreed death for him, naught showed them his death but a creature of the earth that ate away his staff; and when it fell down, the djinn came to know plainly that if they had known the unseen, they would not have tarried in abasing torment.

[34.41] They shall say: Glory be to Thee! Thou art our Guardian, not they; nay! they worshipped the djinn; most of them were believers in them.

Comments: This points to the ability of the djinn to turn one substance into another. During the time of King Solomon copper was highly sought after to make bronze. This passage also tells us of the djinn servitude to Solomon as punishment and that other powerful djinn enforced this action.

The Qur'an—Fatir (The Angels) 35.6

Surely, Shaitan (Satan) is an enemy to you, so take him as an enemy. He only invites his followers that they may become the dwellers of the blazing fire.

The Qur'an—As-Saaffat (The Ranks) 37.158

And they assert a relationship between him and the djinn; and certainly the djinn do know that they shall surely be brought up.

The Qur'an—Fussilat (The Explanation) 41.25, 29

[41.25] And We have appointed for them comrades so they have made fair-seeming to them what is before them and what is behind them, and the word proved true against them—among the nations of the djinn and the men that have passed away before them—that they shall surely be losers.

[41.29] And those who disbelieve will say: Our Lord! show us those who led us astray from among the djinn and the men that we may trample them under our feet so that they may be of the lowest.

The Qur'an—Az-Zukhruf (Ornaments of Gold, Luxury) 43.62

It is only Shaitan (Satan) that suggests to you the fear of his supporters and friends so fear them not, but fear me, if you are believers. And let not Shaitan hinder you, verily, he (Satan or Iblis) to you is a plain enemy.

The Qur'an—Al-Ahqaf (The Dunes) 46.18, 29

[46.18] These are they against whom the word has proved true among nations of the djinn and the men that have already passed away before them; surely they are losers.

[46.29] And when We turned towards you a party of the djinn who listened to the Qur'an; so when they came to it, they said: Be silent; then when it was finished, they turned back to their people warning them.

The Qur'an—Az-Dhariyat (The Winds) 51.56

And I (Allah) created not the djinn and humans except they should worship me alone.

The Qur'an—Ar-Rahman (The Benefit) 55.15, 33, 39, 56, 74

[55.15] And he created the djinn of a flame of fire.

[55.33] O assembly of the djinn and the men! If you are able to pass through the regions of the heavens and the earth, then pass through; you cannot pass through but with authority.

[55.39] So on that day neither man nor djinni shall be asked about his sin.

[55.56] In them shall be those who restrained their eyes; before them neither man nor djinni shall have touched them.

[55.74] Man has not touched them before them nor djinn.

The Qur'an—An-Nas (Mankind) 114.4

From the evil of the whisperer who withdraws. Who whispers in the breasts of mankind, "Of djinn and men?"

Comments: Once again we see how evil, powerful djinn influence humans by whispering in the ears. This characteristic has been ascribed to many other kinds of spirits throughout history. For example, the ancient Greeks believed in daimones ("divine beings"), a type of intelligence or attending spirit. The daimones ranged from good to neutral to bad, and attempted to persuade people to various actions good and bad. Daimones appear in the works of numerous Greek philosophers. Socrates said he had a good daimon (an agathodaimon) who whispered in one ear and a bad daimon (a kakodaimon) who whispered in the other. Plutarch described the daimones as living for centuries, and possessing thoughts so intense in vibration that they could be heard by other spiritual beings and sensitive humans. Spirits whispering in the ear is one of the most common reported paranormal experiences today.

Hadith

As mentioned earlier, the *Sahih al-Bukhari* is one of the six canonical *hadith* collections of Sunni Islam, collected by the Muslim scholar Muhammad Ibn Ismail al-Bukhari (810–870). Most Sunni Muslims consider the *Sahih al-Bukhari* as the most authentic book after the Qur'an. The djinn are mentioned in these writings, and evil djinn are referred to as "devils." Other hadith are quoted as well, including the *Al-Muwatta*, *Sahih Muslim*, and the *Sunan Abu-Dawud*.

Hadith—Sahih Bukhari 4.533

The Prophet said, "Cover your utensils and tie your water skins, and close your doors and keep your children close to you at night, as the djinn spread out at such time and snatch things away. When you go to bed, put out your lights, for the mischief-doer may drag away the wick of the candle and burn the dwellers of the house."

Hadith—Al-Muwatta 51.10

Yahya related to me from Malik that Yahya Ibn Said, "When the Messenger of Allah was taken on the night journey, and he saw an evil djinni seeking him with a torch of fire. Whenever the Messenger of Allah turned, he saw him. Jibril (the Archangel Gabriel) said to him, 'Shall I teach you some words to say? When you say them, his torch will be put out and will fall from him.' The Messenger of Allah said, 'Yes, indeed.' Jibril said, 'Say, 'I seek refuge with the Face of Allah and with the complete words of Allah which neither the good person nor the corrupt can exceed, from the evil of what descends from the sky and the evil of what ascends in it, and from the evil of what is created in the earth and the evil of what comes out of it, and from the trials of the night and day, and from the visitations of the night and day, except for one that knocks with good, O Merciful!"

HADITH—AL-MUWATTA 54.33

The snake stirred on the end of the spear and the youth fell dead. No one knew which of them died first, the snake or the youth. That was mentioned to the Messenger of Allah said, "There are djinn in Madina who have become Muslim. When you see one of them, call out to it for three days. If it appears after that, then kill it, for it is a shaitan."

Comment: This is an interesting passage, for it says that there are good djinn and one should leave them alone and live in peace with them, but beware of the evil djinn. This passage gives instructions on how to tell them apart.

HADITH—AL-TIRMIDHI 350

Allah's Messenger said: Don't cleanse yourself with dung or with bones for that is the food of your brothers from amongst the djinn.

Comment: Once again, the djinn are called the "brothers" of mankind.

HADITH—AL-TIRMIDHI 358

Allah's Messenger said: The screen between the eyes of djinn and the private parts of the sons of Adam as one of them enters the privy is that he should say: In the name of Allah.

HADITH—SAHIH MUSLIM 39.6757

Allah's Apostle said: There is none amongst you with who is not an attaché from amongst the djinn. They said: Allah's Apostle with you too? Thereupon he said: Yes, but Allah helps me against him and so I am safe from his hand and he does not command me but for good.

HADITH—SUNAN ABU-DAWUD 36.5236

Muhammad Ibn AbuYahya said that his father told that he and his companion went to AbuSa'id al-Khudri to pay a sick visit to him. He said: Then we came out from him and met a companion of ours who wanted to go to him. We went ahead and sat in the mosque. He then came back and told us that he heard AbuSa'id al-Khudri say: The Apostle of Allah said: Some snakes are djinn; so when anyone sees one of them in his house, he should give it a warning three times. If it return (after that), he should kill it, for it is a devil.

If Djinn Are Real, Why Are They Not Mentioned in the Bible?

This is a question that comes up over and over again. There are other types of beings mentioned in the Christian Bible who are not humans or angels. In several translated verses of the Old Persian Bible, the words *jinn, jaann,* and *Iblis* are mentioned as the names of the devil and demons. In Cornelius Van Allen Van Dyck's Arabic translation of the Bible, these specific words are mentioned in Leviticus 19:31 and 20:6, Matthew 4:1 and 12:22, Luke 4:5 and 8:12, and John 8:44.

More modern translations—there are dozens in use today—use different terminology. Here are the above verses in the King James Bible, the predominant text used until the mid-twentieth century, and the New American Standard translation made in 1995:

LEVITICUS 19:31

King James—"Regard not them that have familiar spirits, neither seek after wizards, to be defiled by them: I am the LORD your God."

New American Standard—"Do not turn to mediums or spiritists; do not seek them out to be defiled by them. I am the LORD your God."

LEVITICUS 20:6

King James—"And the soul that turneth after such as have familiar spirits, and after wizards, to go a whoring after them, I will even set my face against that soul, and will cut him off from among his people."

New American Standard—"As for the person who turns to mediums and to spiritists, to play the harlot after them, I will also set my face against that person and will cut him off from among his people."

MATTHEW 4:1

King James—"Then was Jesus led up of the spirit into the wilderness to be tempted of the devil."

New American Standard—"Then Jesus was led up by the Spirit into the wilderness to be tempted by the devil."

MATTHEW 12:22

King James—"Then was brought unto him one possessed with a devil, blind, and dumb: and he healed him, insomuch that the blind and dumb both spake and saw."

New American Standard—"Then a demon-possessed man who was blind and mute was brought to Jesus, and He healed him, so that the mute man spoke and saw."

LUKE 4:5

King James—"And the devil, taking him up into a high mountain, shewed [showed] unto him all the kingdoms of the world in a moment of time."

New American Standard—"And he led Him up and showed Him all the kingdoms of the world in a moment of time."

LUKE 8:12

King James—"Those by the way side are they that hear; then cometh the devil, and taketh away the word out of their hearts, lest they should believe and be saved."

New American Standard—"Those beside the road are those who have heard; then the devil comes and takes away the word from their heart, so that they will not believe and be saved."

JOHN 8:44

King James—"Ye are of your father the devil, and the lusts of your father ye will do. He was a murderer from the beginning, and abode not in the truth, because there is no truth in him. When he speaketh a lie, he speaketh of his own: for he is a liar, and the father of it."

New American Standard—"You are of your father the devil, and you want to do the desires of your father. He was a murderer from the beginning, and does not stand in the truth because there is no truth in him. Whenever he speaks a lie, he speaks from his own nature, for he is a liar and the father of lies."

So, it seems that the term *Jinn* does appear indirectly in the Christian bible, but due to the many interpretations and translations over the years the words *djinn, Jinn,* and *Iblis* were replaced by *devils, demons,* and *familiar spirits.* Perhaps the devils and demons of Christianity are really evil members of the ancient race of djinn.

THE DJINN ORDER:
THE GOOD, THE BAD,
AND THE VERY BAD

IT'S A DIFFICULT TASK TO research and obtain information about a race of beings that prefers to remain hidden from us. For the most part, all we have are stories and legends that have been handed down through generations. Most of the information in this chapter comes from information obtained from Phil's trips to several Middle Eastern countries. Information he gathered was in the form of written legends, passages from the Qur'an, and stories from holy men and families he met. Later, we found additional data in a number of books and papers written by Muslim scholars. These references appear in the bibliography.

The djinn are much older than the human race but exactly how much older is unknown. However, if they were around before Adam, the time period from their creation to the present day could be millions of years. A being that could exist for hundreds of centuries could accumulate a great deal of knowledge about the universe and be very powerful. As you might expect, in their long life spans, they have developed a complex society and have evolved with a great deal of diversity.

When compared to a human, a djinni's life span is very long. A person in good health may live to be eighty years old. We consider this age quite elderly, but a djinni of this age is yet a toddler. In a person's life span, an individual learns at his or her own pace. This rhythm is determined not only by the individual's interest level, but also by his or her goals, spiritual development, and intelligence.

Just like their human counterparts, djinn are born with free will and have very little knowledge and power. Humans attend school to learn more about their world, how to function within it, and how to contribute to society. The djinn do the same. The big difference is that a human child may have sixteen years or so of direct schooling, while djinn juveniles may be in training for thousands of years before they can graduate to a higher level.

People mistakenly tend to place all djinn in a single category, assuming all act with a single purpose, controlled by one mentality. This is far from the case; each djinni is an individual, just as is a person. Although djinn are subject to the same laws and morals as humans operating within a social construct, there are renegades who choose to not follow rules. The information the human race has about the djinn not only comes from historical writings and stories, but from djinn who like to talk excessively, another way information about them filters through the dimensions.

Individual djinn react differently to human presence. There are djinn who are harmless and feel indifference toward us and there are djinn who interact with humans, but benignly. Many of the younger djinn are just as curious about us as we are about them and it is in this type of encounter in which a juvenile djinni will take on a different form, such as an animal, fairy, or other type of entity that would surely get our attention and at the same time, conceal its true nature. Shapeshifting appears to be the only way these "youngsters" can get close enough to study us. On a similar note, younger djinn seem to be more attracted to children than adults and will often appear before them in one of the forms mentioned above. They may also stay invisible and communicate using only a disembodied voice. We use the term "youngster" here, but please realize that although the human child may be six years old, the djinn child is most likely thousands of years old.

Some of the very old and powerful djinn have interacted with humans in the past, but they seem to have their own agendas for the most part. A few of these powerful djinn have been sealed in prisons by angels, and in some cases, by King Solomon himself. Although these djinn are not necessarily evil, they have acquired dangerous amounts of power and are unpredictable. They have the free will to act out and may some day pose a threat to humanity. In old Arabian stories, it is this type of djinni that is freed from imprisonment. As the story often goes, the djinni is so grateful that it (usually a "he") grants its human liberator three wishes. After the three wishes are fulfilled the djinni goes on his way, completely free. However, the story doesn't always turn out well for the people involved. The centuries-long imprisonment often makes the djinni resentful, angry, and even psychotic. When finally released from his prison, the djinni sometimes takes his anger out on the human who set him free and then continues to exact revenge on all creatures he blames for his long period of captivity—the human race being enemy number one.

The Thief of Baghdad was a popular movie made in 1940 that features a bitter, angry djinni.[1] The hero of the film is a boy

---

1   *The Thief of Bagdad* (1940) is a British fantasy film produced by Alexander Korda, and directed by Michael Powell, Ludwig Berger, and Tim Whelan. It starred child actor Sabu, in addition to Conrad Veidt, John Justin, June Duprez, and a brilliant performance by Rex Ingram as the djinni.

named Abu who finds a strange bottle washed ashore on a beach. The bottle is old, made of brass and glass, and the top is sealed.[2] Abu breaks the seal and out of the neck of the bottle shoots thick black smoke. The smoke takes the form of a powerful, giant djinni who has been imprisoned in the bottle for more than two thousand years. Recognizing the figure as a djinni, the boy commands him to do his bidding. The djinni answers him with a thundering "NO!" Abu reminds the djinni that he set him free, and according to the will of the king who imprisoned him (King Solomon), the djinni must grant him three wishes. The djinni replies, "For two thousand years I have been in the bottle, imprisoned by the great Solomon himself, master of all djinn. For the first thousand, I vowed that I would serve in gratitude and grant three wishes to any man who freed me, but in the second thousand years, I became angry at all men and vowed to destroy he who set me free to appease my anger, so prepare to die!"

The djinni attempts to crush Abu with his giant foot, and right before he squishes him, the boy calls out to him, saying he is a liar. The djinni pauses and answers, "What do you mean? Take care what you say to me!" Abu says that he doesn't believe the djinni came from the bottle since it is so small and he is so large. They argue, and the djinni proves he was in the bottle by turning himself back into smoke and reentering it, promising that after he proves his point, he will kill Abu. When the djinni is completely in the bottle, Abu quickly reseals the bottle and raises his arm to throw it back out to sea. The djinni pleads with the young man to set him free again. From inside the bottle, he promises not to kill him and will indeed grant him three wishes. He gives his word in the name

---

2 This method of imprisonment was not a lamp as told in *The Book of 1001 Nights* but a brass bottle with a lead stopper and covered with a magnetic iron mesh with the seal of King Solomon or one of his priests,

of the most powerful (Allah), so Abu cautiously opens the bottle. The djinni resumes his giant form and bows down before the boy.

The rest of the story revolves around the three wishes, two of which Abu blunders. After the third wish is granted, the djinni lets out a thunderous roar, "FREE AT LAST!" and flies up into the sky to rejoin his clan in the djinn world.

Though the above film was created for the silver screen, Middle Eastern lore also has many stories of fishermen who dredge up mysterious sealed bottles in their nets. The fishermen usually quickly throw the bottles back into the water without opening them, since they fear that bottles may be prisons confining nasty djinn.

Organization

Now that we have a basic introduction to the djinn psyche, let's explore their society.

Djinn Families

Djinn have families much like humans; however, their immediate family unit is small—usually one child for each set of djinn parents. According to what we discovered, the djinn are able to procreate only once in their lifetime, and male and female djinn can produce only one offspring. As a result, their population is slowly dwindling, and their numbers will diminish. Although this may seem unfair, Islamic teachers will tell you it is the will of Allah and that humans and djinn may not understand this grand plan, but it most likely is the way things are meant to unfold.

It is clear in the Qur'an and some written works of Persian origin that mankind is the second race in the universe, the successors of the djinn. We discussed djinn life spans earlier, and want to relate those points here to progeny: since human life spans are relatively short and prone to disease, we need to have multiple offspring in order to survive as a species.

According to Buddhist belief, a single human life span is much too short to reach enlightenment. A person must return in physical form for many generations before he or she can learn enough about the universe and the true nature of reality to ascend to a higher consciousness and be free of the physical body. Although the djinn apparently do not reincarnate, they have a similar goal, reaching enlightenment. And just like us, some djinn lose their way and are on a different path.

A certain amount of caution and care must be used when dealing with djinn families. Djinn parents are very protective of their children and if you injure or anger any family member—especially a child—its parents and relatives may seek you out for revenge. In ancient Persian teachings, it was mentioned how people could deal with the djinn and give them all the space they require. Readers were also taught not to do certain things that may injure juvenile djinn, such as starting wildfires; throwing old food and human waste into lakes, caves, and the desert; and most importantly, not building in locations where a family or individual djinni shares space with our world. As a djinni's emotions are much more intense than a human's, they are volatile and unpredictable in their reactions to injuries and affronts.

Djinn Clans

Djinn families belong to larger units called clans. The members of the clans include those who are partially or fully related to the djinn family. Each clan has a leader, a powerful older djinn master whom the others obey. Although these clans make for a loosely knit social structure, the clan leader is held responsible for the actions of its members. In most cases, male djinn are the troublemakers and break the rules. Female djinn, known as *djinniyeh*, are responsible for keeping the family structure intact and are quite serious about this responsibility, and most are quite protective of their children and immediate family members. Most djinniyeh will not interact with the human race unless provoked, yet are believed to be responsible for most cases of possession in human beings. In Iran and Iraq, most people will avoid isolated caves because they are afraid they might encounter a djinniyeh with her child. The people of these countries believe a djinniyeh will make the first strike—even unprovoked against a person—to protect her child. It's clear that people are afraid of the djinn, and they seem to mistrust us as well, knowing our violent and unpredictable nature.

Djinn Kingdoms

Clans are thought to be ruled by djinn kings who are able to stay in power due to their abilities. In most cases, these djinn rulers are the oldest, wisest, and the most powerful of this ancient race. According to the holy man Phil met in Saudi Arabia, djinn kings can rule over thousands of other djinn.[3] The djinn who serve a king must give him tribute once a century. What this tribute consists of is unclear, but according to some legends, it involves some type of energy, and in some Arabic stories, a human soul. This belief is also mirrored in Christianity where minions of the devil will collect human souls in exchange for favors, such as money, power, and sex. The lesser demon is allowed to keep a small portion of the collected soul for itself, but the majority must be given to the master. This similarity is interesting, as some Christian and Muslim beliefs share the same roots. The question is: if you've sold your soul, was it given to a fallen angel or a djinni?

Djinn kings can only be removed from power through assassination, a reason Muslim mystics and holy men believe is evidence the kings rule with an iron fist. The highest king of all the djinn is said

---

3 See chapter 2 about Phil Imbrogno's journey to Saudi Arabia.

to be Al-Masjid al-Aswad, a member of the order of black djinn.[4] In Persian mythology, the djinn color was considered the shade or color of its skin. However, since they lack a definite physical form, skin color is technically irrelevant when identifying a particular type of djinn. From what Phil discovered during his journey to the Middle East, the colors of a djinni's skin were ancient Persians' attempts to classify djinn power rather than describe a physical appearance. In Turkey, ancient drawings that are two thousand or more years old show djinn in half human-half reptilian forms with horns, scaly skin, lizard-like eyes, and claws for hands. This depiction is similar to the Christian description of devils and demons. It is also interesting to note that Islamic art dating from only eight hundred years ago shows the djinn as more human-like. It's not clear why the images have changed over the course of time, but perhaps early Islamic artists were trying to present the djinn in a form people felt was more immediately fear-inducing.

Djinn Classes

There are many names for the djinn classes describing their likes and dislikes, or where they live. The Qur'an mentions only three classes: djinn, ifrit, and marid. Other names include jann, ghoul, shaitans, hinn, nasnas, shiqq, si'lat, and a host of others, depending on the local dialect. In western lore, the ghoul is known as a cemetery-haunting, cannibalistic, blood-drinking creature. The hinn are weak djinn, closely related to animals, and prefer to appear as dogs. The ifrit class is cited only once in the Qu'ran, in reference to a djinni who fetched the Queen of Sheba's throne at Solomon's command. As a result, scholars are uncertain if the term "ifrit" definitely refers to a djinn class. The marid are unruly and

---

4 The black king of the djinn, Al-Masjid al-Aswad is mentioned in a fifteenth-century Arabic manuscript known as *Kitab al-Bulhan* (The Book of Wonders).

rebellious. The nasnas are another weak form of djinn, hybrids of human-like and animal-like forms, and may account for some of the reported encounters with mysterious creatures throughout history. The shiqq are lower djinn, appearing as half creatures that are literally only half formed, thus giving them a monstrous appearance. The shaitans are rebellious djinn associated with demonic forces.

For simplicity's sake, we've classified the djinn according to their power and behavior. The classification we use is by color, an easier way to understand this ancient, complex race.

The color order starting with the weakest to the most powerful is: green, yellow, blue, and black. There is also another group, red, which will be described separately; they belong to an order that does not answer to any family, clan, or king—only Iblis.

The only way a djinni can advance in rank and increase in power is to obtain more knowledge. For example, djinn can manipulate the matter in the universe by changing the vibration of strings. This action is much like playing a guitar: the more chords a person knows, the wider the repertoire. Individual string vibrations determine the type of particles and matter formed, and djinn are able to change the "notes" of the strings, thus changing one form of matter into another. This talent for changing matter properties does not come naturally—just like humans who must learn any profession, it is a skill, something developed over a long period of time, usually taught. Some people go through life learning very little, staying on more or less the same intellectual level and the same is true with the djinn. A djinn's progression from green to blue is not something that happens naturally; it is earned with a great deal of practice, study, and hard work. Some djinn are tempted to abuse their power, similar to some people. However, most djinn who achieve high ranks use their power wisely, since they believe they are responsible for their actions in the face of God and will have to answer for their deeds at the Day of Judgment.

Green Djinn

Green djinn have the least amount of power. The majority of green djinn are young and they usually enjoy acts of mischief and pranks played on other djinn and humans. There are some older djinn still at the green level, but for the most part, they keep to themselves and stay away from humans. It's interesting to note that in the 1960s television series *I Dream of Jeannie*, the genie was this green variety, very young and with limited power. As the series progressed, Jeannie became more comfortable performing increasingly amazing feats of djinn "magic" to make the shows more interesting.

Green djinn can shapeshift into animals and humans and have the ability to fly. They can also change one form of matter into another, but their power in this area seems to be limited due to their lack of knowledge regarding the relationship between matter and energy in the physical universe. A similar example would be a child trying to build a computer from a kit. The child does not have the experience and knowledge to complete the task, but an adult who has studied electronics, engineering, and computers would be able to assemble the kit's parts and have a working computer in no time because the adult possesses knowledge and experience, and understands how the device works. Although green djinn are mostly children and young adults, they can be thousands of years old, and their knowledge of human history and the multiverse is much greater than that of any human being. Green djinn are characterized as being playful, vengeful, cruel, and sometimes kind—indeed they are quite temperamental. Among the human race, it's known that some children are more aggressive, smarter, and/or stronger than others. Some are better at science, math, engineering, art, and other things. The green djinn also have different levels of power, knowledge, and talents, but like us, are all different. Some human children are cruel and some are kind. We've all heard about children who use magnifying glasses to burn ants or children who pull the wings off a fly just to see it suffer. Hopefully you'll never encounter a green djinn with the same attitude—to them, *you* are like that fly!

Green djinn often attempt to come into our world simply to explore or have fun, and when they do, they may interact with people of any age. It is an Islamic belief that green djinn live in holes in the ground. Consequently, you should never dump your garbage in a hole, or urinate or jump into one, as it might harbor a temperamental green djinn who won't hesitate to punish you as it sees fit.

Some holes in the ground lead to a subterranean world and it's possible they are actually portals that connect the djinn world to ours. If they are portals to another reality, once you enter, it might be impossible to find your way out without knowing where the door is. These portals are not restricted to holes in the ground, either—similar openings have been reported in outcrops of rock, the sides of mountains, and occasionally, randomly hanging in mid-air.

Many Middle Eastern mystics believe that if you jump into a djinn hole, you'll vanish from our world and enter another plane of existence. The djinn may offer to show you the way out, but for a price. A djinni may ask for your soul, or force you to agree to bring others to the hole so that it can hold you all hostage. They may also ask that you bring certain types of food, alcohol, or tobacco on a regular basis. It must be noted that although djinn in their natural state might be composed of plasma, most of them can take a physical shape for short periods of time. This means that a djinni is able to take in nourishment by absorbing energy or consuming food. It's thought that many djinn enjoy the "taste" of a variety of our everyday foods, especially ice cream and fruits. Human foods only partially provide subsistence, however: djinn must get most of their nourishment by absorbing various types of energy from living things.

The Little Man rrom the Hole in the Ground

The following account has been in Phil's files for twenty years. At the time he received it, he didn't know how to classify it. He was concentrating more on his investigation of the UFO phenomenon, and the report didn't seem to fit in with his current research. He filed the report away and forgot about it until much later, when he went through his old data looking for entity encounters that could have been djinn sightings. This story involves an unusual being "popping" out of a hole and engaging in a short conversation with the witness.

The encounter took place in the summer of 1989 and involved a middle-aged man who was hiking through the woods near Ellenville, New York. It was sometime in the afternoon and the day was clear and warm. While walking on a trail that had several small dirt mounds, the man stepped on a flat rock that rocked back and forth under his weight, making a very hollow sound. The man continued his walk, and a moment later, he heard a voice behind him say, "Hey! What do you think you're doing?" The man turned around and saw a "small man" standing on top of the mound looking at him with a great deal of anger in his eyes. The little man was about two feet tall with a long black beard and dressed in a tight-fitting suit that was black, green, and red. The small man's hair was long, and fell past his shoulders. The hiker turned around and said, "What do you mean? Who the hell are *you*?" The strange little man replied, "You stepped on my home and made a noise that woke me up from a deep sleep!" Pointing to the ground, the little man said, "This is my home right here. How would you like it if I walked over the roof of your home while you were trying to sleep?"

The witness was no more than ten feet from both the hole and the little man—he couldn't believe what he was seeing. As he listened to the little man speak, the witness noticed that the flat stone he stepped on had been moved away to the side of the mound—a perfectly circular dark hole was in its place. In his report, the witness said that the hole was much too dark and deep-looking to account for the bright afternoon.

At this point, the man became fearful. He apologized to the little man, who then said, "Why don't you come in and see my home?" The man politely refused and the creature became visibly upset and said something like, "Then go to hell!" and made a number of obscene gestures with his hands. The little man jumped back into the hole and was gone. The witness slowly and cautiously walked over to the hole and to his amazement, saw that it was gone. All that was left was a small crater in the ground where the rock had rested. The man quickly made his way back to his car and drove home.

In the above story, we see the connection between holes and the appearance of what seems to be a harmless, playful green djinn. Could these holes in the ground actually be portals that open, allowing the djinn and other creatures to enter our world? It's possible that these portals can only be opened in certain areas but they don't seem to be restricted to the mountains and deep woods; we have reports of "dimensional holes" opening up in the homes of people who have had a history of paranormal events since childhood.

Summoning Green Djinn

For the most part, green djinn seem as curious about us as we are about them. As all djinn are shapeshifters, the number of forms a green djinni can take depends on its age and experience. If a green djinni's motive is harmless, it may take on a number of forms that are pleasing to the human eye, hiding its true nature. However, if a djinni is angry or annoyed at a person, it may take on a hideous appearance that would terrify even the bravest human being.

According to Turkish belief, the green djinn are the easiest to summon, due to their already-present interest and curiosity about humanity. If they are open to the communication, the djinn may take on the form of a friendly dog, elf, fairy, or even a beautiful, glowing, angelic-like being. On the other hand, if you summon one or more djinn who don't want to be bothered, you might be in for a great deal of trouble. Several years ago, we received a letter from a woman who grew up in Turkey who tells the story of how her husband and a number of his friends decided to have some fun and try to contact the djinn.

The encounter took place in Istanbul, during a summer evening some time during the late nineties. One of the friends had a brother who was quite religious and lived in a mountain village nearby. The men knew this person had abilities to call the djinn so they all decided to visit him.

There are ancient Arabic rituals pre-dating Islam that can be used in conjunction with the Qu'ran to contact the djinn and bring them into our world. The person who had this ability was reluctant to summon the beings, but the others finally talked him into it, because they didn't really believe the djinn existed.

So, the man chanted Islamic prayers from the Qur'an and after several minutes, the windows blew open. Three glowing orbs entered the room. The light the orbs gave off was so bright, the men had to shield their eyes. The lights were able to move back and forth through the glass without breaking it. The apparently called djinn were very angry they had been interrupted, and asked for what purpose had they been summoned. The men didn't know how to respond, and this angered the djinn even more. The house's lights started blinking on and off, and they heard a loud banging on the door and wall. The djinn finally left, and the frightened men began to calm down. In the middle of the commotion, they didn't notice one of the men had gone missing. The other men figured he got scared and ran somewhere to hide. They looked everywhere, but couldn't find him. Hours later, the men heard a person crying out on the balcony. They walked out to investigate and found the missing friend crouched in a fetal position, soaked with sweat, his face full of fear. He said that as punishment for their act, the djinn had taken him to their world and brought him back. The man said it was a terrible place and was so frightening that he couldn't talk about it. All the men now believe the djinn are real, and they want nothing to do with them ever again.

Blue Djinn

The blue djinn, also called *marid*, are the smallest in number, but are considered the most powerful. The blue djinn rarely interact with the human race and very little is known about them. Stories vary greatly about who the true evil djinn are, but many say the blue djinn are the most heinous of all. On the other hand, other accounts mention that a number of blue djinn were the ones responsible for saving the entire djinn race from extinction by defeating the evil red djinn, the worshippers of Iblis.

The blue djinn are the oldest of the djinn and their power is said to be just below that of an angel. When the race of djinn was ordered to leave the physical universe and give it up to Adam, some of the blue djinn resisted and waged war against the angels. The war lasted a thousand years and in the end, the angels were victorious, an event that resulted in a rift within the djinn race. Many repented and obeyed the order to leave what had become Adam's world, but some refused, including an unknown number of powerful blue djinn and their clans. According to an old Persian belief, if you encounter a very old man alone in the desert, he is most likely a blue djinni in disguise, secretly entering our world. Travelers are warned to be wary of those who travel in the desert alone.

Although the blue djinn are much more powerful than their green counterparts, they can still be manipulated into doing a human's bidding. On rare occasions, these djinn are known to grant wishes to those who summon them, but things always turn out badly for the wisher. If approached correctly and with respect, blue djinn may be persuaded to help a person, especially if that person is troubled by another djinni. Most blue djinn have no trouble tolerating humans, and they aren't as given over to outbursts and unpredictable temperaments as the green djinn. The blue ones lie in wait, accumulating more power as each century passes, hoping that one day, they can once again claim what was theirs and defeat their old foes, the angels, in another war.

Red Djinn

Red djinn have one purpose: the downfall of the human race. They are the followers of Iblis, and from the shadows slowly influence humanity's thoughts over the centuries. Red djinn are the true terrorists of the universe—they whisper in the ears of men and women, causing them to take actions that are against the laws of God and man. Red djinn are also in the business of collecting human souls in order to make them stronger. The Red djinn broke all allegiances to their family, clan, and king. They only follow Iblis, who is their Messiah.

Red djinn usually take on a reptilian form. They are responsible for possession, illness, and hauntings. Many modern-day Islamic clerics believe red djinn are responsible for alien sightings and all other forms of paranormal phenomena. They are the devils and demons of history, and to deal with one courts disaster. They are eager to grant favors and wishes to humans, but their fee for such services is usally quite costly.

Black Djinn

Little information is available about the mysterious black djinn. In the Sunnah tradition, they are associated with evil or black magic. We have found one brief mention of them in one other text: they seem to be leaders of the blue djinn, and are clan leaders or perhaps kings of a large number of clans. Their numbers are unknown. It is possible there is only one, who may be the ruler of all other clan leaders and kings.

According to legend, when King Solomon ordered the djinn to obey him, he had a large black djinni at his side who he was able to control to enforce his will on all of the others. If a green or blue djinni defied Solomon's orders, the black djinni punished them. It's clear this particular djinni king was forced to act as a sergeant of arms for the great king, for he stood by Solomon with his arms folded in a display of power and authority. However, there was a very discontented expression on his face. Who or what the mysterious black djinni represents, their interaction with the human race is extremely limited. It may be that they are too important to deal with us and depend on those who serve them to take care of business.

Yellow Djinn

Arabic stories of a type of djinn described as yellow exist, but not much is known about this classification; they seem to isolate themselves from the physical universe and other types of djinn. Although the term "yellow djinn" has come up more than once in our research, we have little information about this class of elusive beings.

Ascended Djinn

In metaphysics, the spiritual goal of both humans and djinn is to ascend to a higher plane of existence. Ascended humans no longer have a need for physical bodies.

Ascended djinn occasionally interact with people who have not ascended, the latter of which might mistake the former for angels or extraterrestrials.

We believe ascended djinn exist, but the only one we know of is Iblis, most likely the most powerful of all djinn. For the transgression of ascending in order to access the choirs of angels, Iblis may have been demoted and sent to an existence between the physical universe and the realm of ascended beings. From there, Iblis persuaded other powerful djinn who had not yet ascended to fight for what he convinced them was rightfully theirs: the world of human beings. Although all djinn are potentially dangerous, Iblis and his red djinn have only one thing on their minds: our extinction.

DJINN NATURE,
ABILITIES, AND POWERS

THE QUR'AN SAYS GOD GRANTED djinn abilities and powers he didn't give humans. Indeed, some djinn run amok in the world with those powers, creating disharmony and damage in their various guises, sometimes for fun and sometimes for malice. The djinn are made of smokeless fire, and they certainly act like fire, igniting suddenly, behaving erratically, and destroying whatever lies in their path. Humans believe they have ways of containing djinn, much like they try to contain fire itself—but djinn, like raging blazes, have ways of jumping the barriers to burn somewhere else. There is another, tricky element to the fiery nature of djinn: they are not only the blaze itself, they are the arsonist who starts the fire—who laughs while things burn.

Djinn as Tricksters

The Trickster is an archetypal figure found in all mythologies, but is especially prominent in Native American lore. Tricksters operate outside the laws and boundaries of order. Although both a creator and a destroyer, the Trickster spirit is best known for its destructive tendencies: pranks, jokes, and malicious, cruel acts. Trickster has no morals or values, and follows only his desires and impulses. While not inherently evil, Trickster doesn't distinguish between good and evil, for both are means to an end. He has no sexual boundaries, and is even of unclear gender himself at times. He will tell lies if they suit his purpose and follow one lie with another lie that conflicts with the first, such that anyone who listens to him becomes utterly confused and disoriented. Trickster also loves to shapeshift, and his animal nature is expressed in his favorite forms, such as the coyote, snake, raven, spider, or hare.

Trickster plays the fool, but in the end, makes fools of others. Trickster especially enjoys laughing at the expense of the victims he dupes. Though he is sometimes duped himself, he often has the last laugh of chaos and disorder.

Some well-known examples of Trickster figures are Hermes, the Greek messenger god and god of deceit and thieves, as well as all arts and sciences; Loki, the sly gender-changing, shapeshifting troublemaker of Norse mythology; and Coyote, the vulgar, fire-stealing braggart found in serveral Native American traditions.

A strong Trickster element runs through the djinn, and even permeates attempts of humans to define, describe, predict, control, and best the djinn. Although djinn are explicitly acknowledged in the Qur'an, Islamic scholars throughout the centuries have debated their reality. The great Ibn Sina (known to the Romans as Avicenna, 980–1037), a physician and philosopher, was among those who said there was no reality to the djinn. Later philosophers, such as Ibn Khaldun (1332–1406), acknowledged the djinn and said Allah reserved all of the knowledge about them for himself.[1]

The djinn are briefly discussed in Phil's book *Interdimensional Universe*. Shortly after the book was published, he received several letters from people of the Islamic faith from around the word. They found the descriptions and encounters he had with the djinn to be accurate and they offered him congratulations and praise for having the courage to write about a topic that has been largely ignored by the West. These people also stated in their letters that what was covered in the book confirmed their faith in the Qur'an as it proved to them that the djinn are very much alive and active in the modern world.

Recent trends in Islam recognize the undeniable reality of djinn but beliefs about their nature, characteristics, abilities, powers, and lives are, like all forms of supernatural traditions and lore, open to a great deal of interpretation. Modern beliefs blend religion with pre-Islamic folk tales. Some make distinctions between djinn and "devils," who are the evil offspring of Iblis. Some believe in good djinn and bad djinn, while others consider all djinn to be dangerous. Below we discuss traits, abilities, and powers generally attributed to djinn.

They Have Limits to Their Power

Despite the formidable range of djinn abilities and powers, they have limits. Djinn can only operate so much outside of cosmic law and order, for ultimately they are bound by the Qur'anic word of God, as are humans and angels. God gave both humans and djinn power to influence the heavens and earth, but only within the bounds He allows. Those of either race who transgress the limits will be destroyed:

---

1 *E. J. Brill's First Encyclopedia of Islam 1913–1936* (Leiden, the Netherlands: Brill Academic Publishers, 1993), vol. VII, p. 1046.

O company of djinn and men, if you have power to penetrate
(all) regions of the heavens and the earth, then penetrate (them)!
You will never penetrate them save with (Our) sanction. Which
is it, of the favors or your Lord do you deny? There will be sent,
against you both, heat of fire and flash of brass, and you will not
escape.[2]

Muhammad stated that "…whoever intentionally ascribes something to me falsely; he will surely take his place in the (Hell) Fire."[3]
If djinn do not accept their limits voluntarily, they can be forced
to do so, not only by God's wrath, but by taking refuge in the
Qur'an through prayer and recitation. For example, djinn cannot
open doors closed by Qur'anic prayer, nor can they pollute or eat
food similarly protected. Even so, the djinn still have considerable
latitude for destruction in the mortal world—and they use their
Trickster wiles to circumvent prohibitions against them. Apparently, some of them have little concern about answering for their
transgressions on the Day of Judgment, and are instead governed
by their whims and immediate desires.

People who tend to live hedonistic lives in addition to those
who are inclined to be sinful make easy targets for djinn, but they
especially love the challenge of thwarting the faithful. The Qur'an
assures that Satan (Iblis and, by extension, his evil djinn followers)
have no dominion over the pious; however, sometimes the pious
are the most sorely afflicted by djinn.[4] A biblical parallel of such
Trickster treatment is Job's trials at Satan's hands, who asked God
for permission to attack him in order to test his faith. Job was the
most pious and righteous of men—a perfect target. The faithful
may argue that God must allow the attacks of evil, an argument

---

2 Al-Rahman, 33–35.

3 *Sahih al-Jaami*, 8.217. footnote 3.

4 Al-Israa, 65, and *Al-Saba*, 20–21.

made through the ages as attempts to explain why bad things happen to good people. Permission or not, evil has sneaky ways of infiltrating good through its cracks. When Iblis defied God, he vowed he would lead Adam and his kind to perdition.[5]

They Are Untrustworthy and Vindictive

Before people were created, the djinn reigned supreme, building great cities and enjoying God's favor. Egyptian lore tells of this more peaceful time, ruled by a succession of either forty or seventy-two kings all named Sulayman (Solomon), the last of whom was Gann Ibn Gann. The djinn under this last king were said to have built the great pyramids of Egypt, a belief still held by some at the turn of the twentieth century.[6]

The status, nature, and fate of the djinn changed drastically when God created Adam and ordered both angels and djinn to kneel. The defiant djinn were forced to give up their place, and were consumed by resentment and revenge. They became bent on using deceit, evil, and any means possible to strike back at the source of their misfortune: us. By the time the biblical King Solomon had subjected them, they had already made up their minds.

Like Trickster, the djinn are untrustworthy and unpredictable because they make no distinction between good and evil. While technically more amoral than they are truly evil, they can be quite nefarious and deadly at times, as whatever means are at hand justify their ends of revenge. Tricksters lack concern for the welfare of people; if people are harmed or if they die as a result of a Trickster's actions, it's just too bad for them. Similarly, the djinn have little regard for our

---

5 Al-Israa, 62.

6 Edward William Lane, *The Manners and Customs of the Modern Egyptians* (London: J. M. Dent & Sons, 1908), p. 230.

welfare. For sport, they sometimes perch upon rooftops and hurl bricks down on people, wounding and even killing them.[7]

Djinn are vindictive, and will never forgive the person who tries to harm them deliberately. For example, if people try to get rid of a djinni attached to or possessing them, the djinni will take offense. It may leave temporarily, but return with greater force and increased malice.

They Are Masters of Deceit and Illusion

Djinn can never be trusted to tell the truth, no matter how sincere and convincing they appear. If they don't know the answer to a question, they make one up on the spot, with no regard to consequences. They make false promises and abandon people. One story tells of a war in which believers engaged in battle against a band of infidels. Iblis promised to protect the believers and said they would be unconquerable. But when the enemy armies came into view, he fled.[8]

Another story is told about a pious man who was entrusted with the care of a virgin girl while her three brothers went off to war. Iblis gradually persuaded him to seduce her, and she gave birth to a son. Horrified at what the brothers would probably do to him upon their return, the man followed the guidance of Iblis and murdered both girl and infant, burying them in a ditch. When the brothers returned, the man made a great show of sorrow over their unfortunate deaths. Iblis then appeared to the brothers in dreams, taking the form of a traveler, and told them what the man had actually done, and where the bodies were buried. They discovered the corpses and confronted the man, who confessed. The brothers decided to punish him by crucifixion. As the man suffered on the

---

7 *Ibid.*, p. 231.

8 Al-Anfaal, 48.

cross, Iblis appeared to him and promised to save him if he would deny Allah. The man did, and Iblis vanished, leaving him to face excruciating death and divine wrath.[9] One can hear Iblis' Trickster laughter trailing after him as he disappeared into his parallel dimension. Even the djinn who have converted to Islam cannot be trusted. Or, they may claim they have converted when they have not, in order to gain a person's trust.

Sheikhs (a term that applies to both religious authorities and tribal leaders), magicians, and others who dominate and control djinn for the purposes of magic, fortune-telling, and healing are, in the eyes of many, vulnerable to the illusions and lies of the djinn. The Qur'an states that djinn cannot perform miracles, a gift possessed only by the true messengers of Allah.[10] Rather, djinn can only execute the *illusion* of miracles. Thus, they tell lies and perform tricks to give the appearances of magic and miracles, fooling both practitioner and client.

They Possess Invisibility and Superior Speed and Strength

As residents of a parallel realm, djinn are invisible to us unless they choose to appear, giving them a great advantage over us humans. They love to lurk and spy on people, especially in bathrooms, garbage dumps, and dirty, polluted places—but also in homes and intimate places such as bedrooms. They watch and wait for opportunities to strike.

Their invisibility creates many problems for people, who may injure or even kill a djinni without realizing it. The people of the ancient Arabic world believed that you should never cast a stone or even a date pit out into the open, for you may strike an invisible djinni. Never throw water, especially boiling water, out of a window,

---

9 This story has Judeo-Christian roots, but is told also in Islam as an example of the deceits of the devil (evil djinn).

10 Al-Shuaraa, 210–212, and *Al-Isra*, 88.

for the same reason. Driving a stake into the ground may hit a djinni in his subterranean home.[11] Djinn who receive injury rally their clans, who react like a swarm of angry hornets. Together, they rain all manners of disaster, illness, bad luck, nightmares, and even possession down on the offending person and his family.

Their natural form—smokeless fire or plasma—and supernatural power enable djinn to move with tremendous speed. In the story of Aladdin in *The Book of 1001 Nights*, a djinni builds the hero an entire palace in one night. In Egyptian lore, a djinni can travel the distance from Cairo up the Nile to Aswan (982 kilometers, or about 610 miles) in one second.[12] Thus, when they choose to be visible, they can be seen in one spot one second and then vanish and be seen in a distant place almost instantly.

The djinn have superhuman strength and can use their powers to lift and levitate objects of great size and weight, such as the gigantic pieces of marble transported for the building of Solomon's temple. Any person thinking he can best a djinni in a physical confrontation is making a fatal mistake: at the least, he will be severely beaten; at the worst he will be killed in an instant.

They Influence Thoughts and Dreams

Djinn influence a person's thoughts and dreams by whispering temptations and suggestions in their ear. A djinni could be considered the "evil" force sitting on a person's shoulder to counter the good influences of an angel on the other. The ability to hear djinn whispering occurs between the ages of twelve and fourteen. Prior to that, children are protected from a djinni's influence by angels.

---

11 In chapter 5, we noted the cautions against urinating and dumping garbage in holes, and related the story of the little man in the hole whose roof was inadvertently disturbed by an innocent hiker.

12 Barbara Drieskens, *Living with Djinns: Understanding and Dealing with the Invisible in Cairo* (London: SAQI, 2008), p. 96.

Besides whispering, djinn create disturbances such as whistling and strange noises, which distract people at crucial moments. They confuse people by speaking in their own language, Surian, which sounds like a combination of Greek and Latin, or German and Italian. Certain sheikhs are able to understand it.[13]

Djinn can enter peoples' dreams and can influence their thoughts and actions for the worse. They can prey upon desires and weaknesses, and give false counsel. They can appear as figures claiming to be messengers of God—but, as we have noted above, they cannot masquerade as Muhammad himself. Djinn who fall in love with humans come to them in their dreams and whisper in their ears, inciting them to fight with their spouses. They cause nightmares. Djinn can appear in dreams in animal guises, especially as camels, the symbol of evil djinn.

Djinn will also appear in dreams for the illusion of fortune-telling. One method of consulting them calls for taking a piece of someone's clothing—preferably unwashed underwear—and placing it beneath one's pillow, asking for information about the person. The djinn respond with the desired information, delivering it in the dream. Trusting the information is risky, given the djinn propensity for lying and deceit.

They Cast the Evil Eye

One of the most dreaded of evils since ancient times is the evil eye, a withering look that causes illness, misfortune, calamity, and death. Belief in the evil eye is universal. The oldest recorded reference to it dates to about 3000 BCE in the cuneiform texts of the Sumerians, Babylonians, and Assyrians. The ancient Egyptians believed in it, and it is referred to in both Old and New Testaments. Evil eye beliefs are especially strong in the Mediterranean and Middle East.

---

13 *Ibid.*, 121.

The evil eye is powered by envy, a force considered in parts of the Middle East to be the root of all evil.[14] In many cases, the evil eye is cast involuntarily, such as when someone, especially a stranger, admires one's family, business, or possessions; casts anyone a withering glance; or praises anything belonging to another person. Unless immediate preventive measures are taken such as ritual gestures and prayers or invoking Allah's name, disaster will strike. Children will fall ill, possessions will be stolen, or good fortune in business will turn sour. If the evil eye cannot be warded off, victims must turn to sheikhs for help. The evil eye can also be deliberate, like in a black magic spell. Djinn can influence a person to cast the evil eye and if shapeshifted into human form, the djinn can cast the evil eye themselves.

Modesty and avoiding displays of good fortune and wealth are ways to avoid the evil eye, either from other people or djinn. However, djinn know the secrets of people's wealth, their vanities, and their ambitions—all these things serve as ammunition for a weapon such as the evil eye.

They Are Capable of Possession

The djinn can stage a complete takeover of a person by dominating their thoughts and dreams as described earlier, and by entering the body. Their indefinable form enables them to easily penetrate a body and circulate through the blood. They cause all manner of physical discomforts and illnesses, in addition to paralysis, fits, and convulsions. They also cause aberrant and bizarre behavior, such as tearing one's clothes off, laughing hysterically, or dancing wildly in the street. They "come on to the tongue" of a person and speak through them. They cause extreme, even suicidal depression, and insanity. They can incite a person to crime and murder.

---

14 Drieskens, *op. cit.*, p. 70.

In severe cases, djinn take up permanent residence in a body, and must be forcibly expelled through exorcism by a skilled sheikh. Djinn who fall in love with people may enter a person's body in order to be closer to their love. This is not a desirable condition for the person, but in such cases, the djinni will usually not harm the person unless he or she does something to upset or anger them. If an evil djinni takes up physical residence, the danger is much greater—the djinni's intention is maximum damage, even death.

Not all forms of djinn possession are this extreme, however. Some cases involve being "touched" by a djinni—that is, the djinni comes and goes as it wishes and causes mild, temporary possessions. A person may have episodes of unusual behavior and not remember them after the djinni departs.

In some milder possessions, efforts are made to reconcile with the djinni rather than expel it. The djinni is engaged in dialogue. Speaking through its victim, it explains its grievances and what it wants in order to stop its possession. Some of the exorcism rituals are known as *zar*. Victims are usually women who are having problems with their husbands. As a result, they become possessed by djinn. The djinn, who love worldly pleasures, demand appeasement through jewelry and other gifts, sweets, and favors that must be performed by the offending husbands.

Possession is considered a substantial risk of crossing a djinni, or inadvertently injuring one. Sudden emotional and physical shocks rip open a person's natural protection and enable a djinni to breach the mind and body.[15] Exorcisms are not always successful—djinn often sneak back into the body.

15 *Ibid.*, p. 170.

They Magically Grant Wishes

In folk tales, djinn who are imprisoned in vessels and rings must grant three wishes to whomever liberates them, after which they are free. Unfortunately, stories about wish fulfillment are seldom straightforward; usually the wishes backfire, working *too* well, or not at all how the wisher had hoped. As the djinn themselves warn, every wish has a consequence. In most tales, the first wish is usually successful but the next two are not, and the protagonist finds himself in increasing trouble because of the wishes. The wishes must be worded very carefully, for a djinni will find a way to follow them to the letter, but in unexpected ways. Even if he tries to be clever, the protagonist never outwits the djinni, and usually the person's final wish is to undo the first two.

This theme continues to be played out in modern tales of the djinni/genie. Earlier, we mentioned the story *The Thief of Baghdad*, about a boy who finds a genie's bottle on a beach. In the film *Wishmaster* (1997), the protagonist liberates a particularly evil djinni. For one wish, he asks for one million dollars... and receives it in an insurance payout when his aunt dies in a plane crash the djinni had caused.

In "The Man in the Bottle," an episode of *The Twilight Zone* (1960), a down-on-their-luck pawnbroker and his wife are offered an untraditional four wishes by a djinni who comes out of a wine bottle. Dubious, they ask him to repair a broken glass cabinet. When the djinni does this instantly, they get excited and ask for one million dollars. He complies. They give away a lot of the money—and then the tax man comes to claim all but five dollars.

For a third wish, the husband asks to be the leader of a powerful, modernized country in which he cannot be voted out of office. Suddenly, he becomes Adolf Hitler, about to commit suicide in his bunker at the end of World War II. In a panic, the man uses his fourth wish to erase everything that had happened. Everything is back to normal. When he gets home, he finds the wine bottle that contained the djinni is broken. His repaired glass cabinet breaks— everything is as it was before the wishes. He tosses the wine bottle into a trash can on the street. The djinni's smoke reforms the bottle anew, and it lies in wait for someone else to release it.

They Can Shapeshift into Any Form

Shapeshifting is one of the most important abilities of djinn. We have saved it for last so it can be fully discussed and reinterpreted. We believe that some cases of paranormal activity may actually have had shapeshifting djinn behind them.

Artful shapeshifting is a primary Trickster trait. Magical transformations are a great asset in confounding humans, who never know quite what they're dealing with. As a result, people can land in great trouble before they realize it. One must take care not to throw water or stones at dogs and cats, especially black ones, for they are likely to be djinn in disguise. Once doused or hit, they and their clans become angry and will strike back in revenge. Similar precautions apply to snakes, another favored form. Djinn also like to mimic the shapes of birds and goats.

Djinn can take the form of mice to enter homes at night. If the residents have been foolish or absent-minded enough to leave lamps or candles lit, the djinn-mice overturn them, resulting in the home being consumed by fire—an excellent example of their fiery Trickster nature.

Djinn also shapeshift into human form, especially to fool people for the purposes of misleading and persuasion. The one form they cannot ever take is that of the Prophet Muhammad himself. Muhammad makes appearances in visions and dreams for the purpose of guidance. He assured his followers, "...whoever sees me in a dream, he surely sees me, for Satan cannot impersonate me (appear in my figure)."[16] However, nothing prevents a djinni from taking on the human form of a sheikh or an admired authority figure, whom people will mistake as a representative of the Prophet.

It probably occurred to djinn long ago that they could take on the forms of supernatural entities, at least some of whom are real beings in their own right, using them as disguises for interacting with human beings. This masquerade shapeshifting of the djinn has long been acknowledged in Middle Eastern lore. Author Umar Sulaiman al-Ashqar of the University of Jordan comments:

> Many people of our time and the previous times have witnessed something of the djinn, even though many who had seen them or who had heard them were not aware that they were djinn. They thought that they were ghosts, spirits, invisible men, creatures from outer space, and so forth.[17]

Taking on supernatural entity forms appeals to the Trickster in djinn, especially the green djinn, who like to amuse themselves at humanity's expense. The thought of a ghost wandering around a house or lingering on property frightens many people because of sudden appearances, strange noises, disembodied voices, odd smells, and phantom forms with grotesque features. Prevailing beliefs about ghosts hold that they are a type of recording, imprint, or memory left behind by the person who has died, or that they are the restless souls of those stuck between the worlds of the living and the dead. Some ghosts seem to lack intelligence or awareness of the living, while others interact and attract attention. In either case, perhaps they are not remnants of people, but djinn having a bit of fun. Djinn activity may not account for all ghosts,

---

16 Sahih al-Jaami, Ibid.

17 Umar Sulaiman al-Ashqar, *The World of the Jinn and Devils* (Boulder, CO: Al-Basheer Publications and Translations, 1998), p. 18.

of course, but perhaps they have created or piggybacked on the haunting phenomenon. Perhaps some of our most famous ghosts are not ghosts at all. It may be difficult, if not impossible, to ever know the difference.

Another common haunting phenomenon is poltergeist activity—unexplained disappearances and reappearances of objects, banging noises, mysterious rains of stones, lights flicking on and off by themselves, appliance malfunction and/or breakage, property damage, breakage, and disappearance; and other mayhem. *Poltergeist* is German for "noisy spirit," and unexplained destructive activities are often blamed on demons, angry ghosts, other spirits, and black magic spells. Poltergeist activity also befits the Trickster nature of djinn as a way of creating chaos and disorder.

Throughout history, people have reported encounters with mysterious creatures never before seen in the natural world. Sometimes only a few sightings are ever reported, but other times, such creatures seem to exist in a parallel world, popping in and out of ours for reasons unknown. Werewolves, dogmen, Bigfoot, swamp monsters and Jersey Devil-type flying creatures may be entities in their own right—but their forms could also be borrowed by Trickster djinn. Masquerading as a supernatural creature may be for a djinn what donning a costume at Halloween is for humans. The object is to have some fun, perhaps at the expense of others.

The famous Mothman wave of 1966–67 provides a good example of a possible djinn shapeshifting case. Mothman was a winged, red-eyed humanoid that suddenly began appearing in the area around Point Pleasant, West Virginia, (in particular, an abandoned TNT plant) in November of 1966. Mothman was described as being six to seven feet tall. It did not seem to have a head, and its eyes were set near the tops of its shoulders. It shuffled on humanlike legs, and it made a strange, high-pitched squeaking noise. It could take off straight up into the air without moving its wings and flew as though gliding, without flapping its wings.

Mothman terrified witnesses. If they were in cars and sped off, it took off after them, keeping pace in a chase. It never aggressively attacked people, however. It would seem to tire of the chase and break off and vanish. Such behavior is ascribed to green djinn, who sometimes like to toy with people but quickly grow bored and abruptly stop.

Although Mothman received much attention due to its unusual appearance, the real activity in the wave was centered more around UFO/extraterrestrial high strangeness. There were many sightings of mysterious lights, craft, and aliens; electrical and telephone disturbances; poltergeist phenomena; phantom dogs and mysterious creatures; phantom people; and sinister "Men In Black," dark, cadaverous, mechanical-like men who harrass UFO contactees and threaten them to keep silent. A dog disappeared and wild animals were found mutilated. Mothman was blamed for all the phenomena, but was never caught in the act of doing anything but observing and chasing people. The famous paranormal investigator and author John A. Keel traveled to West Virginia to investigate the wave, documenting activity in his book, *The Mothman Prophecies* (1975). Keel said at least a hundred people had sightings of Mothman.

The bizarre activity continued into 1967, declining toward the end of the year. On December 15, 1967, the 700-foot Silver Bridge that crossed the Ohio River at Point Pleasant collapsed, killing forty-six people. Some people linked the bridge collapse to Mothman, though no direct evidence was ever found. The collapse of the bridge was accompanied by a halt in Mothman sightings, and Mothman soon disappeared from the area. Since then, sightings of the creature have continued sporadically in Point Pleasant and all over the world, but there have been no more waves comparable to the one in 1966–67.

Keel believed Point Pleasant was a "window" or portal that temporarily opened to a parallel reality. We also believe in such portals, some of which may be open constantly, not just temporarily. It is possible that a portal did open at Point Pleasant, and many things poured through—including opportunistic djinn. All of the mystery beings—Mothman, Men in Black, phantom dogs, phantom people, and aliens—could have been djinn in disguise. The collapse of the Silver Bridge fits the Trickster motif, a nonsensical but lethal end to a windup of intense paranormal activity.

Sometimes djinn masquerades are more deadly in nature. Folklore and mythologies around the world are filled with supernatural predators of many shapes and names. Their main characteristics are luring unwary people to their doom and ambushing people as they travel, especially at night. In particular, fairy lore is full of such hostile beings, such as the water fairies who drown people, the wispy lights that lure travelers over cliffs and into bogs, and the savage trolls who jump out from beneath bridges. The djinn might make use of these and other nasty forms.

In Egyptian lore, a murderous Nile river entity is known to be a *ginniya*, a female djinni, who takes the form of a beautiful woman with long blonde hair and the tail of a fish—much like a mermaid. She entices people to come to the edge of the river by creating illusions: trays full of glasses of tea floating on the water, balls floating on the water, or an old woman carrying a pot who asks for help. When people come close enough, she grabs them and pulls them underwater. She gives them a choice: marry her or one of her kind, or die. If a person refuses, she strangles him and drowns him; his corpse is found with telltale thumb marks on his neck.[18]

Finally, an excellent example of what may have been a deadly djinn case comes from American supernatural history: the Bell Witch Cave. The Bell Witch "haunting" occurred in the nineteenth century in Adams, Tennessee, and involved spectral creatures, poltergeist

---

18 Drieskens, *op. cit.*, 102.

activity, bedroom invasion, and death. It was blamed on a witch's curse, but has numerous hallmarks that can be interpreted as djinn in origin. We make those comparisons in the following analysis.[19]

Different versions of the story are told, but the main features are consistent. Sometime in the early nineteenth century, John Bell bought a thousand acres of land near Adams and set up a prosperous farm. He and his wife, Lucy, had eight children. In 1817, life went from good to miserable. The first signs were mysterious creatures Bell saw—a large, black dog-like thing on his property that vanished when Bell fired at it with his shotgun, and a turkey-like bird. Both are favored djinn forms.

After that, severe poltergeist outbreaks occurred in the house. Knocking, rapping, and scraping sounds were heard in the home and outside on the doors and windows. Everyone in the family was upset by the sounds of invisible rats gnawing on things, and invisible giant dogs clawing the floors. The disturbances went on for about a year and then escalated to attacks upon the family at night while they were asleep in their beds. Covers were pulled off, invisible hands slapped everyone on their faces and yanked their hair. The Bells' twelve-year-old daughter, Betsy, got the worst of it; she was slapped, pinched, hit, bruised, and stuck with pins. At first, her parents thought she was playing tricks on them, but then became convinced that something sinister was afflicting the entire family.

Word about the problems spread, and the Bell farm became an object of curiosity. It was discovered that the invisible assailant was intelligent, for it responded to communication. When ordered to cease in the name of the Lord, it did—but only temporarily. It often resumed activity with greater intensity. This is characteristic of

---

19 The details of the Bell Witch case are taken from Rosemary's *The Encyclopedia of Ghosts and Spirits*, 3rd. ed. (New York: Facts On File, 2007), pp. 48–52.

djinn, who will temporarily stop their harassment, only to resume it much more powerfully.

After a time, the unknown spirit began to whistle and speak. As we saw above, the djinn are especially known for whistling and whispering. The entity gave different explanations of itself. It said it was a "spirit from everywhere, heaven, hell, the earth. I'm in the air, in houses, any place at any time. I've been created millions of years. That is all I will tell you." This description is a striking fit with the djinn.

The spirit also said it was the ghost of a person who was buried in the woods nearby, and whose grave had been disturbed. Its tooth was beneath the Bell house. The Bells searched in vain for a tooth. A djinn would have laughed to see them on their wild goose chase.

The spirit then said it was the ghost of an immigrant who died and left a hidden fortune, and had returned to tell Betsy where it was stashed. It gave a location, and the Bell boys dug for hours but found nothing. The spirit laughed aloud over that one. Djinn are known for promising riches and then not delivering.

Meanwhile, the local residents were forming their own opinions about the spirit's identity: they decided it was a witch. The spirit said, "I am nothing more nor less than old Kate Batts' witch, and I'm determined to haunt and torment old Jack Bell as long as he lives." Kate Batts was a neighbor with whom Bell had previously had bad business dealings. She threatened to get even. There was no evidence that she ever suited actions to words, but from then on, the spirit was called "Kate." It was a suitable guise for a djinni.

From a djinn perspective, bad business was indeed involved. As we have noted, djinn are extremely territorial and protective of their turf. Like the little man in the hole in chapter 5, they can become enraged if humans invade or damage their property. A djinni could have once occupied the land on which Bell established his farm. The Bells' arrival was nothing less than a home invasion—and the djinni reacted with characteristic anger.

The spirit seemed to spin out of control. It visited other people besides the Bells, blasting them with insults. It made predictions, another hallmark of "fortune-telling" djinn. But most of all, it continued to torment John Bell and his family.

A "witch layer," or professional exorcist, attempted to visit, but his carriage broke down. When he finally made it to the house, he attempted to kill the spirit with a silver bullet, but instead he was slapped around. Frightened, he left. Had he been knowledgeable about djinn, he would have brought iron weapons instead, for djinn, like fairies, are seriously weakened by iron.

The spirit's final action was to make John Bell ill—certainly a favored djinn tactic. John repeatedly fell ill with strange symptoms, and lay in bed twitching and convulsing, as though possessed. "Kate" claimed credit. Bell's health deteriorated. He was found dead in his bed on December 19, 1820, three years after trouble had first began. A strange bottle of liquid never before seen was found in the medicine cabinet. Lucy fed it to their cat, which promptly convulsed and died. "Kate" claimed she poisoned Bell to death, and she laughed hysterically in triumph. The djinni had its revenge.

However, the spirit was not done with the family. It turned full force on Betsy and tormented her over her engagement to a man, forcing her to break it off. Djinn who fall in love with humans are known to do the same. Betsy, however, married another man—but apparently someone the djinni/spirit didn't mind.

"Kate" announced she would leave but would return in seven years. A cannonball-like object then rolled out of the chimney and burst into smoke, and the spirit vanished. Smoke and mist are associated with djinn, as they lack forms in their natural state.

Since then, haunting phenomena have continued on the property, which is now privately owned and operated as a tourist attraction. The original Bell home no longer exists, but has been replaced with a replica. It is said to be haunted as well. The activity may spring from the land itself, which would be characteristic of a place frequented by djinn.

Nearby is a small cave that extends about five hundred feet into a bluff over a river. The cave is renowned for unusual phenomena, including apparitions, photographic anomalies of misty shapes, glowing balls of light, whispering voices, and sounds of breathing. Caves, as we have seen, are a favorite home of the djinn. A disturbed Native American burial site lies above the entrance to the cave. The bones of the woman buried there were stolen, which has given rise to belief in a curse—bad luck will come to anyone who takes anything from the cave, even so much as a stone.

Rosemary has visited the cave with Troy Taylor, founder of the American Ghost Society. Taylor has made numerous trips to the Bell Witch site and believes the cave to be a portal and the home of "an ancient, primeval spirit." It probably is, and it may belong to a djinn.

In Closing

The djinn are the "artful dodgers" of the paranormal, assuming different forms and slipping between dimensions at will. They have the ability to severely disrupt human life. In the following chapters, we compare djinn in more detail to other supernatural entities with whom we in the West are more familiar, and we examine ways to counter their effects.

ANGELS AND DEMONS: THE DJINN CONNECTION

To fully understand the connection between angels, demons, and djinn, we must delve into the Prophet Muhammad's revelation of the Qur'an. According to tradition, Muhammad received the Qur'an in a series of dreams and trancelike inspired states in which he was visited by the archangel Jibril. But was Muhammad actually visited by a djinni instead?

Muhammad is considered to be the last receiver of all divine revelations before the end of the world. His name means "the Praised One" or "He Who is Glorified." In all, there are two hundred names for Muhammad, such as "Joy of Creation" and "Beloved of God." Mention of his name is customarily followed by one of several invocations, such as "God bless Him and give Him peace" or "May peace be upon Him."

Muhammad was born in Mecca around 570 CE; tradition holds that his lineage goes back to Ishmael and Abraham. Some accounts claim he was illiterate, but he had a successful business career and probably was at least semi-literate. In 590, he married a woman twice his age. After twenty years of marriage and a successful career as a merchant of skins and raisins, his spiritual life unfolded. He felt a call to withdraw from the world, and pray and meditate to reach enlightenment. At the root of his spiritual searching was his acceptance of Jesus as the Messiah, the immaculate conception of Mary and the virgin birth, in addition to his conviction that Judaism and Christianity had distorted God's revelations to Moses and Jesus, and that the pagan Arabs lived in ignorance of God's true will.

Muhammad would often leave his wife and children in Mecca to make a four-hour journey to the Cave of Hira, located a short distance from the city on the top of a mountain. Hira is a small cave, about fourteen feet in length by six feet wide. There he would stay in complete isolation for several nights, deep in thought, prayer, and meditation.

In the year 610, while in the cave one night during Ramadan,[1] Muhammad was visited by a "creature" who ordered him in an authoritative, almost threatening voice, *"READ!"*

Muhammad replied to the creature, "I do not know how to read."

The creature grabbed him with such a great force that he almost suffocated. It released him, and repeated the same command three times. On the third time, the creature gave him what later became the opening lines of sura 96:

> Recite in the name of thy Lord who created,
> Who created man of blood coagulated.
> Read! Thy Lord is most beneficent,
> Who taught by the pen,
> Taught that which they knew not to men.[2]

---

1 Ramadan was already a holy month for the Arabs before Islam had spread.

2 Al-Alaq, 96.1–4.

Tradition holds that after issuing its commands, the creature disappeared. Muhammad went to sleep and awakened in the morning to hear words that seemed to be written on his heart: "O Muhammad, you are the Apostle of God and I am Jibril."

According to the *Al-Sira Al-Nabawiyya,* a biography of the Prophet by Ibn Kathir, written in the fourteenth century, Muhammad ran from the cave, all the way back to Mecca, trembling with fear. He ran into his house and found his wife and implored her, "Cover me, cover me." His wife asked him what was the matter. He told her of the creature he encountered in the cave and said he had to leave because he feared for his life. It is not clear at this point whether Muhammad thought the creature was a djinni or angel, but it was obvious he was very afraid of the creature that had accosted him.

From historical accounts of djinn and demons, we know they often make people do things they don't want to by threatening them or using physical force. In Biblical accounts of angel encounters, people often feared the angels because they usually appeared when God was unhappy with a person; the angel was sent to chastise or punish. In the Arabic world, however, djinn would have been even more feared than a powerful angel.

Muhammad was able to see the creature from any angle he looked, implying it was multidimensional in nature. However, there is no record of an exact description of the entity. Muhammad was skeptical of the creature's true identity. He saw it on several occasions after the first encounter, but no one else could see it. The creature followed him from the cave and often appeared in his home. Muhammad's wife, Khadija, wanted to discover the true identity of the creature and so told her husband to inform her when the entity was present. When the creature finally appeared, she asked Muhammad to sit on her left thigh and asked him, "Can you still see the creature?"

He replied that he did.

She then threw off her veil and asked Muhammad to sit on her right thigh. Khadija then asked him, "Can you still see the creature?"

He replied, "No, it is gone."

Khadija then told Muhammad, "Be firm, by the name of Allah, he is an angel and not a demon."

Islamic scholars interpret the test above as meaning that an angel would not stay to look at the uncovered part of a female body, but a demon would. Also, the creature was visible only when he sat on her left thigh and not her right. The pre-Islamic people believed that the proper sequence of things was from right to left. If the creature was also visible on the right, this meant to them that it would have been moving from left to right and against the balanced movement of the universe and against the will of Allah. Only evil djinn can do this—angels can't. This test convinced Khadija that the creature was an angel, and not just any angel, but the Archangel Jibril. Muhammad still remained skeptical.

Three years passed after the first revelation before Muhammad felt ready to call himself a prophet. He preached to his own clan, the Hashimites, that if they did not worship God instead of their idols, they would be punished. The followers of the new religion were called Muslims, which is derived from a term that means "they who surrender to God." His evangelizing was not without conflict and even holy war.

Critics called Muhammad "djinn-possessed" and said he was not a true prophet because God hadn't sent down His angels to him. Later, Muhammad began publicly describing the creature as an angel, but doing so failed to quiet his opponents and critics, who accused him of retro-fitting an angel onto his revelations in order to be accepted as a prophet.[3] Regardless of exactly how it

---

3 Rosemary Ellen Guiley, *The Encyclopedia of Angels*, 2nd ed. (New York: Facts On File, 2004), p. 266.

happened, the first night of Qur'an revelations is referred to as the "Night of Power." According to tradition, the Qur'an was revealed gradually over the rest of Muhammad's life, in nearly daily trance states and frequent dreams at night, with the final revelation coming just months before his death in 632. The transmitting entity is sometimes described as an angel, sometimes as a mysterious man. The holy book totals 6,666 verses and forms the doctrine of Islam. Muhammad himself never explicitly stated how he received all of it. Surah 17:106 states that it was sent from God gradually so that it could be recited to people at intervals.

The "Night of Power" is part of Ramadan, held in the ninth month of the Islamic calendar, a time of fasting, prayer, and pilgrimage. Jibril and other angels descend on the faithful on this night, and will continue to do so until the end of all time:

> We have indeed revealed this (Message) in the Night of Power. And what will explain to you what the Night of Power is? The Night of Power is better than a thousands Months. Therein come down the angels and the Spirit (Ar-Rooh, or Jibril) by God's permission on every errand. Peace! This until the rise of morn![4]

Was the Creature an Angel or a Djinni?

Muslim scholars today still debate whether or not Muhammad actually had a visitation by the angel Jibril; some feel it could have been a djinni. According to Zakara Botrous, a well-known expert on Islam and the Qur'an, the creature Muhammad saw in the cave lacked an angel's characteristics. The angels of the Islamic belief are pure and can do no wrong, and would never try to force someone to do something by strangling them. The entity that appeared to Muhammad greeted him with aggression and threats. We make

---

4 Al-Qadr 97.1–5.

no claims to know whether the prophet Muhammad encountered an angel or a djinni, but whatever attended him in the cave succeeded in its task, for Islam is the largest of the world's major religions today.

In discussing the events surrounding the revelation, we also are not diminishing or questioning the truth of the word of God as revealed to Muhammad. In all great religions, divine word is channeled through prophets who transmit the word to the masses. The stories of how they received the word vary even within their own religions, and become embellished over time with legends that lack historical data. Details of events remain uncertain or obscure, but at the core is the word itself, to which the faithful anchor their spiritual lives.

Contrasts and Similarities Among Angels, Djinn, and Demons

The ancient world that birthed Judaism, Christianity, and Islam teemed with supernatural entities who had the power to intervene or interfere in humanity's affairs, and their characteristics overlap. Numerous similarities and ambiguities exist among angels, demons, and djinn that provide ample opportunities for djinn to masquerade as one or the other. In many ways, djinn resemble some of the descriptions of early angels, in that they are capable of being either kindly and helpful toward people, or coldly righteous and rigid. Djinn also embody the demonic traits of cruelty, deceit, destruction, and chaos.

In the ancient world, angels were God's divine messengers and were morally righteous, but they were capable of destroying entire populations without mercy. Demons were lesser, interfering entities of good, bad, and neutral persuasions, but were usually responsible for anything bad that happened. Djinn were closer to demons in behavior, but with original ties to the angelic realm, as we saw in an earlier chapter. Djinn lore absorbed into the Western tradition tended toward demonic overtones.

The distinctions between djinn and demons are often confusing: djinn can act like demons and have more associations with demons—but they also have similarities to angels. According to M. S. Al-Munajiid, a prominent Saudi sheikh, lecturer, and author, scholars are in disagreement over the difference between djinn and demons. Some of them say that the word *djinn* goes far to encompass the djinn as well as the demons because the word also includes believing and unbelieving djinn. Allah says, "And among us there are righteous folk and among us there are far from that. We are sects having different rules." (Al-Jinn: 11) "And there are among us some who have surrendered (to Allah) and there are among us some who are unjust. And whoso hath surrendered to Allah, such have taken the right path purposefully." (Al-Jinn: 14)

However, the word *shaitan* is used to refer to the unbelieving djinn. Allah says, "…and the devil was ever an ingrate to his Lord." (Al-Isra, 27)

> The world of the jinn is an independent and separate world with its own distinct nature and features that are hidden from the world of humans. Djinn and humans have things in common, such as the ability to understand and choose between good and evil.[5]

In the Western tradition, demons do not choose between good and evil: they are the embodiment of all that is evil, and are completely and totally dedicated to it.

According to Islamic tradition, angels and djinn exist in the world beyond, sometimes referred to as the invisible world. Humans were

5 The World of Jinn and Its Secrets." http://www.islamonline.net/ servlet/Satellite?pagename=IslamOnline-English-Ask_Scholar/FatwaE/ FatwaE&cid=1119503543990

formed from clay, djinn from smokeless fire, and angels from a type of spiritual light called *noor*. This light has structure, and so angels, like djinn and demons, can shapeshift into any form. While djinn follow their own whims and desires, angels take on other forms only when God has directed them to do so.

Parts of the invisible world can be perceived on the human level by babies, animals, saints (including religious authorities) and the simple-minded. Djinn see more of the invisible world than we can, but angels see even more. Evil djinn serve the forces of darkness and destruction, and seek to turn people away from God, dooming them to hell.

As in the Judeo-Christian world, angels in Islam are viewed as positive, protective forces. They are God's messengers and taskmasters, obeying His will. Our modern perception of the shiny, comforting angel of the West evolved over time, however. In early Hebrew lore, some angels didn't look kindly upon humans. In fact, some were downright hostile and didn't want to share Paradise with them, considering it their own privileged territory. When asked by God to bow before his creation, some refused. They were not cast out of heaven as fallen ones, but were incinerated into oblivion. God destroyed these refusing angels until He found those who agreed to honor Adam. Nonetheless, there remained unfriendly angels who attempted to bar access by humans to the various levels of heaven. The mystical merkabah tradition features prayers and secret words that can circumvent such angels.

As mentioned earlier, early Judeo-Christian angels were the "muscle" for enforcing God's rules. When displeased with people, God sent angels to beat, punish, chastise, and even kill them. In the story of the wicked cities of Sodom and Gomorrah, God sent angels to level these cities off the face of the earth. In modern times, westerners have a more idealistic and sanitized view of angels, considering them to be pure spiritual allies in the struggle against evil.

In Islamic tradition, angels are always obedient to God; there are no defiant or fallen angels. When God ordered angels to kneel before Adam, all complied. The role of defiance fell to the djinn.

The defiant djinn and the Western fallen angels have points in common besides their defiance and expulsion from God's presence. The fallen angels followed Lucifer, who committed the sin of pride, and fell from heaven to the underworld. From there, they have reign over mankind to tempt, possess, and cause every illness and misfortune among us.[6] Though they are completely evil in magical lore, they can be forced to aid and educate people, a risky undertaking.

The djinn who refused to kneel to Adam followed Iblis, who by some descriptions was a once-great angel, but now equal to Satan. The evil djinn live in another dimension but also operate on earth, trying to deceive and lead people astray, causing possession and misfortune.

Another kind of wayward Western angel has similarities to the evil djinn: the Watchers. A brief reference to them is made in Genesis 6:1–4, and more information about them is given in the book of Enoch. Called "the Sons of God," they were angels set in heaven to watch over humanity. They coveted women and decided on their own to come down and cohabit with them. In exchange for sexual favors, they taught people the "forbidden arts" of science, metallurgy, chemistry, and divination, among others. Their hybrid offspring, the Nephilim, were cannibalistic monsters, abominations that so offended God that he brought on the Flood to cleanse the earth and begin anew with Noah and his sons.

Evil djinn are credited with teaching humans the forbidden arts, too. Djinn-human offspring are not quite as fantastic as cannibalistic monsters, but they are considered abominations, and such unions are forbidden. In both Western and Eastern traditions, angels act as

6 Isaiah 14:12.

a mouthpiece for God, who does not speak directly to people, with the exception of certain prophets. Angels speak from behind veils or in revelations, dreams, and visionary experiences.

Guardian Angels and the Qur'an

In both Christian and Muslim traditions, people are born with guardian angels that provide protection, guidance, and companionship. The Christian guardian angel evolved from helping and protecting beings such as the *fravashi* of Zoroastrianism (pre-existent souls with human-angel characteristics who reside in homes and communities); the *karabu* of the Assyrians (half-human, half-animal winged guardians of temples and buildings); the *daimones* of the Greeks (personal attendant spirits); and the *genii* of the Romans (guardians of places). The Bible does not refer specifically to guardian angels, but Psalm 91:11–13 does indicate that God provides angels to watch over people:

> He will give his angels charge of you to guard you in all your ways. On their hands they will bear you up, lest you dash your foot against a stone. You will tread on the lion and the adder, the young lion and the serpent you will trample under foot.

In Islam, there are two recording angels who sit on either shoulder, recording all the thoughts and deeds of a person through life:

> Behold two (guardian angels) appointed to learn (his doings) learn (and note them) one sitting on the right and one on the left. Not a word does he utter but there is a sentinel by him ready (to note it). Al-Qaf, 50.17–18.

The record is presented after death in preparation for Judgment Day. In another tradition, two angels appear after death to ask a soul questions about its most recent life, and for the purpose of presenting a life record of good and bad thoughts and deeds. If they give the soul their book to hold in the right hand, it means that soul will go to heaven. If they present it to the left hand, the soul will go to hell.

Another tradition holds that one of the entities is not an angel, but a wicked djinni. The good angel whispers in one ear and the bad djinni whispers in the other, both in a battle for a person's moral conscience. The role of the bad influence in Western tradition falls to the demons, while angels are considered to be solely an influence of good.

In addition to recording angels, Islam also holds that every person has a *qarin*, a special companion spirit or djinni permanently assigned to a person at birth.[7] The qarin combines features of the Greek daimones, who whispered both seduction and advice, and the Christian guardian angel. By some accounts, the qarin is ambiguous in intention, with a primary purpose to seduce and lead its assigned person astray by whispering temptations in the ear. ("Qarin" also refers to a nonbeliever who can lead a Muslim person astray.) By other accounts, the qarin provides companionship, comfort, and protection, including against illnesses and possession by other djinn. The qarin can be of either gender. It is called a double and a brother or sister who lives below the earth.

Some believe that people are assigned qarin of the person's gender, while others believe it is always the opposite gender. An opposite-gender qarin is jealous of any romantic partners a person may have, and will thwart relationships and potential marriages. When humans are said to marry a djinni, it may be with their qarin. Parents warn children not to spend too much time looking into a mirror because the qarin will react in a jealous rage. A qarin who is displeased with its human can cause headaches, illnesses,

---

7 Some Muslims believe the *qarin* is a separate type of entity from the djinn.

nightmares, bruises, and other physical discomforts, insomnia, de-pression and loss of appetite.[8] When the qarin exerts an evil influ-ence, it disavows responsibility for actions on the basis of the free will of the mortal: "His companion (devil) will say: 'Our Lord! I did not push him to transgress (in disbelief, oppression, and evil deeds), but he was himself in error, far astray.'"[9] In other words, the djinni says to God, "It wasn't *me* who made this person sin, I just helped him follow his own desires." Thus, the qarin reveals a Trickster nature in the deliberate and often malicious sowing of discord and chaos.

Muhammad acknowledged the qarin, but said his own converted to the faith, and functioned only in benevolent ways: "'There is no one among you but a comrade from among the djinn is assigned to him.' Sahaba e Karam present in that occasion asked: 'Even you, O Messenger of Allah?' He said: 'Even me, but Allah granted me victory over him and he became Muslim (or: and I am safe from him), so he only enjoins me to do that which is good'."[10] The qa-rin knows everything about its assigned person, including all his or her weaknesses. Giving in to temptation and evil feeds the qarin, enabling it to gain in power and strength. Only leading a righteous life can weaken it.

Knowledge of the Past, Present, and Future

According to Islamic thought, the future is not yet part of the cre-ated world and is known only by God and a select few of his an-gels. Forty days before an event takes place, a message about it is sent down from the Highest Assembly to the heaven where angels

---

8 Barbara Drieskens, *Living with Djinn: Understanding and Dealing with the Invisible in Cairo* (London: SAQI, 2006), p. 181.

9 Al-Qaf, 27.

10 *Sahih Muslim*, 6757.

called *katibin* write it down as destiny.[11] Once written, destiny is irreversible and cannot be changed, even if the person learns about it. Angels do not reveal destiny without God's permission. Certain sheikhs say they are inspired by angels and can know and reveal the future. However, some believe the sheikhs are really talking to djinn masquerading as angels.

Djinn know the past, the present, and what is taking place at another location (clairvoyance or remote viewing), but they do not know the future. Before Islam, they had the power to know the invisible, but they abused it by revealing their secrets to humans in exchange for gifts and control over a person's freedom.[12] God took their power away and shut them out of the seventh heaven. They climb up stairs or fly up to sit at the door and eavesdrop on the angels, who chase them away with stones. If hit, the djinn fall like burning stars (meteors).[13]

King Solomon proved the djinn have no knowledge of the future by concealing his death, in order to show people that they should not let the djinn fool humanity into thinking their ethereal counterparts ever had such knowledge.

It is said Solomon died leaning on his stick, and his corpse remained propped up on it for an entire year. Meanwhile, the djinn, thinking he was still alive, went on as slaves building his temple and city. At last, ants ate through the stick and the corpse collapsed. The djinn suddenly realized he was dead and had no more hold over them, and they fled.[14] In Western tradition, angels are consulted for fortune-telling, although it isn't an official function.

---

11 http://www.thewaytotruth.org/metaphysicaldimension/angels.html. Accessed October 2010.

12 Another similarity to the Watchers.

13 Al-Jinn, 8–9.

14 This story shows the gullibility of djinn, and has parallels to stories in Christian lore about how easily the devil can be fooled.

Theirs is not to reveal the future—unless God tells them to—but to stand by to provide aid when called upon by people as they go through the trials and experiences that are the results of choice.

Western demons are said to be clairvoyant, and able to know and tell the future. They know the secrets of people past and present, and are capable of commanding any language. In cases of possession, demons reveal these abilities; the speaking of dead languages or claims of the ability to tell the future are taken as proof of possession.

Possession

In ancient times, illnesses, afflictions, aberrant behavior, and misfortune were blamed on demons who were said to have the power to enter the body and take over one's body and mind. Djinn have this ability, too, and the traits of their possession described in the previous chapter can be applied to demons as well.

In Islamic and Christian traditions, the invading entities find ways to sneak into the body. The djinn often enter when a person's aura is weakened or split from trauma. In Western lore, demons enter through the breath, such as when a person sneezes, or hiding on bits of food. Giving in to temptations and sin will, of course, make one susceptible as well.

Certain individuals—religious authorities and healers—have the ability to exorcize demons through prayers, incantations, fumigations, and issuing holy commands. Exorcisms can easily go wrong when an unskilled exorcist challenges powerful, crafty demons or djinn; a person who performs this sort of task must be knowledgeable and powerful in his or her own right. In the Western tradition, the Catholic church has strictly ritualized exorcism, with rules governing how and why demons can possess people, and how they must behave in exorcisms. Demons do not just upset life, but use possession as a way to mock the Church and God, spewing forth blasphemies and obscenities through His most beloved creation.

Sexual Union

Angels and demons do not marry and have families, but the djinn do, just like us.

It is interesting to note, however, that angels, demons, and djinn are all capable of having sexual relations with human beings. Such unions are not considered desirable for mortals, and the offspring are usually oddities, if not downright monstrosities. Demons are considered to be sterile, but can impregnate women through a bothersome and awkward process of first using a female form to seduce a man to collect his sperm, and afterwards changing to a male form to impregnate a woman.

Both djinn and demons can approach humans sexually as seductive lovers in beautiful or familiar forms. Certain demons, the incubi (male) and succubi (female), are more sexually aggressive, especially in cases of hauntings and possession.

Eating and Drinking

The angels and demons of Western lore do not eat. In Genesis 18 and 19, two angels who are shapeshifted into the guises of men visit Abraham and tell him he and his elderly wife, Sarah, will bear a son. Abraham and Sarah offer them a meal and the strangers eat, and then depart to destroy Sodom and Gomorrah. Whether or not the angels actually consumed the food was a subject of great theological debate in Christianity. Theologians opined that angels, being non-corporeal, cannot eat, and so they only gave the illusion of eating in order to conceal their identities. Djinn eat and drink. They are allowed the bones over which the name of Allah has been said, and they can give animal dung to their own animals to eat.[15] There are many more points of intersection among djinn, angels, and demons, and we have summarized the most important ones in the table on the next two pages:

---

15 *Sahih al-Bukhari*, vol. 5, book 58, no. 200.

DJINN	ANGELS	DEMONS
Have gender	Have no gender	Shapeshift their gender
Live for thousands of years, eventually die into oblivion	Live until end of universe	Live longer than humans, eventually die and wither to their primordial state
Had original ties to angels	Closest beings to God	Had original ties to angels
Outcasts from God's favor	Enjoy God's favor	Outcasts from God's favor
Inhabit dirty, polluted places	Inhabit heavenly realms	Inhabit dirty, polluted places
Eat and drink	Do not eat or drink	Eat and drink
Organized in families and clans	Organized in hierarchies of powers and duties	Organized like the military
Have sex with each other	Do not have sex with each other	Have sex with each other
Have sex with humans; can impregnate	Some have sex with humans; can impregnate	Have sex with humans; can impregnate
Shapeshift to any form	Shapeshift to any form	Shapeshift to any form
Usually invisible unless they choose to be seen	Usually invisible unless they are directed to be seen	Usually invisible unless they are directed to be seen
Follow their own wills; some the will of Iblis; converted follow the will of Allah	Follow the will of God	Follow the will of Satan
Duty is to self and own agendas; some to Iblis; some to Allah	Duty is to glorify God	Duty is to Satan to subvert humans
Do not speak directly to God	Speak directly to God	Do not speak directly to God

DJINN	ANGELS	DEMONS
Deceitful, Trickster nature	Messengers of God	Deceitful, Trickster nature
Opportunistic interference in human affairs	No intervention without direction from God	Opportunistic interference in human affairs
Cause illness, bad luck, misfortune	Provide support and help	Cause illness, bad luck, misfortune
Possess humans and animals	Do not cause possession	Possess humans and animals
Can enter dreams	Can enter dreams	Can enter dreams
Knowledge of present and past but not future	Knowledge of past, present, and future	Knowledge of past, present, and future

In Closing

Making distinctions among supernatural entities and drawing boundaries is problematic at best. The problem increases in complexity when concerning the strongest and most prominent forces who represent the absolutes of good and evil. The nature, characteristics, and traits of entities often blur together. They are not "either-or," but "both-and." For example, can we confidently recognize an angel as an angel, certain it is not something else in disguise? The djinn are renowned for masquerades, and so are demons in the Western supernatural world. Saint Paul observed, "And no wonder, for Satan himself masquerades as an angel of light."[16] Theologians wrote that demons could also appear as the Virgin Mary, saints, and even Jesus himself. The literature of the saints contain numerous accounts of holy men and women being deceived by demons. If the most dedicated holy people can be so deceived, how can ordinary mortals hope to know exactly what they are dealing with when they have entity encounters?

The answer is not easy, and we suggest that we often do not know—we think we are dealing with one particular entity when in fact we may be dealing with djinn.

---

16 Corinthians 11:14.

8

DJINN, FAIRIES, AND LEPRECHAUNS

ONE OF A DJINNI'S FAVORITE disguises is that of a fairy, an intermediary being found in mythologies around the world. Fairy beliefs are universal and strikingly similar across cultures. In all places, and at all times in history one can find fairies in mythology and folklore. Usually, they appear in stories as small, supernaturally gifted beings that live inside the earth and harbor longstanding grudges against the human race.

Though Western fairy lore predates Christianity, much of it has acquired Christian elements. In Western lore, fairies seem cute, pretty, and harmless. In modern depictions, they are usually small beings (usually with wings) that tend to things in nature. Modern fairies of this type occasionally interact with humans, usually in good or sometimes comically mischievous ways. Traditionally, however, fairies are not as innocent, not even in Western lore. Underneath their gossamer glow lies a dark side that crosses into djinn territory.

Popular Western notions about fairies have been increasingly sanitized since Victorian times, before which they were among the most feared of supernatural entities. In earlier times, even the good-natured fairies were believed to use their supernatural powers against people more than for help, and people went out of their way to avoid them or, if they absolutely couldn't, at least placate them. Fairies offer a good disguise for the stealthy, shapeshifting djinn, enabling them to hide in plain sight in a supernatural part of our world. This masking in no way negates the existence of fairies, the varieties of good and bad fairies, or anyone's experiences with them. But have all our encounters with fairies been with them—or with djinn?

The use of fairy disguises probably appeals most to green djinn and red djinn. The green djinn are fascinated with people, as are many fairies, and both can fall in love with humans and follow them around. Green djinn love to play, and fairies are renowned for their nocturnal dancing, singing, and bewitching brews. Green djinn also love pranks and jokes, a trademark fairy activity.

The guise of ill-tempered fairies suit the red djinn, the ones looking for ways to cause serious strife with humans. Most of the fairies documented in Western folklore have a dim view of humans at best. Like many blue djinn, they avoid people, believing them to be inferior and not worth their attention. But cross them—especially those who have mean streaks and bad tempers—and disaster strikes. Angry, wronged fairies will destroy homes, fortunes, and health, using some of the same tactics employed by angry, terrorizing red djinn.

Fairies have already been compared to extraterrestrials, most notably by the folklorist Thomas E. Bullard, and by ufologist Jacques Vallee in *Passport to Magonia* (1969). In our research, we found an even stronger connection to the djinn. The connections shared by djinn and fairies that also link to extraterrestrials add even more intrigue if it can believed that a masquerade of shapeshifting is indeed in effect.

We have identified numerous similarities and links between djinn, fairies, and leprechauns. We mention leprechauns separately because it is uncertain whether or not they technically belong to the class of fairies. In some descriptions, they are called fairies—even "Ireland's national fairy"—and in other descriptions, they are separate entities that interact with fairies.

Origins of the Word *Fairy*

Fairy is generally thought to come from the Latin word *fata*, or fate, which refers to the Fates of mythology: three women who spin, twist, and cut the threads of life. *Fairy* came into usage in medieval times and was often used to refer to women who had magical powers. *Fairy*, originally spelled *faerie*, referred to the state of being enchanted.

According to lore, fairies themselves do not like the word, but prefer such labels as "the Good Neighbors," "the Good People," "the Gentry," "the People of Peace," "the Strangers," "Themselves," "the Seelie (Blessed) Court," and similar terms. Compare them with the djinn, often referred to by similar names, such as "God's Other People," "Them," "One of Those," and "Those Other People." Fairies are also called "the Little People" because of their diminutive size: most are described as two to three feet in height. However, in some accounts, fairies do not care for the term "Little People" either, considering it and "fairy" to be disrespectful.

A connection between fairies and Persian lore was made by Lady Jane Wilde (1826–1896), an Irish poet and wife of Sir William Wilde. Lady Wilde was interested in Irish fairy stories, and wrote extensively on them. She said the word *fairy* originated in ancient Persia, and in these passages described characteristics shared by both fairies and djinn:

The belief in a race of supernatural beings, midway between man and the Supreme God, beautiful and beneficent, a race that had never known the weight of human life, was also part of the creed of the Iranian people. They called them *Peris,* or *Ferouers* (fairies)... Every nation believes in the existence of these mysterious spirits, with mystic and powerful influence over human life and actions, but each nation represents them differently, according to national habits and national surroundings...

The Sidhe, or Fairies, of Ireland, still preserve all the gentle attributes of their ancient Persian race, for in the soft and equable climate of Erin there were no terrible manifestations of nature to be symbolized by new images; and the genial, laughter-loving elves were in themselves the best and truest expression of Irish nature that could have been invented. The Fairies loved music and dancing and frolic; and, above all things, to be let alone, and not be interfered with as regarded their peculiar fairy habits, customs, and pastimes. . . but the fairies were sometimes willful and capricious as children, and took dire revenge if any one built over their fairy circles, or looked at them when combing their long yellow hair in the sunshine, or dancing in the woods, or floating on the lakes. Death was the penalty to all who approached too near, or pried too curiously into the mysteries of nature.[1]

Lady Wilde believed the Irish names for fairies, *sidhe,* or *fead-rhee,* is a modification of the Persian term *peri.* The sidhe and the peri were comparable to the Egyptian and Greek concepts of demons, she said, and all were "a race midway between angel and man, gifted with power to exercise a strange, mysterious influence over human destiny." Her descriptions certainly fit the djinn as well.

---

1 Lady Wilde, *Ancient Legends, Mystic Charms, and Superstitions of Ireland* (Boston: Ticknor & Co., 1887), p. 1.

They Were Early Inhabitants of Earth Who Lost Their Dominion

Fairies, like the djinn, preceded humanity as a sentient race that inhabited the earth. In Irish lore, the original fairies were the Tuatha Dé Danaan ("the people of the goddess Danu"), said in some accounts to be directly descended from the gods. The fairies took up residency in Ireland, and possessed supernatural and magical powers. Over time, they lost battles to invaders and used their powers to retreat into the earth, into a parallel world where they could remain invisible and undisturbed.

They Are Outcasts from Their Realms

The djinn were cast out because they did not bow down to Adam, but rebelled under Iblis. Fairies have a number of origins, according to lore. In addition to being the original inhabitants of earth, they are said to be nature spirits, the souls of the pagan dead who cannot enter heaven, the ancestral dead, the guardians of the dead, supernatural creatures who are part human and part monster, and fallen angels. When Lucifer and his followers were thrown out of heaven, some didn't become demons of hell but fell to earth and became fairies. Although there are no equivalents of fallen angels in Islam, the fall of the djinn, and the transformation of Iblis into an evil parallel of Lucifer/Satan, has strong associations with the "fallen angel" explanation of fairies.

The belief that fairies were fallen angels is particularly strong in Irish and the Scottish Highland lore, where folklorist Alexander Carmichael recorded an oral version of the fallen angel story in which the fairies are cast out with the "Proud Angel," Lucifer.

In October of 1871, Carmichael and his traveling companion, the folklorist J. F. Campbell, were forced to wait out a storm on the island of Barra. They spent their time listening to the local folklore.

One of the storytellers was a ninety-two-year-old man named Roderick MacNeill, who had never worn shoes and never been ill, and who climbed about the sheer cliffs like an expert. MacNeill's account of the fairies follows:

The Proud Angel fomented a rebellion among the angels of heaven, where he had been a leading light. He declared that he would go and found a kingdom of his own. When going out at the door of heaven the Proud Angel brought *dealanaich dheilgnich agus beithir bheumnaich*, prickly lightning and biting lightning, out of the door-step with his heels. Many angels followed him—so many that at last the Son called out, 'Father! Father! The city is being emptied!' whereupon the Father ordered that the gates of heaven and of hell should be closed. This was instantly done; and those who were in were in, and those who were out were out; while the hosts who had left heaven and had not reached hell, flew into the holes of the earth *mar na famhlagan*, like the stormy petrels.

These are the fairy folks—ever since doomed to live under the ground, and only permitted to emerge when and where the King permits. They are never allowed abroad on Thursday, that being Columba's Day, nor on Friday, that being the Son's Day, nor on Saturday, that being Mary's Day, nor on Sunday, that being the Lord's Day.

God be between me and every fairy,
Every ill wish and every druidry,
To-day is Thursday on sea and land,
I trust in the King that they do not hear me.

On certain nights when their *bruthain*, bowers, are open and their lamps are lit, and the song and the dance are moving merrily, the fairies may be heard singing light-heartedly—

Not of the seed of Adam are we,
And Abraham is not our father,
But of the seed of the Proud Angel,
Driven forth from heaven.[2]

Variations of the fallen angel story are told in Western fairy lore. In some, the angels who become fairies were the unwitting dupes of the Proud Angel, and they fall into a netherworld where they are too wicked for heaven and too virtuous for hell; over time, they become increasingly dark and demonic in nature.

In these stories, we find strong parallels between the djinn and fairies: the fairies were angels in heaven who rebelled and vowed to form their own kingdom and they fell into holes on earth. The djinn rebelled and were banished and formed their own kingdoms, preferring to live in holes in the ground and caves. Deprived of their place and status, both djinn and fairies developed deep and long-standing grudges and the desire for revenge.

Some fairies and djinn removed themselves deeper into their own realm, content in the knowledge that foolish humans would at some point bring about their own demise, and they would be able to reclaim their places in the world. Others find opportunities to strike out against humans.

They Are Linked to the Demonic

As we see in the sections above, both djinn and fairies have become associated with the demonic and devils. As punishment for disobeying God's order to bow before Adam, Iblis was thrown out of paradise and became Shaitan, or Satan, and his djinn followers came to be regarded as demonic in nature. In fairy lore, fairies are

---

2 Alexander Carmichael, *Carmina Gadelica* (Edinburgh: T. & A. Constable, 1900), p. 353.

sometimes described as servants of the devil and witches, helpers in the carrying out of hexes, curses, and harmful magical spells.

Both djinn and fairies are also agents of possession.

They Are Hidden

The djinn are called the Hidden Ones because they are obscured from human sight. The Qur'an states, "He [the devil] and his tribe see you, while you do not see them."[3]

A story given in Celtic lore says that fairies are the offspring of Adam and Eve,[4] and earned their nickname "the hidden people" because of Eve's sin. After the fall, Adam and Eve have a great many children. One day, God was walking through the world, and he called on Eve and asked her to present her children. Ashamed at the great number of them, Eve sent half of them to hide, and presented the ones she thought were the best. God was not fooled, and said, "Let those who were hidden from me be hidden people."[5] So the fairies became invisible and hidden from sight—just like the djinn.

They Believe They Are Superior to Humans

Iblis proclaimed to God that the djinn, made of smokeless fire, were superior to humans, made of mere clay. Iblis went to Adam and made his attitude clear: "[Adam] if you are given mastery over me, I will surely disobey you. And if I am given mastery over you, I will destroy you."[6] After Iblis was cast out of Paradise, he sized

---

3 Al-Araf, 7.27.

4 In Norwegian lore, the fairies are the offspring of Adam and his first wife, Lilith, rather than Eve.

5 "Theories of Fairy Origins," http://waeshael.home.att.net/origins.htm#17.

6 Umar Sulaiman Al-Ashqar, *The World of Jinn and Devils* (Boulder, CO: Al-Basheer Publications and Translations, 1998), p. 69.

up Adam and found him to be hollow and without self-control; in other words, an easy target. He vowed revenge on Adam's descendants and told God: "Now, because You have sent me astray, verily I shall lurk in ambush for them on Your right path. Then I shall come upon them from before them and from behind them, and from their right and from their left, and you will not find most of them beholden [to You]."[7]

Fairies consider themselves to be superior to humans and know they have the ability to destroy them. Y.W. Evans-Wentz, an American anthropologist who collected fairy lore in the British Isles, Ireland, and Europe, heard many such descriptions. In the area around Ben Bulben Mountain in County Sligo, Ireland, a man gave him this description of fairies, who called themselves the Gentry:

> The folk are the grandest I have ever seen. They are far superior to us and that is why they call themselves the Gentry. They are not a working-class, but a military-aristocratic class, tall and noble-bearing. They are a distinct race between our race and that of spirits, as they have told me. Their qualifications are tremendous: "We could cut off half the human race, but would not," they said, "for we are expecting salvation." And I knew a man three or four years ago who they struck down with paralysis. Their sight is so penetrating I think they could see through the earth.[8]

They Have Long Life Spans, But Not Immortality

Time is something that fairies and djinn have in plenty. Both have much longer life spans than humans, though no one knows to what extent. As we noted in chapter 2, djinn live for thousands of years. In fairy lore, fairy life spans are much longer because of the

---

7 Al-Araf, 15–16.

8 Jacques Vallee, *Passport to Magonia* (Chicago: Henry Regnery Co., 1969), p. 27.

different passage of time in their world than on earth. Time passes much more slowly for fairies, and a day to them can be a year to humans.

There is no immortality for either djinn or fairies, however, and at some point, both must die. Their fate in the afterlife is uncertain, since, according to lore, both are damned in the eyes of God. Djinn and fairies await their fate at the Last Judgment.

According to Lady Wilde, when that day arrives, the fairies "are fated to pass into annihilation, to perish utterly and be seen no more."[9] Some of them nervously await salvation. Irish and Scottish stories tells of fairies asking a sympathetic human to inquire on their behalf about their fate. The human consults a sympathetic saint or priest, who always gives an unhappy answer: the fairies are doomed and have no hope of ever reentering heaven. Upon hearing this, the fairies always break out in great cries and lamentations.

When Iblis and the djinn were cast out of paradise, Iblis asked for reprieve until the Last Judgment Day when the dead are raised. However, he openly acknowledged that he would spend his time subverting and corrupting humans: "Do you see this [creation] that you have honored above me? If you give me grace until the Day of Resurrection, I will verily seize his seed, save but a few."[10] Even so, God granted his request.[11]

As for the fate of the djinn, the Qur'an states that djinn who become believers, that is, convert to Islam, will be taken to paradise while evil-doers will be sent into the hell fires along with evil-doing humans.

---

9 Wilde, *op. cit.,* p. 208.

10 Al-Israa, 62.

11 Al-Asaaf, 14–15.

They Are Organized Into Societies and Families

Djinn marry and have families that are organized in clans, and who are ruled by kings. Fairies also marry and have families, work at jobs, and are ruled by kings and queens. Both djinn and fairies keep pets, most notably dogs and cats.

They Must Pay Tributes to the Devil

In chapter 5, we noted that the djinn who serve a djinn king must pay him a tribute once a century. There are different kinds of tributes, but one of the most commonly cited is a human soul, which the djinn ensnare with enticements of physical pleasures, money, and power.

In fairy lore, fairies must pay a tribute to the devil every seven years, usually one of their own who is chosen by the devil himself. To avoid this terrible payment, stories tell of fairies kidnapping a human infant or sometimes a young child and offering it instead.

The famous story about Thomas the Rhymer, a Scottish laird and poet who lived in the thirteenth century, features this element of the Devil's tribute. According to the *Ballad of True Thomas*, which circulated in various versions through the sixteenth to nineteenth centuries, the handsome Thomas was kidnapped by the Queen of Elfland, who became infatuated with him. For seven years, he enjoyed himself in the beautiful realm of the elves. Toward the end of the seventh year, the fairies grew worried, for the devil's tithe was soon due, and they feared that the devil would choose Thomas because of his good looks. Reluctantly, the Queen of Elfland sent Thomas back to the Land Above (earth), and bestowed upon him the gift of prophecy.

They Have Supernatural Powers

Djinn and fairies possess supernormal strength and the power to be invisible at will. They can levitate themselves and whatever they carry and fly through the air. They materialize, pass through walls and solid objects, and can vanish into thin air. A woman in Ireland told Evans-Wentz about fairies, "When they disappear they go like fog; they must be something like spirits, or how could they disappear in that way?"[12] Fairies especially do not like to be seen by humans, and will punish those who accidentally espy them. Evans-Wentz tells the story of an Irish man who noticed a group of small fairies playing hurley while he was watering his cow. They saw him watching them, and immediately beat him so badly he could barely speak. During the night, however, they took pity on him and rubbed his face with a magical ointment to heal him.[13] In other stories, fairies will temporarily or permanently blind the person who sees them, by striking them across the eyes.

One of the most famous powers attributed to both djinn and fairies is the ability to grant wishes: as the imprisoned djinn is bound to grant three wishes to whomever frees him, fairies grant wishes to humans who do them good deeds. For example, an Irish story tells of a woman who finds a fairy dog in a state of exhaustion. She takes it home and nurses it back to health. Eventually the fairies find out where their dog is and come to fetch it. In gratitude, they ask the woman if she would like a dirty cow yard or a clean cow yard. She answers "dirty," because a cow yard would have to be empty in order to be clean. The fairies multiply the number of cattle she owns.

Djinn wishes seldom work out well, and fairies have been known to rescind their wishes, owing to their capricious nature. A com-

---

12   W.Y. Evans-Wentz, *The Fairy Faith in Celtic Countries* (New York: Carroll Publishing Group, 1990. First published 1911), p. 36.

13   *Ibid.*, 49.

mon story in fairy lore is of the fairy bride who bestows wishes and favors upon her human husband as long as certain conditions are met. If the conditions are broken—no matter how long they have been married—the fairy spouse and all the wishes, usually goods and livestock, vanish back into fairyland. Sometimes, the punishment seems impulsively devised. For example, fairies will pay for services rendered by humans, but with odd conditions, such as "do not look at your money until you get home." Of course the foolish person peeks at the money to see how much he has been given. Immediately, the money turns to something worthless, like dead leaves or ash.

Both djinn and fairies have supernatural healing abilities, and if motivated, may use them for our benefit, sometimes even granting us powers. Fairies sometimes give powers as an outright gift. Djinn are more likely to use powers as bargaining items in pacts, an exchange of favors for a soul.

They Are Masterful Shapeshifters

The djinn assume any form they wish, from animals to humans to angels. It is thought that instead of whispering to people directly, Satan will instead appear in human form, though usually with a strange-sounding voice or an indescribably strange appearance. Likewise, djinn may appear in front of humans and inform them of their nature, but they have been known to lie, often claiming to be angels. Sometimes they call themselves "invisible men" or they claim to be from the spirit world."[14] The "invisible men" perform miracles in order to look like servants of Allah, and some of them aid the infidels against Muslims.[15]

---

14 Al-Asqhar, *op. cit.,* p.131.

15 *Ibid.,* p. 136.

Fairies also can assume any form they wish. They often shape-shift into extremely attractive humans, especially when trying to lure a man or woman as an object of romantic desire. In Ireland, a story is told about fairies who assumed the forms of flies to engage in great battle among themselves. When the battle was over, the number of dead "flies" could have filled baskets.[16]

They Live in a Subterranean World

The djinn prefer to live in caves, holes, and other remote locations where they will not be bothered by people. In chapter 5, we saw the case of the man who was hiking and stepped on the "roof" of a hole occupied by a small man who may have been a green djinn. The description of the tiny man and his home in the ground might also be interpreted as a fairy emerging from his underworld den.

If mortals enter a djinn abode, they become trapped unless the djinn take pity and permit him to find his way out.

Fairies live beneath the ground in a secret land where they, too, will not be disturbed. The doorway to their world is often in a mound or fort, called a *howe* or *knowe* in Scotland, and a *rath* in Ireland. The doorway—akin to an interdimensional portal—is usually closed to mortals, but the occasional person may accidentally stumble through. Once through the door, the unlucky traveler becomes lost to the physical world, and is unable to find a way out without help. While in the fairy realm, people are subjected to fairy time, which is much slower than the way time passes for us normally. If the trapped people succeed in returning to the Land Above (as the mortal world is called), they may be shocked to find that their families and everyone they knew are long dead, while for them it would seem that only a week or two had passed.

16 Evans-Wentz, *op. cit.*, p. 39.

Sometimes fairies forcibly bring people to their realm, such as in the case of Thomas the Rhymer. Sometimes they grant access to people they like. In 1692, a Scottish minister named Robert Kirk of Aberfoyle was said to have been given repeated entry to the fairy realm. He enjoyed great favor until he broke one of their cardinal rules by traveling into the court of the evil fairies. As punishment, he was sentenced to permanent captivity in the fairy realm.

The area of Cnoc Meadha in western Ireland was renowned as a fairy stronghold. Inside the hill was reputed to be an entrance to their underground realm, where cave-like excavated passages led to the palace of Finnbheara, the king of the Connaught fairies.

Some fairies live among rocks, and some like to live in mines. Mine fairies are called kobolds, knockers, and Tommyknockers, and are heard knocking away in the tunnels with their hammers. Sometimes they help miners, and sometimes they hinder them.

There are few descriptions of the djinn world; those who have been there describe it as a horrific, terrifying place. Fairyland, on the other hand, is usually described as beautiful and pleasant, with a dreamy, ethereal quality to it. All who live there have nearly eternal youth. However, the evil fairies of Irish lore, such as members of the Unseelie Court (Unblessed Court), live in a dark and gloomy realm.

Fairies who live in dismal places often glamorously disguise them if they are able to entice humans into them. A Welsh story concerns an elderly couple whose maid disappeared, and was believed to have been abducted by the fairies. When the maid gave birth, fairies summoned the elderly woman to come to their realm and attend her. She was led to a cave that opened into a fine and beautiful bed chamber. She was given a magical ointment to rub on the infant's eyes, and was cautioned not to let any of it touch her own eyes. She accidentally touched her left eye with the ointment:

And now a strange thing happened: with the right eye she saw everything as before, gorgeous and luxurious as the heart could wish, but with the left eye she saw a damp, miserable cave, and lying on some rushes and withered ferns, with big stones all round her, was her former servant girl, Eilian. In the course of the day, she saw a great deal more. There were small men and small women going in and out, their movements being as light as the morning breeze. [17]

When the old woman was returned to the mortal world, she was warned not to tell anyone that she could see fairies. Every day she saw them, moving invisibly in the world right next to humans. One day she spied Eilian's husband stealing from the market and she confronted him. He took a bulrush and struck her left eye, blinding it for the rest of her life. Her fairy sight was gone.

They Are Territorial of Their Turf

Both djinn and fairies prefer privacy and do not appreciate humans trespassing on their territory, especially their homes. Both are found in remote areas—the caves, holes, and deserts characteristic of the Middle East, and secluded lakes, mountains, caves, forests, and glens elsewhere in the world.

Fairies are especially fond of certain kinds of trees on their turf, including elder, oak, ash, blackthorn, and hazel. They guard them jealously, and woe betide the person who cuts them down.

A cottager in Ireland once tried to cut a branch of a sacred elder tree that was hanging over a saint's well. The fairies who looked after the tree became angry. Twice they stopped the man by sending him a false vision that his house was burning. He raced home, only to find nothing amiss. He should have realized fairies were

---

17 "The Welsh Fairy Book," http://www.sacred-texts.com/neu/celt/wfb/wfb29.htm. Accessed November 2010.

intervening, but he was determined to cut the branch, and he succeeded on his third try. Again he had a vision that his house was burning, and he went home. He found his cottage burned to the ground.[18]

Similarly, but with less harsh consequences, is a story about Heart Lake near Sligo, Ireland. The lake was renowned as a portal fairies used to travel between worlds. A group of men once tried to drain the lake, but stopped when they had visions of their homes burning down. Like the cottager, they went rushing home, only to find everything intact. However, they had the sense to stop, and they left the lake alone.[19]

An example with dire consequences concerns a man foolish enough to violate fairy turf and insult them as well. Around 1920, plans were made to clear land for a hospital in Kiltamagh, Ireland. Among the trees to be cut down were two hawthorns everyone locally knew belonged to the fairies. Not one of the residents would touch the hawthorns, so the task fell to a man from out of town. When warned that the fairies would punish him if he cut the trees down, he angrily replied, "I'll be back, never fear, and to hell with your bloody fairies!" That night, the man suffered a stroke and was crippled. He died within a year. He returned to the town as he had vowed—but in a coffin. The hospital was built, but it never opened.[20]

The invisible paths that fairies use for their travel in the mortal world are called fairy tracks. It is especially risky to disturb them by building something upon them. The fairies will come right through the structure and create poltergeist-like phenomena, such

---

18 Briggs, *op. cit.*, pp. 159–60.

19 William Butler Yeats, *The Celtic Twilight: Men and Women, Ghouls and Faeries* (London: Lawrence & Bullen, 1893), p. 93.

20 D. A. McManus, *The Middle Kingdom: The Faerie World of Ireland* (London: Max Parrish), 1959, pp. 62–63.

as sudden openings and closings of doors and windows. Furthermore, the occupants will sicken, their crops will fail, and their animals will die. [21]

They Engage in Tricks and Acts of Malevolence

Both djinn and fairies punish people who displease them in many ways. Punishment may be slight, in the form of mischievous tricks that in older times meant things like stealing firewood, spooking livestock, or hiding lamp oil. In modern times, these creatures continue their pranks, affecting electricity in houses and interfering with lights, appliances, computers, and car batteries.

More serious punishments can adversely affect the health of people, animals, and crops. In the most extreme cases, djinn and fairies are not above murder. Acts of aggression against humans are usually the result of provocation, but some will strike on a whim.

Fairies and green djinn are both playful by nature and they love jokes and pranks, most of which are relatively harmless. They enjoy confusing travelers and leading them astray, causing worthless objects to look like great treasures, and wasting people's time. An oral account from the Isle of Man, a place rife with fairies, involves a postman making his deliveries in his horse-drawn cart in 1884. He was on a lonely road at about one o'clock in the morning when suddenly a swarm of red-suited little men came out of the bushes and surrounded him, halting his horse. They jumped aboard his wagon and started throwing the mail bags off. The man loaded them back on, only to have the little men throw them off again, laughing with great glee. Other little men danced wildly in the road. This went on for hours until dawn broke. The little men vanished and the postman was exhausted. Neither he nor anyone

---

21 Rosemary Ellen Guiley, *The Encyclopedia of Demons & Demonology* (New York: Facts On File, 2009), p. 85.

else could explain why this attack took place, except that the fairies enjoyed upsetting people.[22]

Other acts are harmful to people, sometimes in deadly ways. The djinn lift people up into the air and toss them like toys. According to the scholar Al-Asqar:

"They have been known to carry people through the wind and take them from place to place ... but this is only done with the evildoers who do not believe in Allah as the Lord of the Heavens and the Earth, or those people who do sinful acts."[23]

Fairies who feel wronged by people punish them by ripping them through the air at great speed, dropping them down into brambles and brush until they are bloody. A Welsh fairy tale tells of a farm wife who once found a fairy dog, and took it home but treated it cruelly. When the fairies found out, they picked her up and sent her on harrowing flights through the air. She was dipped into bogs and swamps and tossed through briars, until all of her clothes were torn off and she was scratched and bleeding.[24] The Sluagh, or "the Hosts," are wicked fairies renowned for their murderous nature. They swoop down and capture mortals, carrying them over land and sea. Then they drop their victims into mud and bogs, sometimes killing them. A Scottish account tells of a child snatched up one night by the Sluagh. It was returned the next day, lifeless, with the palms of its hands stuck into holes in the walls of its house.[25] The Sluagh also levitate cattle and abduct them for their food. When they have consumed all the meat, they take the hides and roll up old men in them, and let them fall to the ground.

---

22 Martin William, "Collecteana III In the Isle of Man" (*Folk-Lore*, vol. 3, 1902), p. 186.

23 Al-Ashqar, *op. cit.*, p. 131.

24 "The Welsh Fairy Book," *op. cit.*

25 Katharine Briggs, *The Vanishing People* (New York: Pantheon Books, 1978), p. 151.

They Cause Possession

Since ancient times, illnesses and afflictions—including strange behavior that today would be diagnosed as mental illness—have been blamed on spirits who have entered a person's body and possessed him or her. Both djinn and fairies are among the types of entities who possess people.

Sometimes both engage in possessions because they want to experience a human form. Fairies abduct humans during sleep and take them over; they are especially fond of beautiful children. The changeling is such a possession. Lore says that fairies have ugly children, and like to steal attractive human children at night, leaving their own infant in its place. The exchange is more like a possession, however, because the human child undergoes a transformation for the worse that includes physical and mental deteriorations and marked changes in personality. In some folklore accounts, such fairy-possessed children were called "demonic" and "evil."[26]

Certainly, some cases of alleged possession in earlier times can be explained by a lack of understanding of disease and illness. However, cases of entity possession seem to be on the rise worldwide. They are usually attributed to demons, but djinn and fairies may also be responsible.

They Are Weakened by Iron

In folklore, iron is one of the best and most universal weapons against anything evil: demons, djinn, fairies, vampires, the demonic offspring of Lilith, and a host of other bad supernatural entities. Iron saps strength and power. It is unknown exactly where this belief originated, but it was widespread even in ancient times. One reason may be the fact that human blood contains iron and has an

---

26 Guiley, *op. cit.*, pp. 85–86.

ironlike smell. Iron weapons and tools thus held the sympathetic magic of the life force, and could be used against things not human.

In some cultures, such as the ancient Babylonians, Egyptians, and Aztecs, iron was sacred and was believed to come from heaven—perhaps because iron is found in meteorites. The ancient Greeks and Romans would not allow iron in their temples or sacred rituals because it would repel spirits. For the same reason, ancient Saxons did not use iron rune wands in cemeteries in order to not disturb the dead.

Both djinn and fairies loathe iron. Recall the earlier story of the enslaved djinn who built King Solomon his temple: the djinn were afraid of having to work with iron tools. Solomon commanded them with a magical ring made of copper and iron, engraved with a talisman, a pentacle. The great king also imprisoned even the most powerful of djinn in bottles made of brass laced with magnetic iron (magnetite) to neutralize their "magic."

In Arabian lore, great desert whirlwinds were said to be the flights of evil djinn, and could be warded off with the cry of "Iron! Iron!" In India, iron amulets are worn to repel djinn.

According to the minister Robert Kirk, fairies told him that they were uncertain how their weakness against iron developed, but they knew it could burn them. In the old days when fairies still lived above ground, they discovered they had no protection against the iron swords and weapons of the early human invaders, much to their horror. Worst of all was cold iron, that is, pure iron not smelted from ore and hammered without melting. It was easier to retreat than to confront such weapons. Evidently there were some fairies who were never bothered by iron, or who gained immunity against it, for there are iron-working fairies in lore, especially among the mine fairies.

To keep fairies away, people used to put sharp iron scissors and tools in their homes. They tried to prevent fairy kidnappings of newborns by putting iron scissors underneath pillows or hanging them over beds. Iron nails and horseshoes were hung over doorways of homes and stables, and sometimes buried beneath thresholds.

They Mate with and Marry Humans

Djinn are capable of sexual intercourse, and they marry and breed among themselves. They also intermingle with humans. Not only is this undesirable from a human perspective, it is forbidden according to Muslim law. The Qur'an states that Allah "created for you mates from yourselves that you might find rest in them, and He ordained between you love and mercy."[27] This prohibition especially applies to djinn, because they are the closest entities to humans. The offspring of djinn-human unions are considered abominations: they are said to be sterile and aggressive to such a point that they exhibit sociopath behavior. Such children also are said to exhibit great psychic powers and have a strong influence on human beings. The children of a female djinni are said to be invisible, like her, but the children of a male djinni appear more like humans.[28]

One alleged offspring of a djinni-human union is the famous Queen of Sheba, who captured the interest of King Solomon. Although the Qur'an never mentions her by name, Arabian stories refer to her as Bilqis.[29] According to lore, her father was a human king by the name of Al-Hadhad and her mother was a djinni named Marlis. The story goes that Marlis was pursued by evil djinn (red

27 *Ibid.*, p. 29.

28 Drieskens, *op.cit.*, p. 99.

29 No one knows precisely where the kingdom of Sheba was located, but modern historians believe it was in or near modern-day Yemen.

djinn) and was injured in a battle. Al-Hadhad found her wounded, and rescued and hid her. They fell in love and had a child together.

When Bilqis was fifteen, she was quite aggressive and uncontrolable. She quickly rose to the position of queen by eliminating all those who stood in her way. It was said that her methods of persuasion were only surpassed by her beauty, and because of this, Solomon was enchanted by her. The great king's advisors told him he shouldn't become involved with the queen, as she was the daughter of a djinn and a relationship was forbidden by God. Solomon wouldn't let go of his interest, and thought of a way to secretly find out if Bilqis was indeed half-djinn.

The offspring of a human and djinn were believed to have a great amount of hair on their legs and feet that would give away their true identity. When Solomon invited the queen to his palace, he had the floor that led to his throne made of a shiny, glass-like material. When Bilqis entered the great hall, she thought it was water, so she raised her skirt, enabling him to see her feet and ankles. He was relieved to see them hairless. However, in an Arabian tale—which many scholars feel is embellished—Bilqis craftily removed all the hair from her legs and feet before visiting Solomon's palace.

In another version of this story, the djinn spread the lie that Bilqis had the feet of an ass. They knew she was the daughter of a djinni, and if she married Solomon, their children would be even more cunning and powerful than Solomon himself, as they would have djinn blood. The enslaved djinn were afraid that any djinn-human offspring would further enslave them.

It is clear from the sparse historical accounts of the Queen of Sheba that, djinn or not, she had considerable power and influence. She influenced the other rulers, including the pharaoh of Egypt, not to attack Israel because she wanted the kingdom for herself. Today, this type of power might be considered a kind of psychic mind control.

Since the days of the legendary Queen of Sheba, Middle Eastern people of both sexes have claimed sexual unions and marriages
with djinn. In the United Arab Emirates is a clan that claims descent from a female djinni, despite their normal appearance. The
claim is unsupported.[30] Other modern accounts of human-djinn
marriages exist. Young men who cannot afford to marry women
sometimes visit a priest or sheikh who will marry them to a female djinni. They know the djinni will be jealous and will insist
on strange conditions within the marriage. These husbands cannot talk about their djinn wives, or else they will drive them in-
sane or possess them in unpleasant ways. The men cannot look at
any mortal female, and they must always knock before entering
a room. Stories resembling urban legends are told of the horror
that awaits the man who enters a room occupied by his djinni wife
without knocking:

> Amira told me about her cousin who was married to a djinni.
> For a year, he and his djinn-wife had lived happily together,
> and they even had a son. One day, the man forgot about the
> stipulation of knocking before entering, and he stumbled upon
> a horrifying scene. The *ginniya* had taken on a different shape.
> She was hairy and ugly with vertical eyes in her black face. She
> was cooking and their child was crying hungrily in the other
> room. The moment the man entered, he saw her breast, black
> and ugly, passing by on its own to feed the baby. The *ginniya*
> disappeared, taking her son with her, and never returned again.
> In Amira's story, her cousin came away relatively unscathed. In
> other similar cases, the human lover ends up blind or loses his
> mind.[31]

30 Al-Ashqar, *op. cit.*, p. 22.

31 Barbara Drieskens, *Living with Djinns: Understanding and Dealing with the Invisible
    in Cairo* (London: SAQI, 2006), p. 182.

Sometimes the djinn marital partners are described as the qarin, the djinn companion assigned at birth, or a *makhawi*, a term for djinn who fall in love with humans. If a woman marries a makhawi, they live together as a normal husband and wife. The makhawi appears only at night to sleep with his mortal wife and has certain conditions that must be met. In exchange for having all her needs fulfilled, the wife is forbidden from disclosing the true nature of her husband. If she does, he will mistreat her. It is believed that the most beautiful women of all will be chosen for wives by a makhawi.[32]

Green djinn can develop fascinations and romantic attachments with humans. While sexual or legal union may not always be the result, the green djinn's infatuation can interfere with normal relationships.

Fairies are renowned for falling in love with humans and marrying them, producing hybrid children. A love-struck fairy will follow a human around, much like an infatuated green djinn. Fairies try to lure their beloved into their own world, where they can be imprisoned. Sometimes if they cannot succeed with enticement, they resort to kidnapping. In fairy lore, if a young mortal wife or husband dies, they are believed to have been carried off by the fairies. They die to the mortal world, but remain alive in another form in the fairy kingdom.

Humans may fall in love with fairies and can marry them, for fairies bring many blessings to such a union. A human husband-fairy wife union is more common in lore than the reverse. Sometimes, humans can convince fairies to live in our physical world. Like the djinn-human marriages, human-fairy relationships have conditions. If the human spouse fails to live up to the requirements set by the fairy spouse, the blessings, the marriage, and the fairy vanish.

---

32 *Ibid.*, pp. 182–83.

One story tells of a husband who is warned by the father of a fairy bride to never strike his wife. If he does so three times, she and all her blessings will disappear forever. In some versions of this story, the husband minds his manners, sometimes for many years, but inadvertently strikes his wife on three separate occasions.

In fairy lore, the hybrid fairy-human offspring are considered strange, but they are not necessarily abominations. Like djinn-human offspring, they possess unusual supernatural powers.

Leprechauns

Leprechauns are among the most famous creatures of Irish lore. They are often called fairies, but may be in a class of their own. Their name derives from the Gaelic *luacharma'n,* ("pygmy"), or *leith brogan* ("maker of one shoe"). Originally, the name was used only in a part of northern Ireland, but over time the leprechaun became "nationalized" as one of the most familiar of Irish fairies.

Leprechauns are described in appearance as old men about two feet tall, often dressed in green or like a shoemaker, with a cocked hat, leather apron, and upturned toes on their shoes. They are jovial when left to their own devices, but are hostile toward humans. Like many djinn, they prefer solitude. They spend their time making shoes for fairies—always one shoe, never a pair. The sounds of their cobbling can be heard in remote areas. They like to drink intoxicating brews.

Leprechauns are famous for guarding their hidden treasure, usually a pot of gold buried in a secret cache or at the end of a rainbow. Leprechauns are usually invisible, but if one of them is seen and captured, he will promise to take a person to his treasure if allowed to go free. In djinn-like fashion, the leprechaun's promises turn out poorly for humans. En route to the treasure, the person must never take his eyes off the leprechaun, not even for a second, or the leprechaun will vanish. Or, the leprechaun will bargain with false money from one of two leather pouches that he always carries. One holds a silver shilling or coin that returns to the pouch each time it is paid out. The other holds a gold coin the leprechaun uses for bargaining its way out of tough situations. However, the coin turns to leaves or ashes after the human takes it and lets the leprechaun go.

The tale of Patrick O'Donnell and the leprechaun bears striking resemblance to stories about tricky, wish-granting djinn. Out in the woods one day, O'Donnell found a leprechaun caught on a long black thorn. He offered to help the little fellow in exchange for being taken to his pot of gold. The leprechaun agreed. He took O'Donnell through the woods, trying to trick him into looking away, but O'Donnell was wise to that trick and kept his eyes on the leprechaun. Finally, the leprechaun took him deep into a swamp filled with hundreds of blackthorn bushes. The leprechaun stopped at one, and said the gold was buried beneath it. O'Donnell realized he now had a problem, for he did not have any tools for digging up the treasure. The leprechaun declined further help, pointing out he had fulfilled his end of the bargain. O'Donnell decided to go home and fetch a shovel. Before leaving, he tied his red scarf to the bush so he would be able to find his way back. The leprechaun laughed, knowing he has outwitted the man. Free to go, the leprechaun disappeared. O'Donnell fetched his shovel—but when he returned to the swamp, he found that every thorn bush had a red scarf tied to it. He never found the treasure.[33]

In the *Leprechaun* horror films (four have been released since 1993), the leprechaun becomes even more djinn-like. In the first film, a man steals gold coins from an evil leprechaun, who exacts revenge by killing the man's wife by causing her to fall down stairs. The man imprisons the leprechaun in his basement, using a four-leaf

---

33 Kathleen Krull, *A Pot O' Gold: A Treasury of Irish Stories, Poetry, Folklore, and (of Course) Blarney* (Hyperion Books for Children, 2004), pp. 147–151.

clover as the seal that nullifies the little man's supernatural powers. He attempts to destroy the leprechaun with fire, but collapses of a stroke. He is taken to a nursing home, and the leprechaun is left in a crate. Ten years later, others discover the crate and accidentally release him. The leprechaun goes on a marauding spree of violence in revenge against his imprisonment. He is finally destroyed in a fire explosion—but only temporarily, for he can be revived at some point in the future as long as his gold is missing.

The leprechaun's supernatural abilities mirror those of the djinn: the granting of three wishes that get twisted, levitation, and supernormal strength. In subsequent films, the leprechaun has the power to start fire, bend reality (in earlier times this was called bewitchment or glamour), enter and possess human bodies, regenerate damaged body parts, and create mysterious force fields. Like the djinn in the *Wishmaster* films, he can survive most attempts to destroy him. Ultimately, however, the human protagonists find a fatal weakness.

In Closing

There is considerable overlap between djinn and fairies, and we have touched only on the major similarities. We believe the djinn use many entities as "fronts" for interacting with humans, but fairies, with their diverse traits and rich lore, provide some of the best disguises. Certainly many human involvements with fairies are with fairies. However, the gray and shifting territory shared by fairies and djinn should cause us to reexamine and reevaluate our contact experiences.

ALIENS, DJINN, AND UFOS

THE PHENOMENA OF UNIDENTIFIABLE OBJECTS seen in the sky have been with the human race since the dawn of history. Although most modern "investigators" are more interested in searching for alien spaceships from other star systems, the answer to at least part of the UFO mystery may not be as easy or apparent. The late Dr. J. Allen Hynek, who was considered to be the world's foremost authority on UFOs, once stated, "I would be disappointed if they (UFOs) all turned out to be someone else's spaceships from another planet. I believe the explanation to the total sum of the UFO experience to be more exotic."[1] Dr. Hynek spoke of visitors originating not from another planet or galaxy, but from a parallel reality. A parallel reality could also be interpreted as another dimension, and to us, this sounded like the home of the djinn.

---

1 Dr. J.Allen Hynek (1910–1986) was an astronomer best remembered for his UFO research. Hynek acted as scientific adviser to UFO studies undertaken by the US Air Force under Project Sign (1947–1949), Project Grudge (1949–1952), and Project Blue Book (1952–1969). Hynek coined the term "close encounter."

This is not to say that all or even some UFO reports are not extraterrestrial in origin, but we must consider that a certain percentage of these encounters could be djinn manifestations. The UFO experience is quite inclusive in its material, and it is our opinion that some sightings and close encounters are more phantasmic than solid and physical in nature.

Many of the UFO "saucers" described by witnesses are characterized as being discs of light that change shape and have the ability to pop in and out of vision. Reports about UFOs such as these are more paranormal in nature and are often ignored by investigators because they fail to fit the alien "spaceship" theory.

There are many close encounter UFO cases that involve contact with some type of intelligence that will often identify itself as an extraterrestrial, angelic, or sometimes the devil. It is in experiences like this that we should suspect an interdimensional being that is trying to cover its true identity. Islamic scholars describe the djinn as glowing objects that can change their shape and at times take on a physical form. We have many "UFO" cases in our files that describe encounters like this; for years they were labeled as "High Strangeness."[2] However, when the idea of the djinn is placed into the equation, these bizarre cases seem to make more sense.

The Voice of Deceit

A Qur'an passage says evil djinn will try to persuade humans by whispering in their ear.[3] That "whispering voice" in the ear can be also interpreted as a form of telepathy. This phenomenon is common not only in cases involving UFO contactees and other para-

---

2 The term "high strangeness" was used by Hynek to describe those UFO cases that did not fit the normal bulk of reports. They include electromagnetic effects, abductions, the appearance of strange beings, and psychic communication with an alien intelligence.

3 An-Nas, 114.

normal experiences, but also in religious or mystical visions. Priests and other Christian clerics of the late medieval period in Europe believed angels whispered in the ears of men and women with a familiar voice to influence or guide them. It seems obvious these heavenly visitors chose not to appear, but only to speak, so as not to cause panic or fear. However, we must ask ourselves: are angels really the ones communicating with these "special" people, or are they really djinn? It could be argued that because angels and djinn use the same methods, one can't be entirely sure.

Since 1983, Phil has investigated countless UFO sightings and claims of "alien" contact in New York's Hudson River Valley. These are documented in his book *Night Siege: The Hudson Valley UFO Sightings*. At the time, Phil did not know what to make of the related contact cases—they did not fit into the overall "UFO sighting" picture. They were labeled as "high strangeness" and filed away. After reviewing them twenty years later, it is obvious some of these cases were in fact dimensional rather than extraterrestrial encounters, and may have involved djinn. One must remember that when we speak of "dimensional beings," we are referring to the djinn. In the case below the experiencer had a UFO sighting and later, contact with an unknown intelligence that was particularly careful to withhold identifying information.

Night Fright and Missing Time

The witness, whom we will refer to as Sam, was a thirty-year-old computer programmer at the time of the experience. On April 23, 1990, at about 10 PM, Sam was driving home on Route 164 in Patterson, New York, from a friend's house in nearby Fishkill. This particular road is very dark at night, as there are no street lights and very few homes. As Sam drove along the dark, winding road, he began to feel uneasy, like something bad was about to happen. He slowed down and looked into the woods on both sides of the road, expecting a deer or some other animal to dart out in front of him. Sam often got feelings like this in the past, and on more than one occasion, he would listen to this inner voice and take the appropriate action, only to nearly miss what would have been an injurious accident or otherwise unpleasant encounter.

On this night, Sam noticed a solid glowing object on his left, just above the tree line. The object was pulsating, and was yellow-red in color. The lights seemed too low to be a plane, and appeared to be several hundred yards away. The pine trees along the road partially obstructed his view, so he continued to drive, but slowly. He came to a clearing and stopped his car and noticed that the object had gotten much closer to him. As he watched, the object moved directly over his car. Sam rolled down his car window and watched the object for about a minute or so. He decided he wanted to get a better look, and stopped the car and got out. He sat on the hood and watched this object, which he described as about the same size as a "minivan" and about a hundred feet above his head. The object changed in shape from an oval to a perfect circle. Sam reported feeling heat coming from the object as well. He was surprised to see five small figures gathering around the edges of the light as if they were looking at him. He got the impression that this object was some type of window, and although he saw only silhouettes, he was certain they looked humanoid in shape. The object dipped lower and seemed to grow in size. Eventually, it became so large and low that it blocked all of Sam's view of the sky. The object then began to move very slowly, and Sam was amazed that something of that size could move so slowly and be as silent. Sam's amazement gave him the sense that the object "was not part of our universe and [was] peering in from another dimension." Then, something strange took place: the next thing Sam remembered was driving down the road, the object completely gone. He did not remember getting back into the car, seeing the object completely pass over, or finding the road again.

When Sam finally arrived home, he discovered it was much later than he had thought. He estimates the entire sighting was under ten minutes, yet the trip home took him three hours. He had a difficult time sleeping that night and felt as if something was watching him from the dark corners of his bedroom. For the next week, he woke up in the middle of the night feeling very confused, in a cold sweat, his heart pounding. He somehow knew these episodes of night terror had something to do with the UFO he had seen. As the weeks passed, Sam found it very hard to concentrate on his work and was fearful of going out at night—he felt the UFO was waiting to get him alone in an isolated place. Sam also said that sometime after the sighting, he would wake up in the middle of the night and stare into the dark. He said he felt as if something was in the corner of the room, waiting for him to fall asleep so it could come and get him. This type of fear is not uncommon in such cases—many witnesses report feeling a personal connection with the UFO they see and feel strongly that some kind of entity is out in the night waiting for them to fall asleep so it can enter their homes and take them. This feeling may actually be some type of psychic connection with this dimensional intelligence.

For several weeks, everything seemed to return to normal. Then one night, near the end of June, Sam woke up to find his whole bed vibrating. He looked at the wall across the room and saw a circular hole forming that was jet black. Sam tried to get up, but to his horror, realized he was unable to move. He claims he was "levitated" off the bed and floated into the opening of some type of "vortex." Sam then found himself lying on a table in a dark room. Several beings were standing around him; the one near his left side was moving some type of instrument around his head. Sam tried to move, but every part of his body was paralyzed. He described the beings as short, with gray skin and round eyes. As he watched, the beings all changed in shape to a glowing light, then into a form that horrified him: they looked like demons with long pointed ears and very "ugly, gargoyle-like faces." They inserted something into his nose and navel that caused him a great deal of pain.

After the insertion procedure was finished, Sam was allowed to get up. One of the beings escorted him through a passage that glowed red. Sam got the impression he was in a cave, but thought that perhaps he had died and was in hell. At no time was there any spoken communication, but Sam knew where the being wanted him to go and what it wanted him to do. He was shown a panel composed of a grayish material that had "many projections" coming out of it. He looked around. Although the room he was in was dimly lit, he was able to see a corridor to his right that led to another room. The being then looked at him, and he got a strong feeling that he was not allowed to go there.

The entity who escorted him then put thoughts in his mind. Sam now knew that they were from another dimension and he received information that they were once on earth a long time ago and were in the process of working to come back. Their reason was because unless they did so, their race would become extinct. Then, without warning, Sam found himself back in his bed.

Sam believes the beings will come back for him some day, and when they do, he will not be allowed to return. His entire life has changed and he claims to be in some type of mental contact with the dimensional entities. Sam feels he is gathering information for them, and what he sees and experiences is somehow being transmitted. Sam said that although the beings were hesitant to give him detailed information, he knows they come from a desolate plane of existence, and they envy us because our planet is so beautiful. Sam said the beings are angry that humans are polluting earth as they themselves made the same mistake a long time ago, and have no real place to call home as a result. Sam said living here would be problematic for them, but they are slowly adapting themselves so that future generations will be able to live in our environment.

Sam said these creatures have considerable trouble understanding our emotions. They consider us an immature race that is bent on self-destruction. He feels the beings are using him in order to understand humans and how we react in different situations. Sam is convinced the beings he encountered that night are "emissaries from the devil," and they are out to destroy the human race and take over our world so that they can live here. As of the writing of this book, Sam has become a born-again Christian and refuses to have any further involvement in UFOs or other types of paranormal phenomenon. Sam's case is one of many in which the experiencer who was once an atheist scared or indifferent to embracing a religious belief, comes to fervently believe in an all-loving and protecting God.

Djinn seem to take the guise of alien extraterrestrials to hide their true nature. This is not to say that all UFO experiences are caused by djinn, but some experiences, like Sam's, may be ultraterrestrial rather than extraterrestrial.

A Master Trickster

The following case study involves "Ben," a man in his late thirties. At the time of his encounter, Ben had a family and a good job, and an interesting history of contact—he had experiences as a child. At the age of six, he once woke up in the middle of the night to see a creature standing at the foot of his bed. He described the entity as tall, with scaly skin that looked like an "alligator" with a green glow around it. He watched in total terror, too afraid to scream for his parents. The entity then looked at him and said, "In the future, I will come for you again and then we shall talk about how you may serve me." The creature's eyes flashed red. It turned into a cloud of black smoke and went right through the bedroom's closed window without breaking it. As soon as the "smoke" left the room Ben was able to move again. Crying in terror, he screamed for his parents. His parents told him what he had seen was nothing more than a nightmare and that it was not real. He wanted to believe them, but deep down, he knew the visitation really had happened. For the next five years, Ben had to sleep with several nightlights on, as he was dreadfully afraid the "monster" was going to come back for him.

After the initial paranormal experience as a child the rest of his life was normal, and as he got older he forgot about the threat of the entity to return. He got married at twenty-five, landed a job as a building inspector for the State of New York, and led a normal life. On his thirty-fifth birthday, he woke up in the wee hours of the morning and was shocked to see the same creature he had seen as a child, once again standing at the foot of the bed. He was so terrified he couldn't move—he was again paralyzed with fear. Ben couldn't so much as scream to wake his wife, who was sleeping soundly right next to him. The creature looked exactly the same, and when it spoke, its eyes flashed red. It was wearing what looked like a very thick suit made of some type of rubber. In an interview, Ben told us the creature was so horrible-looking, he was sure it was the devil. The being then said in a coarse, deep voice, "I am from another place, another planet if you wish. Do you remember me? I have returned and will be with you until the transition is made." Ben did not understand what the being meant, and still has no idea today.

The entity said his name was Orlis and that he was part of an ancient group of beings who have been around since humans were nothing more than "monkeys." Orlis said he would make amazing things appear in the sky in the next few days. Just before the creature vanished, Ben heard a voice in his right ear give a number of dates: September 28, September 30, and November 6, all at 8:30

PM. Sure enough, on all three dates, a large, glowing "egg" shaped object appeared in the sky over his hometown of Kingston, New York. Dozens of people witnessed the UFO, which was described as yellow in color and hovering and making circular motions in the sky. One witness said that "at times, the object would move so fast that it looked like a bright glowing 'infinity sign' (a lemniscate) in the night sky. In anticipation for the next two dates, Ben called his neighbors just before 8:30 in the evening to watch for the "UFO" he knew would appear as the being promised. He was correct all three times: he and his neighbors watched the sky on those dates and at those times and saw the "glowing yellow egg" make its strange maneuvers.

The fact that Ben was able to predict when this object would appear was remarkable enough to warrant a visit by us. During our visit, five different neighbors corroberated his story. This was the first time in Phil's thirty-plus years of investigating UFOs that someone was able to accurately predict when a sighting would take place. Over the next few weeks, we would visit Ben quite frequently and with each interview, his story would get more incredible.

In our first conversation with Ben, he told us he was in mental contact with a being from another universe. He said this being purposefully arranged for the UFO to be seen by him and multiple witnesses. The being did this, he said, to prove the contact was real and he was not crazy. Ben was told he was contacted from a very early age and was specially selected to bring information to the human race from a race of ancient people that once lived on earth. Although the being never told Ben exactly where he was from, he did tell him he was part of a race that was non-physical, composed entirely of energy, existing in another dimension. The being that identified itself as Orlis told Ben that they were "responsible" for the human race and were trying to straighten things out because an experiment had gone wrong. They were correcting their mistakes by contacting certain people like Ben to give information to help our species.

Ben was in contact with the being on a mental level for several months, never actually seing Orlis in person. The communications became more frequent after photographs were taken. Orlis would wake Ben up at all hours of the night to "talk" and give him information about future events and UFO sightings around the world. These conversations became a major concern for his wife and two children, who would witness Ben having a conversation with nothing but the air. Eventually, Ben learned that he did not have to talk—Orlis could read his thoughts. Soon after, all their conversations were on a telepathic level, Ben thinking the questions and Orlis giving him an immediate answer.

Unfortunately, the information Ben received never really checked out. For example, one night Ben called Phil very late to tell him there were going to be massive UFO sightings over France and major earthquakes and natural disasters within the week, but nothing happened. At that point, it seemed the only correct information Orlis gave Ben was in his initial contact about the UFOs that would appear in the sky. As stated above, this was indeed verified—a number independent witnesses verified the sightings and the local paper carried a number of stories.

After a time, communications with Orlis became so frequent they began to interfere with Ben's job. While driving his car, Orlis would tell Ben he was going the wrong way, and so Ben would turn around, only to get lost and go on wild goose chases for hours before reaching his destination. One night, Orlis told Ben there was going to be a starship landing in Connecticut, and they would finally meet face-to-face. Ben got into his car in the wee hours of the morning, and began driving to the location Orlis had given him. He did not really want to go, but by then, he knew that if he disobeyed Orlis' "command," he would torment Ben all night and prevent him from sleeping.

Ben drove in circles for an hour until Orlis directed him to a dirt road and a fenced area just outside Pawling, New York. He was instructed to climb the fence, ignoring the "No Trespassing" signs posted around the perimeter. After climbing the fence, he walked through a field, eventually seeing some structures and huge antennas ahead. He made his way toward them when he suddenly heard a noise and was blinded by a brilliant white light. The light was so bright, he couldn't see anything; he stood motionless, waiting to find out who had found him. Ben was sure the light was coming from a ship and that the outline of the figure approaching him was Orlis, but it was not. Ben had actually been stopped by a military security patrol. Orlis had directed Ben to a secret government installation we later found out was partially operated by the National Security Agency. Ben was arrested for trespassing and his wife was called to come and get him the next day. When Ben told his fantastic story about his communications with Orlis, he was forced to get psychiatric help and was placed on several drugs. Ben told us that when he started taking the drugs, communications with Orlis stopped, but he can still feel his presence. He knows that if he does stop taking his drugs, the communications will continue where they left off.

Ben's case is bizarre, but not unique. The whispering voice in his ear, the mixture of true and false information, the torment—all point to contact with djinn. Often, djinn entities may approach selected individuals and use extraterrestrial guises. To gain a person's confidence and interest, the djinn may say the individual was specially selected to help the human race save itself from some worldwide catastrophe or other form of widespread destruction. The combination of urgency and trust opens the person up, allowing a djinni to continue its link with this reality and in the long run, assume direct control of the person.

Glowing Orbs, Aliens, and Djinn

Earlier, we gave an account from Turkey wherein six friends wanted to have some scary fun and summon a djinni. To their surprise (and misfortune), the djinn appeared, but refused to take on physical forms; the witnesses described the djinn presences as looking like several brilliantly glowing orbs. The following case comes from the United States and also involves orbs of light, but this time they took the form of the "gray aliens" common in UFO stories.

On October 29, 2007, the witness, a twenty-eight-year-old man whom we shall refer to as Ted was returning about eleven in the evening to his home in Lake Carmel, New York, from a friend's house along Route 52 near Stormville, a nearby town. Route 52 becomes quite isolated around the Storm King Mountain area. The main danger is hitting a deer or other animal as it crosses the road—but in this case, the witness would have something more to worry about. As Ted drove south on 52, he saw a large, lit object in the sky. He stopped his car and got out and observed an object he described as being the size of a large commercial jet pass directly overhead at low altitude. What surprised him the most was that although this aircraft was quite large and flying quite low, it made no noise at all. The object consisted of twenty or so bright white, yellow, green, and red lights in a V shape formation. As he watched, the UFO slowed down almost to a halt and he suddenly felt scared. He felt a pressure in his head he interpreted as the object (or someone inside it) trying to communicate with him. Although Ted claims to not have heard a voice, he felt a strong presence he described to us as being "not human." Without warning, Ted felt as if "ants were crawling" up and down his back, and a strange blast of heat went around him. After ten seconds or so, the sensations ceased and the object vanished in the sky, right before his eyes. The rest of the trip home was uneventful.

The next day, Ted called the state police and was told he probably saw nothing more than a group of private pilots who enjoyed flying around at night, faking the appearance of a UFO. The officer asked Ted if he wanted to file an official UFO police report, but he declined. Although he didn't really believe the officer's explanation for his encounter, Ted thanked him for his time and attention. Ted told us, "I wanted to argue the point that this couldn't have been any type of conventional aircraft, but I decided it was a good idea to just drop the issue, especially when the officer wanted to bring me in to headquarters to make an 'official statement.'"

In the week that followed the encounter, Ted strongly felt something was in his bedroom late at night. He would wake up at about the same time, between two and four in the morning, and felt as if someone was watching him. Ted reported to us that the presence he felt was "evil" in nature, and was so strong that he got out of bed several times to search the house, including all the closets and under the bed, to make sure no one was hiding somewhere. In an interview, he told us, "It was strange—for a week after that sighting of the UFO, I felt uneasy. Usually, I'm a very sound sleeper, but I kept waking up. In the morning, I would feel drained of energy, as if some type of vampire was visiting me at night and taking my blood or life force."

When we asked if he ever woke up with marks on his body or nose bleeds, he replied that nothing like that ever took place; he only felt tired and weak. Despite his willingness to talk, it seemed to us that Ted was holding back and much more happened than he was letting on. When Phil asked him if indeed this was the case, Ted replied, astonished, "How did you know? I was afraid to tell you, but I should tell you about what happened if we're ever going to find out what's really going on." We encouraged him to continue with his story. With a considerable amount of hesitation, Ted proceeded to describe a late-night visitation he had with an alien force that still had him stricken with fear.

Was It Aliens or Djinn?

Ted told us that in mid-November, he opened his eyes one night and noticed a faint greenish glow on the wall that faced the foot of the bed. He tried to get up, but was unable to move his arms and legs. As Ted watched, the glow became brighter until three balls of light came through the wall with a "whooshing" sound. The lights were all about the same size, approximately the "size of a large cantaloupe." As Ted watched them, the lights began to pulsate from orange to white, emitting heat. The globes of lights stayed motionless for five seconds or so, and then began to change form. As Ted watched in fear, the globes of lights changed into three small "gray aliens" that were only a few feet tall and very thin. He told us, "They were classical aliens you see in the movies, television, and magazines, with the large heads and big eyes, in some type of dark, tight-fitting outfit."

The "aliens" threw glances at each other and began to walk toward the bed. Ted knew they were going to do something very bad to him, so with all of his focused energy, he broke the paralyzing hold and sat up in the bed. Ted then pointed his finger at the beings and yelled, "I now know you are not aliens, but sent from the devil and in the name of Jesus Christ, I order you to leave me alone!" The beings stopped in their tracks, looking quite caught off-guard. They morphed into their glowing orb forms and retreated through the wall. To our knowledge, this was Ted's final experience, as he never called us again. Perhaps once they were unmasked, the djinn no longer wanted to bother with him.

Glowing orbs are often spotted in areas where UFOs are seen, but can also appear in haunted or cursed areas, and other locations rife with paranormal activity. In recent years, thousands of people have been coming forward with photographs of strange orbs of all shapes and colors they have digitally captured. Although imaging scientists and photographic experts have a multitude of explanations for a good number of them, there are an equal number that baffle even the most skeptical. Ghost hunters believe the orbs are discarnate spirits; UFO hunters think they represent some type of alien probe; some channelers and spiritualists believe they are angels; and some paranormal investigators think they represent a phenomenon called a "spook light." Perhaps none of these theories are correct.

It could very well be that the glowing lights are green djinn. A possible reason why they are appearing more and more is because our reality is merging with the djinn world. In many cases, these orbs are invisible to the naked eye and can only be occasionally picked up on digital cameras. These so-called invisible orbs have been imaged in and around the mysterious stone chambers of New York, and also around places Native Americans believe are sacred. Whatever they are, they seem to be dimensional in nature and most likely are always around us, but out of our limited range of perception.

The Cursed Estate: A Djinn Portal

The following case came to our attention in the fall of 2007, shortly after Phil did a radio interview for a syndicated show that broadcasted over most of northeast America. It involved a retired man named Martin who purchased a house in Holmes, New York. Martin's wife had passed away a number of years ago from a long-term illness, and his children were all adults, married and with children of their own. Martin said he was ready to spend some time alone and continue with his life. His home was on several acres of property, and despite being built in 1830, was in pristine condition. He remarked that he was surprised he was able to purchase the four-bedroom home plus the land at a phenomenally low price. The deal seemed too good to be true, and it immediately made him suspicious. However, the building inspector said the home was sound, so he went ahead and purchased it. After Martin moved in, he would discover the *real* reason why the house had so many owners since its construction, and why it was always offered well below market value.

Martin moved into the new home in the fall of 2006 and was quite excited—it was in a beautiful location and had quite a bit of room for a study, library, and workshop. From the first day Martin moved in, strange things began to happen. Lights would turn off and on by themselves, objects such as loose change, car keys, books, food, and even furniture would disappear overnight and never return. During the night, he heard footsteps in the house and unusual sounds he thought were electrical in nature. Doors would slam in the wee hours of the morning, causing him to jump out of bed in fear of home invasion. He never found anything. On numerous occasions, the faucets in the kitchen and bathrooms would be left running overnight and while he was out of the house, resulting in floods that damaged floors and ceilings.

On more than one occasion, Martin saw shadowy images in the rooms and heard sounds like a group of people chanting in some ancient language he could not identify. One winter evening while downstairs having coffee with two friends, they all heard heavy walking in the bedroom above. He told us, "It sounded like someone had boots on and was pacing back and forth." Martin and his friends ran upstairs to investigate, but found nothing.

Objects such as plates, pictures, and even candlestick holders would jump off tables and fly across the room, striking him. Despite all of these events, Martin decided to stick around, hoping that perhaps the strange occurrences would eventually stop. He was sure the activity was due to an angry ghost that would eventually give up and leave him alone, but his mind would change after one night and one experience that had him packing his bags.

A Nighttime Visit from the Lizard People

In the spring of 2007, Martin woke up from a deep sleep at about two in the morning: he heard sounds coming from the next room as if someone had broken into the house. He was very concerned because he was completely alone—the nearest neighbor was much too far away to hear anything. He immediately picked up the phone in his bedroom to dial 911 but was shocked to find the phone dead. Martin then heard the sounds getting closer and closer. He jumped out of bed waiting for the intruders to enter the bedroom. He tried to turn on the light, but there was no power. Then, four small "lizard-looking people" entered the room, stood motionless, and stared at him. He said their eyes were reptilian and their skin had the appearance of being dark, rubbery, and scaly. The four beings approached him. Being an ex-marine, Martin was not going to go down without a fight. He grabbed one of the creatures, telling us its arm felt like a "dead fish, cold and slimy." He took a swing at another creature. The creature turned into smoke and his arm and hand went right through it. The creature then reformed into the lizard being. Martin yelled, "I am not going with you!" He picked up a lamp on a small table by the bed and threw it at them, along with everything else he could find, including a small hammer. The objects had no effect—they bounced off the creatures "as if they had shields."

One of the beings raised his hand and a yellow light came from his palm. Martin was instantly paralyzed and fell back on the bed. The beings approached him and did something with their hands. Another yellow light appeared, followed by some type of instruments that materialized in mid-air. The next thing Martin knew, it was nine in the morning and he woke up with a severe headache. He couldn't find any evidence of his nighttime visitors, but he was sure the previous night's experience was not a dream.

One week later, nearly exactly the same experience took place, except this time, Martin did not get out of bed and fight. He awoke to see the beings enter the room and was unable to move. Having had enough, Martin soon sold the house, taking a loss on the property. As of the writing of this book, the house's new owners have not reported any strange happenings; they thought our inquiries were ridiculous and they did not want to be bothered with "such nonsense."

The characteristics in the cases mentioned in this chapter appear to be more like close encounters with djinn than aliens. Although many UFO investigators may consider experiences such as Martin's to be alien abductions, we believe what actually took place was contact with a dimensional intelligence (the djinn). The creatures Martin encountered appeared solid, yet at least one was able to turn into "smoke" and re-morph into a physical being. Also once again, the preferred appearance was reptilian. We like to note that the reptilian manifestation nearly always induces more fear than the beautiful, angelic appearance; perhaps this is the reason the djinn choose to appear as such. Fear is a powerful emotion that generates a great deal of energy: it raises a person's pulse, and sends the brain into a "panic" mode. Remember that according to Islamic belief, djinn can subsist on physical food and energy, although judging by their "costumes," they seem to prefer the latter.

In Closing

Many encounters with what people believe are aliens could actually be djinn. It can be argued that the djinn prefer using the extraterrestrial guise in order to hide their true identity. As for the abductions, we do not know why they could be abducting people. Abductees' reported "medical tests" could be a diversion that hides something more sinister. Since the 1950s, stories of contact with aliens have changed from benevolent (involving beings that were merely curious about the humans) to frightening stories of horrible monsters that want to experiment on the people of earth like laboratory animals. It seems the days of "We Come in Peace" are over.

DJINN AND
SHADOW PEOPLE

SHADOW PEOPLE ARE ONE OF the most terrifying, yet least understood, of all supernatural experiences. Shadow people exhibit the characteristics of all the negative entities we have discussed in this book—but no one knows exactly who or what they are. We have been studying shadow people in-depth for several years, and believe that djinn are behind them—or behind at least many so-called shadow people experiences.

Since 2005, we have compiled an extensive database of shadow people experiences and lore. Rosemary was inspired to start the project after receiving a continuous stream of emails and letters from people who described similar, unusual experiences and wanted explanations. In the years since, she has given numerous presentations and media interviews on the subject, and each time she does, we receive a new wave of letters from more people about their experiences. Hundreds have poured in, indicating to us that this phenomenon is far more widely experienced than most paranormal researchers realize. Clearly, something strange is going on in the dark corners where dimensions intersect.

All the descriptions of shadow people given in this chapter come from reports in our database. The phenomenon is broad and complex, and we can hit only the highlights here—but they amply demonstrate the case for djinn involvement.

Shadow People Experiences

Our examination of hundreds of cases shows that there is a dominant, "core" shadow person experience: A person wakes up in bed to see a tall, solid, black silhouette of a man in the bedroom. It may be standing right beside the bed, or in a corner or the doorway. The person may actually see it slide out of a closet, come in the door, materialize through a wall, or slide out from beneath the bed. It does not walk—it glides, and it moves incredibly fast.

Its shape has the form of a human with what appears to be legs, arms, a torso, and a head, without any features. It is as if a person's shadow is moving along the wall and through the room.

The figure usually appears to be wearing a coat or cloak, and often a hat or something rumpled on its head. Again, there are seldom facial features, details, or colors—everything is pitch black, or "blacker than black," as many experiencers say. If the room is dark, the shadow person's blackness stands out against the darkness. It seems solid, thick, and with physical mass, for it blocks out whatever is behind it. Even though the entity has no facial features, the victim knows it is staring at him with great intensity. Said one experiencer:

> This shape had the form of a human with what appeared to be legs, arms, torso, and head but there were no features to be seen. It was as if a "shadow" was moving along the wall with the shape of a human but featureless. It was watching me.

The shadow man radiates powerful hostility, anger, malevolence, and even evil. People usually react with great fear, panic, and hysteria. They scream, jump out of bed, and tear out of the room, or turn on a light. Often, the shadow person disappears, sometimes into thin air. Other times, it slips back into the closet or beneath the bed, or melts through a wall or window. What at first seemed solid suddenly has no solidity at all.

In addition, shadow people are silent. They do not communicate, though sometimes people mentally pick up on an intention, as does this man, a repeat experiencer:

> There's this black figure, kind of like a three-dimensional shadow. It doesn't really talk, but it always makes its intentions clear to me. Well, not really its intentions. I'm not sure how to explain it. The thing sends off vibes of pure malevolence. It's like evil incarnate. It always starts out the same. It's like I'm awake in bed and this thing (shadow) comes to visit me. It's usually outside my front door trying to get into my house. Sometimes it gets to my bedroom door. And once in awhile, it makes it to the foot of my bed. Words cannot explain the complete evil that emanates from this thing. It causes absolute panic and terror, like it knows just how to get to you.

The man said the shadow man never physically harmed him, but the psychological and emotional terror took a heavy toll on him.

Sometimes people feel paralyzed in bed. They manage to pull the covers up over their heads or they squeeze their eyes shut. When they look again, the shadow person usually has vanished. When the are seen disappearing, it is like smoke or mist. Prayer sometimes sends them away. Sometimes they linger, much to the victim's terror.

There are, of course, variations to these details. Some shadow people are much shorter, three to five feet in height. Sometimes they have facial details, usually red eyes, though we've received a few cases of white or blue eyes. Sometimes the shadow person acts aggressively toward the person, grabbing, sitting on, choking, or breathing on him or her (experiencers have the intuitive feeling that the shadow person's breath is toxic). Said one man:

> The suffocation felt as if I were pinned down. I couldn't move. I had the physical sense of weight on my chest. My shoulders were pinned down. It felt as if "it" was holding a pillow over my face, preventing me from breathing. Getting it off and being able to take a breath was both physical and spiritual. I was pinned down like from a wrestling move with physical weight on top of me. I tried pushing, rolling, and thrashing about. I thought someone had broken into the apartment and was attacking me. As well as trying to fight it off me, I was praying for my life. I didn't have the strength to get it off. Suddenly, the weight lifted off me and I was able to see my attacker, the shadow image. It was so real, that I checked all doors and windows after the attack to see how anyone could have gotten into the apartment. Everything was locked from the inside.

The following was reported to us from a man who once worked a midnight shift and slept during the day. He awakened to find himself under terrifying assault:

> At the foot of my bed was a shadow figure. This figure, as best as I can describe it—and I will never forget it—had the shape of a man. It was tall, as tall or taller than I am, over six feet tall. There were no details of features that can be described, clothing, facial features, etc. The color was the most unique detail. It would require you to experience it to understand. It is best described as blacker than black without really having a true color. It was more like a void of all color, with maybe a hint of a bright blue around the outline, similar to the color of an electric arc.

Any of that blue I saw was only present as it faded or more accurately, receded from site.

The event happened in the early afternoon. It started as a physical, and I believe, spiritual attack. The presence was trying to suffocate me. I remember trying to fight it off physically. Whatever it was, was well beyond my strength. At the time, I was twenty-two years old and in good physical shape. The fight lasted probably only a few seconds, but it seemed like an eternity to me. I fought it off with every ounce of strength I could muster, and prayer as well. It was one of the few times I was seriously afraid for my life. Whether it just let go or I managed to fight it off is still a mystery to me. I don't want a rematch.

Shadow people experiences happen to people of either sex and every age. We have found a fairly even distribution of them through age and gender. Most experiences occur at night, when most people are sleeping. But many occur during the day, including times when people are awake and at home or at work. Some people have only one or two terrifying, unforgettable encounters, and others are visited by shadow people repeatedly. Some shadow people seem to "shadow" entire families, plaguing them wherever they live through generations.

We have found a significant overlap of shadow people and ET encounter/abduction experiences—people who seem prone to both. The victims never know when either type of entities will come—or why.

While most shadow people encounters happen in bedrooms and homes, some take place in haunted locations with a high intensity of activity. Rosemary has observed shadow people in her investigations of diverse places. Some have a distinct human shape, while others are more like blobs or pillars of black, and even clouds of swirling black that look like ink or liquid smoke.

Who are the shadow people and what do they want? No one really knows—but we have some ideas. They seem to be intensely interested in observing us. And they are not a new phenomenon. Old Native American lore speaks of "watchers" with this appearance who live in remote areas. Similar accounts of "dark ghosts" and "phantom hooded monks" going back to the Middle Ages are strikingly similar to modern-day accounts of shadow people.

To arrive at our conclusion that the djinn are behind at least some shadow people experiences, we went through a process of elimination, analyzing the phenomenon from different perspectives. We considered ghosts, poltergeists, incubi/succubi, nightmare hags, demons, Men in Black, extraterrestrials, ultraterrestrials, and thought forms as possible sources. None of these are a good fit, although shadow people have characteristics of nearly all of them. They haunt places and appear and disappear like ghosts. Animals are aware of them and do not like them. Their appearances are sometimes accompanied by poltergeist effects. They act in a malevolent way, and their malevolence, combined with their dark appearance, convinces people they are dealing with demons. However, prayer and invoking the names of God and religious figures do not always work against them. They come at night like ETs, materializing through walls and rendering people paralyzed in their beds in fear. They resemble the dark-suited, hostile Men in Black who harass ET/UFO experiencers. They can sexually attack people like incubi and succubi however, this is rarely reported. They do not abduct people like the gray ETs—that we know of. Some shadow people experiencers feel the entities want to kidnap them. We don't know if this takes place, for the people we have interviewed say they have used considerable will power and energy to prevent their kidnapping. Shadow people also seem to be ultraterrestrials, in that they originate from another dimension and bend the physical rules of ours by materializing and dematerializing at will.

In our initial report analysis, we leaned toward extraterrestrial and ultraterrestrial explanations. We wondered if the shadow people were a little-known type of entity or race with a particular agenda concerning human beings and earth. We were intrigued by the overlap of ET and shadow people experiencers, and by the similarities in their behaviors.

The deeper we went, however, the more evidence pointed to djinn. It seemed unlikely to us that the form of the shadow people is natural to them; rather, it is probably a disguise. The coat or cloak may conceal another shape. Experiencers often wonder, why the hat? The hat is usually out of style, like the mid-twentieth-century Dragnet or Dick Tracy hat, or the stovepipe hats popular in the nineteenth century. Sometimes the hat is large and floppy. We believe the hat conceals something about the entity's head—or perhaps it hides equipment. Some experiencers volunteer that they have the "feeling" that the true form of the shadow people is so hideous that humans would not be able to stand it. Another expla-nation may be simply the djinn's Trickster nature, the taking on of a form that makes no logical sense.

Other types of entities sometimes visit shadow people experi-encers as well, though not necessarily at the same time. These are often small creatures—another favored form of djinn. The follow-ing is one such case, reported by a woman who started having ex-periences when she visited a friend. The shadow person followed her to her own home and began appearing there. Then it was re-placed by a creature:

> I awoke at approximately 3:30 in the morning. The room was completely dark. Across the room, to the left end of my bed, at the foot, in the corner, I saw what appeared to be a man dressed in a black trench coat and a fedora hat pulled down on his forehead. It had no facial features, or any arms, or legs, but somehow I knew it was male. There was a red glow like that of a cigarette near where

his mouth should have been. He just stood there, staring. I felt as if I couldn't move; sleep paralysis, I think, is the name for it. I told my friend the next day and she reported she had never had any sightings at her house before. I visited her a month later and again awoke at approximately the same time of night. When I woke I purposefully didn't open my eyes. I knew he was there and this time I was afraid. I turned over to my right and quickly turned on the bedside lamp. There was nothing in the corner when I looked back.

A month later, in my own house, 250 miles away, I awoke to find him leaning in the corner of my room. Again, at the foot of my bed on the left. The same night my fourteen-year-old son, whose room is next to mine, reported seeing the man standing in his doorway. Interestingly enough, the shadow man hasn't been back to my house. Instead, I've been visited by a cat-sized gargoyle that sits on top of my dresser.

We have collected other stories of strange small creatures, including one that resembled a cross between a cat and a rabbit, and a creature that seemed like a mole, with fleshy claw feet. We have often seen and heard about what Rosemary calls "the little gray scurrying things," cat-sized gray shapes with no definable heads or tails and multiple legs and feet, which move rapidly along walls and up and down stairs.

What Is the Shadow People's Agenda?

The shadow people seem interested in observing us and spying on us. Why do they come when we are asleep? Perhaps we are vulnerable to having our minds and bodies probed. If the djinn are intent on regaining their place in the physical world, it stands to reason that they need information about physical bodies. Their natural plasma state may not be well suited for long periods of time in this dimension.

Like ET abductees, shadow people experiencers usually have no idea why they are visited. Sometimes place seems to be a factor, for people cease to have experiences when they leave or change residences. This would indicate that geophysical properties may be at work creating portals between dimensions. In some cases, we have found emotional turmoil to be a factor. Perhaps the energy generated by intense emotions attracts and "feeds" the entities. Fear may feed them as well; hence their radiation of malevolence to get the emotional response they desire. Also, the generation of fear may protect their true identities and purpose. When we are afraid, we simply want to escape—we do not want to ask questions or probe too deeply. Fear is definitely a tactic we would expect from djinn.

Are the djinn working in cooperation with at least some of the abducting ETs? Are they providing reconnaissance and monitoring—or even mind programming while we sleep? Or are the abducting ETs another form of djinn themselves, as we considered in the previous chapter? Whatever their agendas, both the shadow people and the abducting ETs seem to have hostile intentions towards human beings.

Remedies Against Shadow People

Almost everyone who writes to us asks how they can send shadow people away or prevent them from returning. Even a single experience can leave deep psychic scars, and a fear and conviction that "it" will come back, especially if the person thinks about "it." As mentioned earlier, many people have found prayer to be effective. The most common remedy that works for the most people is turning on lights. Some repeat experiencers have spent years sleeping with lights on just to keep the shadow people at bay. In fact, electricity—and electromagnetism—may provide keys to defenses against shadow people.

Electromagnetic Interference

The generation of electrical and electromagnetic fields of energy may disrupt the ability of shadow people to maintain a form in our reality. The operation of lights, televisions, radios, computers, and even cell phones may break apart their shapeshifted "bodies." Perhaps shadow people are trying to learn how to avoid or nullify negative electrical and electromagnetic effects. They may be scanning our brains and nervous systems while we sleep to get information that will be of use to them.

Interestingly, we found a news item from October 14, 2001, in which a leading psychical researcher in England opined that the electromagnetic effects of increasing cell phone usage were depressing ghost activity:

> LONDON (Reuters)—Mobile phones are killing off ghosts, an expert who has spent years researching the occult has said. Tony Cornell, of the Society for Psychical Research, told the Sunday Express newspaper that reports of ghost sightings had started to decline when mobile phones were introduced 15 years ago.
>
> "Ghost sightings have remained consistent for centuries. Until three years ago we'd receive reports of two new ghosts every week," said Cornell, of Cambridge in Eastern England.
>
> "But with the introduction of mobile phones 15 years ago, ghost sightings began to decline to the point where now we are receiving none."

According to the paper, haunted tourist attractions in Britain could be under threat if the number of cell phones continues to grow from the present figure of 39 million.

Apparently, paranormal events, which some scientists put down to unusual electrical activity, could be drowned out by the electronic noise produced by phone calls and text messages. Judging from the reactive behavior of shadow people, they are affected in the same way.

One of our cases provides supporting evidence for this possibility. The case involved a salvage company that operates out of a large commercial building. The company salvages old computers and components from cell phone towers. Shortly after the company landed a big contract from a major cell phone carrier, a tall shadow man began showing up in the workplace. It stood by them and watched them work as they stripped components. The shadow man sometimes watched them work on computers, but it seemed the most interested in the pieces of cell phone towers.

The figure seemed to radiate evil and was unnerving. It would speed around and suddenly appear and disappear. The employees also noticed some of their tools began disappearing. They would come to work in the early morning to find tools that they used on the cell phone tower components misplaced or completely gone. If missing, the tools were usually returned within a few days, but to a different spot in the workplace.

After months of nearly daily appearances by the shadow man, one employee took remedial action. He brought a crucifix and a portrait of the Virgin Mary, and hung them on the wall by his workbench. Every morning, he said prayers for protection. Soon afterward, the shadow man stopped coming. Was it religious intervention—or had the shadow person gotten all the reconnaissance it needed?

More Connections

In our investigations of highly active sites, we have found shadow people to be part of a much bigger picture that includes other phenomena and entities. There may be certain areas or portals where the djinn can be comfortable and relatively stable, leaving and entering our dimension at will. Perhaps they assume a wide variety of shapes—maybe, to paraphrase the late John Keel, just to confound us.

THEY WANT OUR WORLD
AND THEY WANT IT NOW!

IT MUST BE REMEMBERED THAT except for those djinn who are in between dimensional rifts, the majority of this ancient race exists in another reality very close to our world. According to recent theories in theoretical physics, this other reality is located at a right angle to a right angle from any position that we are facing. Thus, we three-dimensional beings would not be able to turn and look into that area of space. This is because as we move, that area of space also moves with us, and so we can never move fast enough to peer into this other reality. The only possible way that this could be achieved is to bend space itself or perhaps move faster than the speed of light.

For centuries, the djinn seem to have been quiet. Only in the past forty or so years have they once again become more active in our world. There could be a variety of reasons and explanations as to why the djinn are increasing their activity in this reality. The theory that makes the most sense to us, and could explain why the appearance of djinn in this world is cyclic, is that they are composed of plasma and are greatly affected by changes in magnetic fields. They seem to avoid intense magnetic fields and appear irritated when in close proximity to devices that might be able to divert, disrupt, or slightly change the polarity of plasma. For centuries, the magnetic field of our planet may have protected us from the djinn by closing off their reality from ours. Recently, scientists have discovered that Earth's magnetic field changes over a period of time; since the nineteenth century, its strength has decreased by ten percent.[1] Due to this decline, areas of negative magnetic anomalies have increased, creating loops or portals through which the djinn can once again enter our world.

It must be further noted that our sun is very quiet despite the fact that we are in a period of maximum solar flare activity. The peak of solar activity is set for 2012, and solar astronomers at Kitt Peak National Observatory expect (or fear) that the sun may make up for its inactivity and balance itself out.[2] This would result in massive solar flares and coronal emissions. The particles and energy reaching earth would strike our magnetic field and weaken it considerably, causing life on our planet to be subjected to intense solar radiation. The weakening of the magnetic fields may be what the djinn are waiting for so they can safely enter our dimension

---

1 NASA/AMES Research Center: http://www.nasa.gov/vision/earth/ lookingatearth/29dec_magneticfield.html. Accessed October 2010.

2 Kitt Peak National Observatory supports the most diverse collection of astronomical observatories on earth for nighttime optical and infrared astronomy, and daytime study of the sun. Kitt Peak is located 56 miles southwest of Tucson, Arizona.

by coming through vortexes or holes in our planet's natural defense shields. The legends about the djinn returning to take back what they believe is rightfully theirs may not be all fairy tales and amusing stories from ancient Arabian mythology—they may in fact contain a considerable amount of truth. If our suspicions are correct, in the years that follow 2012, we should continue to see an increase in paranormal activity and a great change in our perception of what we consider to be reality.

Return of the Djinn

As we progress further into the twenty-first century, the djinn race are once again manifesting in our world after a long absence. In the past, they have appeared as human-like genies, angels, demons, gargoyles, and other mythological creatures. However, this time they are taking the form of UFOs, aliens, fairies, ghosts, spirits, shadow people, and creatures that seem out of time and place. They may be responsible for a great deal of channeling, visions, and other forms of psychic contact. It is evident from our research that the djinn are intensely interested in the current human condition and want to learn more about the technologies we have developed over the past century. They also appear to need human beings and other life forms in this reality to help them make the transition into our world. Perhaps the many stories of aliens from other worlds that are creating hybrid species in order to live on our planet are not merely the tales of over-imaginative peoples' minds or flights of fancy. The "aliens" from other star systems may actually be dimensional beings trying to create a new race—a sentient race with free will that can exist not only in our reality but also the world of the djinn. Like Bilqis, the Queen of Sheba, such a race would be quite formidable, as they would combine the power of the djinn with the aggressive, creative mind of a human.

Judging from the increase in paranormal activity around the world, it is apparent that the djinn are not restricted to the Middle East. Over the past ten years, we have investigated many claims of "haunted homes" and other places, and it is clear that in a fair percentage of these cases, something else is at work rather than (or in addition to) ghosts. The activity in many of these places is more Trickster-like, which has always been an identifying djinn quality. In some cases, people have been driven from their homes by activity that takes a sudden, malevolent turn. This paranormal activity may include disembodied voices in the night, apparitions of human-like beings or monsters, strange lights and flashes, poltergeist activity, missing objects, electrical malfunctions in the home, shadow people and figures, nightmares (especially of hideous creatures), and adverse animal reactions. Dogs and cats seem to be able to sense and perhaps see a djinni that is invisible to the human eye, which always induces fear in the animal. In addition, humans who live or spend a lot of time in environments occupied by djinn may experience harmful health symptoms that defy medical diagnosis, as well as negative psychological effects such as depression, suicidal thoughts, irritability, aggression, and excessive paranoia. In some cases, married couples begin fighting with each other, and may even separate. This is how the djinn work: if they can't scare the people out, they may resort to trying to turn couples and family members against each other. In the Middle East, couples will often go to religious counselors when they are having difficulty since they feel a djinni is trying to break up their marriage.

Phil has concentrated his research in the northeast United States, while Rosemary has conducted investigations in other states and foreign countries. When we compare notes and findings, many cases bear striking similarities. The experiences mentioned earlier seem to provide a foundation for understanding the relationship between humans and djinn.

We now consider the possibility of djinn in our paranormal investigations, and encourage other investigators to venture beyond their conventional explanations of ghosts, poltergeists, ETs, demons, and supernatural creatures. Djinn are everywhere, sometimes hiding in plain sight. The following are a few cases we believe involve djinn.

Skinwalker Ranch

A ranch in Utah has become famous in paranormal circles—the "Skinwalker Ranch," named after one of the dominant phenomena said to command the area. So much negative activity occurred there that owners left and sold it to the National Institute for Discovery Science (NIDS).[3] The story of the NIDS investigations at the ranch is documented in *Hunt for the Skinwalker* (2004) by Colm A. Kelleher, former deputy administrator of NIDS, and George Knapp, a broadcast journalist. We stress that the interpretation of djinn is our own, and is not made in the book.

In Native American lore, skinwalkers are evil, shapeshifting sorcerers who travel about very rapidly, especially at night. They cause illnesses, incite people to violence, rob graves, and can even kill people. The ranch is situated on land in the Uinta Basin, an area renowned for supernatural lore and activity. The ranch is said to violate skinwalker pathways, making it a particularly unlucky place. Locals either avoid speaking of skinwalkers or talk about them in hushed tones so as not to attract unwanted attention. We believe skinwalkers may actually be djinn in disguise: their activities and powers fit the descriptions, and humans fear them in the same ways.

---

3 NIDS was created by real estate developer Robert Bigelow of Las Vegas in 1995 as a privately funded organization to scientifically investigate UFO and paranormal phenomena, and to advance fringe science. It was discontinued in 2004. NIDS involved teams of scientists and researchers.

Activity witnessed at the ranch includes intense poltergeist activity; strange orbs of light that seem to possess intelligence; supernatural, bullet-proof wolves; dark entities; mutilated cattle and missing animals; large, black triangular objects in the sky; other UFO activity; crafts or objects that glide around and land on the property; and sightings of the Men in Black.

One of the most peculiar sightings was of an orange mass that repeatedly appeared in the western sky, seemingly a window into another reality. One night, the mass appeared in the nighttime sky, and Tom (the pseudonym of the ranch owner who sold the property to NIDS) looked at it through a telescope:

> In the middle of the orange mass, Tom could see what looked to him like "another sky." Through the magnifying scope he distinctly saw a blue sky... like it was a window into somewhere else where it was still daylight. Tom felt like it could have been a tear or rent in the sky about a mile away, and through the rent he could see a different world or perhaps a different time. It was nighttime as he gazed through and it was daytime "on the other side." [He] began to think that the strange events on the ranch might be explained in terms of different dimensions, alternate realities, and such.[4]

Flying, fast-moving objects, including one described as black in color, were observed emerging from this hole in the sky. Tom became convinced that "his ranch was the site of some kind of dimensional doorway through which a flying object entered and maybe even exited this reality."[5]

On another occasion at night, one of the NIDS investigators witnessed a yellow light manifest on the property, which turned

4 Colm A. Kelleher and George Knapp, *Hunt for the Skinwalker* (New York: Paraview/Pocket Books, 2005), p. 6.

5 *Ibid.*, p. 64.

into a tunnel. A large black humanoid creature about six feet tall with no facial features crawled out of the tunnel and walked away. The tunnel shrank and disappeared, leaving behind a pungent smell of sulphur. The creature resembles descriptions of shadow people, and sulphur could indicate its origin as subterranean, a preferred djinn dwelling place. It seems the investigator, like Tom, observed an actual interdimensional opening, as though an unknown intelligence had thrown open a door in order to access our world.

The NIDS investigators witnessed other phenomena, but were never able to capture any of it on camera, due to mysterious malfunctions and destruction of equipment. It seemed as though whatever was causing the phenomena played a cat and mouse game with them—another hallmark of djinn. Some of the investigators experienced health issues while at the ranch, such as intense migraine headaches, which also is characteristic of djinn.

After several years of investigation, NIDS had "very little physical evidence of anomalous phenomena, at least no physical evidence that could be considered proof of anything. This was in spite of hundreds of days of human monitoring and several years of camera surveillance."[6] The investigation was officially ended, but we do not doubt that phenomena there and in the area continue.

The ranch and surrounding environs sit on a negative magnetic anomaly, according to US Geological Survey maps. As mentioned previously, negative magnetic anomalies are often found in paranormal hot spots.

---

6 *Ibid.*, p. 209.

The San Luis Valley

Similar activity occurs in the San Luis Valley, another hot spot, the world's largest alpine valley stretching from approximately Villa Grove in southern Colorado to Taos in northern New Mexico. Since 1989, researcher Christopher O'Brien has investigated more than a thousand reports of unusual activity, including UFOs and mysterious lights, cattle and animal mutilations, ghosts and hauntings, mysterious creatures and hitchhikers, shapeshifters, and skinwalkers, evidence of alleged underground bases, and encounters with devilish or djinn-like entities.

O'Brien received a report of a djinn-like encounter from the police chief in Questa, New Mexico. In 1993, the police chief's uncle was driving home late one night north of Questa, heading south on Highway 522. He saw a woman dressed in fancy red evening clothes walking alongside the road, and so he stopped to offer her a ride. She got into the pickup truck and said nothing, only staring straight ahead. The uncle turned to ask her why she was walking along the road by herself so late at night, and got a shock—she had goat's legs and cloven hoofs! Before he could react, she vanished right before his eyes.[7]

The police chief's story is reminiscent of the tale of the half-djinn Bilqis, the Queen of Sheba, reputed to have donkey legs or extremely hairy legs and feet. The "phantom hitchhiker" is a common phenomenon found everywhere in the world. It is often tied to ghost lore concerning a tragic death. A female is spotted walking along a usually lonely road late at night. She accepts a ride, and sometimes communicates where her home is. She always vanishes from the vehicle. These mystery hitchhikers do not seem dangerous or harmful, so perhaps the shock they give those who try to help is the payoff!

---

7 Christopher O'Brien, *Stalking the Tricksters, Shapeshifters, Skinwalkers, Dark Adepts, and 2012* (Kempton, IL: Adventures Unlimited Press, 2009), pp. 158–159.

Mothman or Djinn?

In an earlier chapter, we discussed the possibility of djinn involvement in the Mothman wave of sightings in the 1960s. West Virginia is an active state from a paranormal perspective, and the Appalachians are full of strange lore and stories about the supernatural. Some of the more remote mountains and hollows may provide ideal places for djinn to exist with little human interference. We have seen how fiercely territorial the djinn can be, and that when disturbed, they can react with great hostility. They can reside quietly in a dimensional intersection location for long periods of time—but if stepped on, they put on a display of power.

Every year, Rosemary attends the annual Mothman Festival in Point Pleasant, West Virginia, where she gives presentations, conducts investigations, and mingles with festival-goers. In 2009, she met a West Virginia resident who told her about a frightening paranormal experience he had in the field of his own farm, with an invisible but palpable entity.

Robert (not his real name) was inclined to interpret the entity as Mothman, but with due respect to Robert, we think a djinni may be a closer fit. As we noted previously, Mothman might have been a shapeshifted djinni. Interpreting paranormal experiences is often highly subjective, much like dream interpretation. People arrive at an explanation that makes sense to them.

Robert's terrifying encounter began with a series of lower-key, unusual phenomena in the early 1990s. He and his wife would be in states of deep meditation and absentee healing inside their farm home when the sounds of something heavy walking on the roof would creak the ceiling. Robert had an intuitive feeling that he was being "warned off" from going outside to investigate when these episodes occurred.

One night, he and his wife had friends visiting. He stepped outside alone to enjoy the fine night air. It was quite dark outside.

Suddenly, he became aware of an invisible presence standing on the ground about ten to fifteen feet away from him:

> The thing had faintly glowing red eyes, maybe three times as large as mine, spaced three times as wide. They were elongated— meaning perhaps twice as wide as they were high. They emitted a faint, almost infrared glow, which was in itself a bit frightening. The being must have been about seven-and-a-half feet tall. I could not determine its shape or size but it seemed massive.

Robert rushed back inside but did not say anything so as not to alarm his wife and friends. Although the presence was unsettling, he did not detect any "bad vibes" from it.

Two years later, he experienced what he later described as "the most frightening and stressful experience" of his life. He was in the habit of going way out into his rear field on summer nights and bedding down in a sleeping bag beneath the stars. He took along his dog, Tanya, and a .38 revolver with him in case he encountered any "rowdy dogs." The nights were usually peaceful, and sometimes he saw UFO activity. On this night, however, things took a much different turn.

Robert was almost asleep when he was woken up by a ringing thump sounding in the ground. He recognized it as a deer warning—when the deer are alarmed, they strike the ground with their hooves, and it creates a ringing sound that other deer pick up. Robert heard the sounds of deer very swiftly moving away from his vicinity. Immediately his senses went on high alert.

Suddenly a strange and intensely strong energy hit Robert's body unlike anything he had ever experienced. It was painful and penetrating, and terrified him:

> It resembled a massive psychic attack but hundreds times more powerful. I tried to reduce the effects on me but my best efforts had no effect on the energy experience or the physical, psychic,

or emotional damage effects. I tried in vain to counter the attack…This was the most alien feeling in my life and it filled me with unreasoning terror beyond anything I had experienced or even imagined. I believe it might paralyze an average person.

Tanya went unconscious and the batteries in his flashlight went dead. Robert felt the source of the attack was about fifty to a hundred meters distant from him and about twenty degrees up from the horizon. He was unable to see any form or shape.

For four to five hours, Robert sat tensely, trying to ward off the attack, holding his revolver, knowing the gun was not enough for whatever was out there in the darkness. He forced himself to perform mental exercises that would ease his fright and stress. The malevolent energy maintained a constant, nearly intolerable level, and he felt a genuine physical attack could happen at any moment. Then, when the first streaks of dawn lit the sky, the energy vanished as abruptly as it had started, and he was relieved when Tanya came to. That night was the last Robert ever slept outdoors. He also reported suffering from post-traumatic stress disorder for years.

What attacked him? Perhaps Robert's land is inhabited by a djinni who stays in the outer reaches where it is seldom disturbed. His excursions to sleep out in the field may have finally irritated the djinni, who regarded him as a squatter or home invader. It made a show of force as a way of scaring him away.

"The Farm"

We have been working on a case since early 2009 that involves a wide variety of phenomena much like Skinwalker Ranch, the San Luis Valley, and the Hudson River Valley. We are unable to disclose the location because the property is privately owned, but it is a typical farm in a rural area. The surrounding region has been known for UFO activity, sightings of mysterious creatures, and hauntings. There is a small house on the property. The land was farmed in the nineteenth century. In the late twentieth century it sat idle for about twenty years, and several years ago was purchased and turned into an active property again. We do not know if previous owners experienced anything unusual on the property. Since farming resumed there, paranormal activity has been experienced almost daily.

Phenomena include apparitions of people believed to be previous occupants during the farm's earlier days; mysterious creatures such as an "imp" with a leathery, cat-like face that looks into a window of the house, the "little gray scurrying things" we described in an earlier chapter, menacing shadow people, a mole-like creature that attempts to burrow into human bodies; poltergeist effects; malfunctions of household and farm equipment and the land line telephone; footsteps in parts of the house where no one is present; and a shapeshifting black blob that races about in the field. The employees who work on the property often feel an invisible but hostile presence inside the house and on the land that gives them the impression that they are not welcomed and should leave.

Rosemary put together a team of investigators that has conducted numerous investigations on the farm indoors and outdoors, including all-night surveillances. Team members collectively have experienced all of the above phenomena. Some of the staff and all of the investigators except for Rosemary have suffered adverse health problems; Rosemary has had an unusual degree of car problems. Phenomena have followed some of those involved to their homes. Rosemary has experienced apports of coins at her home— pennies, nickels, and dimes—since commencing the investigations. The apports are the sort of Trickster phenomena one might expect from an entity that likes to switch from serious activity to pranks. People involved with the case, including Rosemary, have had nighttime entity visits in which an unpleasant and predatory presence enters the room.

The entity—we believe it is a single one and not multiple—goes through periods of high activity followed by periods of low activity or dormancy. It especially acts up in advance of a planned investigation, as though it is aware and tries to scare any investigators away.

We believe this land is occupied by a djinni who may have been on the land long before people ever arrived there. It was enjoying solitude until the farm was reactivated several years ago. It is clearly displeased with the disturbances, and reacts by creating the phenomena. Will it ever go away? Probably not. It obviously does not like to be investigated or examined; every investigation has been accompanied by a marked increase in (and severity of) activity. It seems to like to remind the people there that it is boss. A Native American tactic to appease spirits was performed: an offering of ceremonial tobacco, sprinkled around the house and property, and burned in a small cauldron. The tobacco offering was followed by a decrease in activity, but not a cessation. It is difficult to assess the long-term potential danger for humans in cases such as these. Where unpleasant paranormal activity is continuous, people either learn to tolerate it, or they become worn down and leave.

"I Was Here First!"

A medium we know who works in paranormal investigations was called to an odd case in the eastern part of the country. The site was a home in which a family was experiencing escalating unpleasant activity. The other investigators were convinced a demon was to blame, and they were ready to arrange for a religious exorcism.

Ann (not her real name) offered to try to communicate with the entity to assess the situation. When she mentally tuned in, she was surprised—the energy did not "feel" like a demon, or a ghost—or anything she was familiar with. The entity seemed ancient, almost primeval. It explained to her that the house was located on its turf. It had been present long before humans arrived. The Native Americans understood its territorial rights, and had honored it and left it alone. But the white settlers who came in built on its land and created irritating disturbances. The entity said it "owned" one square mile. For reasons that were not clear, it was acting up now. Perhaps it had acted up in the past as well with previous residents. Or, perhaps there was something in particular about the present occupants that the entity especially did not like. It communicated to Ann that it was providing a warning to the people in the house. It wanted them out.

The entity also said that there was nothing the people could do to kill or destroy it. An exorcism would not work. However, it said, Ann herself might be able to send it away, but only to certain locations on the earth. Images sprang into her mind. One was somewhere in Africa. These locations seemed to have some sort of elevator in them, in that there was access up and down from the surface of the earth to below the surface.

Due to a number of circumstances, Ann wound up removing herself from the case. The fates of the entity and the people in the house are not known. This case also has characteristics of djinn: an ancient entity that preceded humans on the planet, is territorial, and is powerful enough to resist most attempts to send it away. The images of the certain places on earth seem like interdimensional portals with subterranean access—a favored place of the djinn.

Severely Haunted Homes

Nearly every paranormal investigation group has one or more cases that fit the following profile: A family moves into a house, usually priced at below-market value, and soon experiences unpleasant phenomena that escalate in intensity. Phenomena include mysterious sounds and footsteps, shadows and shadow figures, black dogs and cats, hideous shapes, poltergeist activity, electrical problems, nightmares, apparitions of people and hooded figures, unexplained illnesses, unexplained accidents that injure the occupants of the house, tension and arguments, bad luck, and more. Sometimes research reveals that the house has a documented history of paranormal activity, bad luck, accidents, and unusual number of deaths in the house, and so on.

The usual approach of paranormal groups is to bring in a psychic or a priest who declares that the house is haunted by a demon or an elemental, a type of low-level spirit that exists in nature. Religious exorcism rituals, blessings and prayers are performed. The paranormal activity diminishes or ceases—but not for long. Eventually it returns. Weeks, months, even years may pass before it does. Meanwhile, if the house changes ownership, the sensitivity to the phenomena varies. Some people are more vulnerable than others.

Some of these cases may indeed be caused by infesting demons, but in persistent cases, the occupying entity may be a djinni. The house may sit in a portal area, which is not likely to close, especially upon the religious commands of people. Dealing with djinn has little to do with "good" people versus "evil" spirits. Rather, the conflict is racial: humans versus djinn.

In Closing

We believe there are many places all over the planet where djinn have a strong presence. We are re-evaluating cases in our files, and we find many that fit a djinn profile. In some cases, djinn may create mild haunting phenomena, and in others, they may make life quite miserable for humans. Conventional exorcisms against demons, "elementals" and ghosts will not work on them, for they are far more powerful than humans. If they retreat, it is at their own volition. For example, a djinni can masquerade as a demon or any other kind of entity and pretend to be exorcized—just to go into hiding and reappear at a later time. Perhaps this might explain some of the more resistant possession cases.

Some djinn are not interested in peaceful coexistence. As an analogy, if your home is invaded by ants or rodents, you do not care how "nice" the invaders think they are, or that they want to share space with you—you want them *out*. This attitude is how many djinn regard humans—as pests. A frequent refrain in negative hauntings is an entity's warning—"Get out!" When the djinn say it, they mean it!

HUMAN–DJINN CONTACT:
IS IT POSSIBLE?

ONJURATION IS TRICKY BUSINESS. REGARDLESS of a spirit's type and nature—good, bad, or indifferent—all are difficult to summon and even more difficult to control. If a ritual is not executed properly, or the summoner lacks the proper power, a spirit may wreak havoc, including damaging or draining the summoner's physical and mental health.

The djinn are no different than other spirits and entities when it comes to being summoned. As they have free will, calling upon a djinni can be very dangerous; just how it will react to the conjurer is anyone's guess. Like humans, djinn have their own rules that govern their behavior. In most cases, a djinni will ignore anyone trying to call upon it unless it has something to gain in return. Djinn also have been conjured to manipulate, possess, and do harm to others. This can be a dangerous prospect, because like us, not all djinn are good—some are evil, and a small number are downright psychotic.

The Prophet Muhammad was able to call upon the djinn, and when he did, they challenged his claim that he was the chosen prophet of Allah. In every version of the story, Muhammad is able to control the djinn and convince them he is indeed the Prophet, resulting in the djinn converting to Islam. Of the many stories told, the most popular and our favorite appears below.

The Prophet Muhammad's Contact with Djinn

It is stated by Imam Baihaqi in *Dala'il-al-Nubuwaat* that the Prophet Muhammad once said to his companions in Mecca, "Whosoever from amongst you desires to see the djinn, he should come to me tonight."[1] One of his followers, Hadhrat Abdullah Ibn Masood, was the only one who came that night, for all others were fearful of the djinn. The Prophet took him to a high hill in Mecca on a clear, moonless night. Muhammad drew a circle and told Ibn Masood that no matter what happened, he was to remain seated and motionless within its confines. Hadhrat Abdullah Ibn Masood sat within the circle and began reciting the Qur'an. Suddenly, a large number of djinn appeared out of smoke and encircled Muhammad, who was outside the circle. The djinn seemed to be creating a barrier around the prophet, captivating him.

Ibn Masood heard the djinn say to Muhammad, "Who gives evidence that you are the Prophet?"

Muhammad pointed to a nearby tree and said, "Will you accept my claim if this tree gives the evidence?"

The leader of the group of djinn said, "Yes, we shall accept it."

On that, the Prophet called the tree and it moved toward the djinn. This gave evidence to the group of djinn that Muhammad was indeed the prophet chosen by Allah. The djinn were so im-

---

1 A book of Muslim short stories.

pressed that they gave praise to Allah and his prophet and converted to Islam.

How did Muhammad know to place his companions within a circle for protection? Perhaps he was familiar with the concept of a magic circle. Circles have had a magical, protective significance since ancient times, when they were drawn around the beds of sick persons and mothers who had just given birth to protect them against demons. If a person summons spirits, a magic circle protects him against any negative influences, and creates a symbolic barrier against his own lower nature.

The story about Muhammad provides no clues as to whether or not he used any magical symbols or rituals in casting the circle, such as found in the magical lore attributed to King Solomon.

Solomon's Control over the Djinn

Ever since the days when King Solomon forced the djinn into slave labor, individuals have sought to harness their supernatural powers, usually for acquiring secret knowledge, power, the ability to tell the future, procurement of love, and riches and treasure.

Solomon used a power granted him by God, a dominion which was to be given to no one after him. His power was channeled through a magical ring that nullified the djinn's ability to resist him. That legendary ring has vanished into the mists of time, but in its place are numerous manuals of magic, some said to be written by Solomon himself. In the Western magical tradition, these handbooks came to be known as "grimoires," and supposedly they were available only to the initiated. As with anything supposed to be "forbidden" or "secret," however, they found their way into the masses. Many claimed roots of antiquity and lineages going back directly to Solomon, but most of the principal ones were written in Europe (especially France) in the seventeenth and eighteenth centuries during a period of renewed interest in magic. They are heavily derivative of Hebrew magical lore, as well as Egyptian, Hellenistic, and Greek magical texts.[2]

The most famous and oldest text attributed to Solomon is the *Key of Solomon*, also called the *Greater Key of Solomon*. The manual contains incantations and instructions for summoning djinn, (called demons in Western translations). According to lore, Solomon wrote all of his magical secrets in this book, and ordered that upon his death it be sealed in an ivory casket and placed in his tomb. Some time later, his tomb was opened and the casket and book were discovered.[3]

The Jewish historian Flavius Josephus referenced such a book in the first century CE, but it's not clear whether he was referring to this grimoire or to the Testament of Solomon, which tells the stories of Solomon's djinn subjugation:

> God enabled Solomon to learn the skill which expels demons, which is a science useful and sanitative to men. He composed incantations also by which distempers are alleviated. And he left behind him the manner of using exorcisms, by which demons are driven away, so that they never return.[4]

The *Key* probably was written by one or more anonymous authors; it circulated as a magical text in Europe from about 1100 on, the earliest date of a known manuscript.

Another Solomonic magical text is the *Lesser Key of Solomon*, also called the *Lemegeton*, a term of unknown meaning. Although it, too, claimed a direct lineage from Solomon, it probably was written in stages by different anonymous authors from the sixteenth cen-

---

2 Rosemary Ellen Guiley, *The Encyclopedia of Demons & Demonology* (New York: Facts On File, 2009), pp. 100–104.

3 John D. Seymour, *Tales of King Solomon* (London: Oxford University Press, 1924), p. 58.

4 *Ibid.*, p. 57.

tury on. It is derivative of the Testament of Solomon and the book of Enoch, as well as the *Key*. The *Lemegeton* has four parts; the *Ars Goetia* describes the 72 "fallen angels" Solomon evoked and how they can be conjured. Whether or not the entities are actually fallen angels, djinn, or something else remains uncertain.

In Islamic belief, the books of magic attributed to Solomon are lies the djinn invented, in an attempt to make Solomon come off as a sorcerer—a disbeliever. After his death, the djinn wrote books of magic and disbelief and placed them beneath Solomon's throne, claiming they were the texts he had used to subjugate them. The djinn then spread the lies throughout humanity, fooling people into thinking they could learn genuine magical secrets.

Summoning the Djinn

Another Western text of interest in relation to summoning djinn is *The Black Pullet*, probably written in France or elsewhere in Europe in the late eighteenth century. It is one of the few grimoires that does not claim to be ancient—but it does feature the djinn, though they are not called by that name. It evokes the Solomonic legend, centering on the use of talismanic rings and inscribed circles as the channels of magical power.

According to the legend told in *The Black Pullet*, the magical secrets were discovered by an anonymous soldier in Napoleon's army sent to Egypt. Near the pyramids in Cairo, he and several companions were attacked by Arab soldiers. All but him were killed, and he was left for dead. By sunset he feared he too would soon expire—but suddenly a stone rolled back in the Great Pyramid and a turbaned Turk came out. The Turk took the solider inside, where there were vast halls, huge galleries, subterranean chambers, and piles of treasures, all ministered by spirits (we may assume them to be djinn). The attendant to the Turk was a djinn (also called a spirit in the text) named Odous.

After the soldier recovered his health, the Turk took him into his confidence. All the riches in the pyramid were the product of eighty years of occult and magical practice, which the Turk wished to pass on to the soldier, as he was nearing death himself. To demonstrate his power, the Turk showed him a magical ring. He blew on it three times and said an incantation. Attendant spirits (djinn) and whatever else the Turk wished appeared. He manifested a sumptuous feast of fine food and wine in this manner.

The Turk showed the soldier *The Black Pullet*, described as like a version of the Arabian folk tale *Aladdin and the Enchanted Lamp*, but with an extra inner spiritual meaning. The text told how to acquire magical power with twenty-two talismans embroidered on silk and etched on rings made of bronzed steel. The Turk said he was the only one who possessed this knowledge. He guided the soldier through all twenty-two talismans. At the end, he summoned Odous to bind him over to the soldier. Odous, the soldier reported, appeared as "a young man of the most beautiful stature; the remainder of his person shone with all the charms, and on the summit of his head shone a flame of which my eyes could not sustain the brilliance."[5] (From this description, it is easy to see how this entity might be interpreted as an angel or guardian spirit.)

The Turk had another gift for the soldier in addition to the magical manual: a black hen ("pullet" coming from the French term for chicken, *poulet*) trained to find gold. In fact, a ritual to create a "gold-finding hen" was one of the most important parts of *The Black Pullet*.

After being taught the secrets, the soldier lost consciousness. The Turk died and was cremated, and Odous became the soldier's dedicated servant. They departed for Europe, taking the book, the Turk's ashes, the black hen, and the piles of treasure. In France, the

---

5 *The Black Pullet*, http://www.scribd.com/doc/11062300/The-Black-Pullet-Science -of-Magical-Talismans, p. 13. Accessed November 2010.

soldier published the book. He used the black hen to find great hidden riches.

The connections of these Western magical ritual guides to the djinn are quite clear: the claims to a Solomonic heritage, the djinni-like servants, the evoking of the Arabian lore of wish-granting djinni, and the lure of great treasure, one of the specialties of the djinn. The entities in the Western grimoires may be called spirits, demons, fallen angels, or angels, but the djinn lurk behind them. Material from the various grimoires has found its way into many books and texts on magic, mixing in some cases with Christianized material. Magical rituals continue to be reinterpreted in modern times, with additions from modern Paganism and even shamanic traditions. The result is that origins become increasingly obscure— something the djinn would appreciate and encourage in order to mask their presence.

Some Western rituals have been specifically adapted from Middle Eastern sources to conjure djinn, not "demons" or "spirits." Many in the Islamic world disapprove of westerners meddling with djinn, believing that non-believers (infidels) do not have the right—or the proper knowledge—for doing so.

Middle Eastern texts and rituals for summoning the djinn have existed for centuries and are still available for use in modern times. Muslims may not think others have the "right" to engage the djinn, but the djinn pre-date Islam, and they are, in some form or another, everywhere.

Some djinn-conjuring rituals are taught orally, and others are written in magical handbooks. Like Western grimoires, djinn magical manuals are for sale everywhere, in marketplaces and on the Internet. One can even buy rings, pendants, and bottles allegedly holding djinn who are waiting to be released in order to grant wishes; it is more than likely many of these objects have little or no value.

Some djinn rituals that have made their way to the West come from the Sufi tradition. The djinn can be conjured in various ways: through child mediumship; through mental clairvoyance and dreams; and through manifestation in mirrors, water, and other objects.[6] Gazing into a reflective surface such as a mirror is called "scrying" in the Western tradition, and is a time-honored method of remote viewing, seeing into the future, and getting spirits to manifest. *The Book of 1001 Nights* also tells how to summon djinn.

Like demons, djinn are difficult to summon and control. According to lore, their natural form is hideous and few people can tolerate it, so God decreed that when they appear to people, they must morph into a more pleasing human or animal form. We have noted that two of the favored animal forms of the djinn are a black dog and a snake. Once summoned, the djinn must be bound to the practitioner, which may be accomplished through binding into an object such as a bottle. For example, *The Book of 1001 Nights* tells of inscribing the name of God in Hebrew on a knife, and drawing magical symbols with incantations written around them. Similarly, a tradition exists in Western magic of capturing small demons called imps into rings, vessels, and other objects. The imps are summoned out to do the bidding of the practitioner, a magician or a witch.[7]

Justification for Summoning the Djinn

Islam considers it acceptable to call up the djinn in order to educate them on Islam and convince them to convert and worship Allah. Asking the djinn to attack others or aid humans in committing sins and disobedience, however, is forbidden. For the most

---

6 Children up to the ages of twelve to fourteen are considered immune to the influences and dangers of djinn.

7 Rosemary Ellen Guiley, *The Encyclopedia of Witches, Witchcraft & Wicca*, 3rd ed. (New York: Facts On File, 2008), p. 172.

part, it is believed that consorting with djinn leads to trouble, and should not be undertaken. The medieval Islamic scholar Ibn Taymeeyah (1263–1328) regarded the djinn as "ignorant, untruthful, oppressive, and treacherous."[8] Djinn, he said, will lie to their summoners and will not necessarily do as commanded. If they are ordered to harm a person or a djinni whom they hold in high regard, they will ignore the command: "Neither the one chanting incantations nor his incantations have any power to force the devils to help them."[9] Furthermore, djinn are fond of creating illusions, appearing in visions and speaking in voices that conform to a conjurer's expectations. They are the ultimate deceivers, masquerading as other spirits such as angels and even religious figures. From that perspective, Christian visions of saints and the Virgin Mary could be djinn illusions—a view the Christian faithful would vehemently reject.[10]

Sheikhs (religious authorities) have the knowledge and skills for summoning and controlling djinn—but any one sheikh may not be able to control all djinn. Some learn their skills in a shamanic fashion, through healing themselves in an initiatory illness, in which they identify the djinni responsible and expel it from their bodies.

Islamic sorcerers (male and female) are said to traffic with evil djinn, the children of Iblis. They use "red magic" to summon them for such tasks as fortune-telling and procuring love and money, and they use "black magic" to summon them for evil purposes such as harming people through the evil eye, illness, misfortune, and even murder. Witches use djinn to "tie" spells, and also consult djinn for untying spells cast by other witches.

---

8 Abu Ameenah Bilal Philips, "Visions of the Jinn: Ibn Taymeeyah's Essay on the Jinn," http://islaam.com//Article.aspx?id=75. Accessed November 2010.

9 *Ibid.*

10 *Ibid.*

Some of the rituals for conjuring djinn are simple, and some, like Western magical rituals, are quite complex, involving fasting, meditation, supplications, and incantations over long periods of time, such as forty days. Any break in the ritual dooms it to failure.

One method of djinn summoning involves a combination of the Qur'an and a magical text. The text has incantations for summoning djinni in a progressive manner, from weakest to most powerful. The Qur'an is read in conjunction with the summoning. The practitioner begins with the weakest djinni. If that djinni can be subdued and bound, the practitioner moves on to the next higher djinni. He keeps going until he reaches a djinni too powerful for him to bind, and then he moves back to the previous and last djinni he was able to bind. This is the one he will work with.[11]

A Dangerous Game

The risks of djinn conjuring are substantial, even if the practitioner intends to only work with a "good" djinni for a purpose such as healing. The same risks apply to any magical practice involving any type or pantheon of entities. A spirit invited to enter the energy space of a human being has the potential for takeover, a prospect that includes insanity and possession. Inexperienced practitioners can quickly find themselves in deep trouble, and may have difficulty finding someone with skills powerful enough to banish a djinni who has attached to a person.[12]

Dealing with and conjuring one's *qarin,* the djinni companion assigned at birth, is dangerous and risky, as it is with most other

---

11 Author interview.

12 The authors know of a case involving a youth who attempted this method and was mentally destabilized by the djinni. Details cannot be divulged to protect privacy, but the youth was institutionalized, and a great deal of money was spent to hire an adept in another country who could command a powerful enough djinni to cast out the one afflicting the youth.

djinn. Trying to command or enslave the qarin can jeopardize one's health or even one's life, according to lore. If a qarin becomes problematic by exerting too much negative influence over a person, relief may be sought from a professional to perform a banishing ritual, but this, too, is considered a risky undertaking. If the ritual is not successful, the qarin may become vindictive and cause more problems.

It is possible to summon djinn with little effort, which can land a person in trouble. Even talking about djinn can summon them, and so one must speak of them in whispers or refer to them with euphemisms, such as "them" and "those other people." According to Turkish beliefs, green djinn are easy to summon because they are very curious about us and will take any opportunities to get closer. The different forms a green djinn can take will depend on its age and experience. If their motive is harmless contact or curiosity, they may take on a number of forms pleasing to the human eye and to hide their true nature. However, if a djinni is angry or annoyed at a person, it may take on a very hideous appearance that would terrify even the bravest.

If open to communication, a green djinni may take on the form of a friendly dog, elf, fairy, or even a beautiful, glowing, angelic being. On the other hand, if you summon a djinni who does not want to be bothered, you might be in for a great deal of trouble.

Can djinn ever be conjured for beneficial purposes? The Qur'an states that God gave humans authority over all things in creation, which implies inclusion of the djinn:

> Do you not see that God has subjected to your (use) all things
> in the heaven and on the earth, and has made his bounties flow
> to you in exceeding measure, (both) seen and unseen.[13]

---

13 Al-Luqmaan, 20.

Sheikhs are able to conjure djinn for mediumship, and to learn about a person's illness. For example, a sheikh will ask his personal djinni to talk to the djinni of a sick person in order to find out valuable information about the affliction.

It has been suggested that the djinn's abilities of invisibility, rapid movement, flying, and penetration of the human body and material objects could be harnessed for surveillance, intelligence gathering, crime investigation, weather reporting, transport of objects, and medical diagnosis and treatment.[14] Given the inclinations and temperament of the djinn, however, the feasibility and even desirability of a cooperative relationship is questionable.

Djinn Sorcery

According to Islamic views, djinn attach themselves to disbelievers and enable them to perform miraculous feats that amaze others, such as predicting the future. This is considered sorcery, and the lies of the djinn influence the disbelievers themselves to lie to others. The Qur'an states that the lies are based on the information the djinn glean from eavesdropping on angels:

> Should I tell you upon whom the shaitan descend? They descend upon every forging sinner. They cast to them the hearing (which they "snatched" from the heavenly assembly), and most of them are liars.[15]

Disbelievers beguiled by such glamor become themselves the servants and allies of Iblis.

We cannot leave the subject of conjuring the djinn without giving more consideration to their possible influence on Western

---

14 Mahmood Jawaid, *Secrets of Angels, Demons, Satan and Jinns: Decoding Their Nature through Quran and Science* (self-published, 2006), pp. 57–59.

15 *Ibid.,* 221–223.

culture. As we have noted, the distinctions between djinn and other entities are often blurry. Western magic is syncretic, that is, it blends diverse sources, among them Egyptian, Greek/Roman, Judeo-Christian, and pre-Islamic Middle Eastern influences absorbed into the culture of the early Hebrews. So, we must consider the hidden role of the Hidden Ones, who are part of that mix. Perhaps the entities who answer the call of magic and who arise in the imaginations of artists and writers are really djinn. We do not have space to examine all of the influences in detail here, but the following examples show the complex picture that emerges when one starts tracking down all of the interwoven connections that trace back to the hidden djinn.

Did H. P. Lovecraft Know the Djinn?

Strange, unnamed entities who may be djinn populate the fictional works of the famous American horror writer H. P. Lovecraft (1890–1937). An atheist, rationalist, and scientific materialist, Lovecraft disavowed any personal belief in the supernatural. However, he was steeped in fascination with the supernatural, and created his own original mythos, Cthulhu, based on his knowledge of Egyptian and Arabian mythologies and occultism. His extensive knowledge of Arabian lore brought him into contact with the djinn. Did he weave the djinn into his horror stories? He certainly excelled at evoking a sense of dread of unknown and unnamed horrors dredged up from dark depths, evocative of the djinn.

Of particular note is Lovecraft's *Necronomicon*, a fictional grimoire of powerful magical rituals. *The Necronomicon* was born in his 1936 essay, "A History of *The Necronomicon*." Lovecraft said the grimoire was originally titled *Al Azif* and was written by "the mad Arab Abdul Alhazred," a fictitious name he derived from *The Book of 1001 Nights*, and an epithet he used to call himself. According to

Lovecraft, the mad Arab was a poet who lived in Yemen and wrote the ritual book in 950 CE.

Lovecraft said a copy of the book existed in his fictitious city of Arkham. He referred to it in some of his other stories, but never produced an actual book. As interest in his works grew, cult status around the mysterious *Necronomicon* arose as well. Whether or not such a manuscript ever did exist, versions of it have been "found" and published. Some Lovecraft enthusiasts believe he knew genuine secret rituals for conjuring the dreaded entities he called the "Old Ones" or the "Great Old Ones," an ancient race older than humans beings, huge in size, and of immense power. The Old Ones have a physical form composed of a different kind of matter than exists in the human universe. They are imprisoned beneath the sea, inside the earth, and on far-flung planets. They either removed themselves, or they were banished by the gods for using black magic. They are waiting for the opportunity to rise again and rule the world. The Old Ones have been compared to extraterrestrials, demons, archetypes, "Aristotelian elementals," and "specters of a future mentality."[16] But they could very well be based on djinn, banished for their transgressions and residing in remote and far-flung places in this and other dimensions until they can return and reclaim the earth.

One of the central Old Ones is Cthulhu, whom Lovecraft introduced in 1926 in "The Call of Cthulhu," describing it as "a monster of vaguely anthropoid outline, but with an octopus-like head whose face was a mass of feelers, a scaly, rubbery-looking body, prodigious claws on its hind and fore feet, and long, narrow wings behind." Cthulhu lived in R'lyeh, an ancient city that had sank beneath the sea. This is an interesting cross-correlation to djinn, for according to Muhammad, the throne of Iblis lies beneath the sea, surrounded by sea serpents:

---

16 Anton Szandor LaVey, *The Satanic Rituals* (New York: Avon Books, 1972), p. x.

Jabir reported: I heard Allah's Messenger (may peace be upon him) as saying: The throne of Iblis is upon the ocean and he sends detachments (to different parts) in order to put people to trial and the most important figure in his eyes is one who is most notorious in sowing the seed of dissension.[17, 18]

As noted earlier, some of the djinn conjured by King Solomon came up out of the sea, specifically Abezithou, a one-winged djinni who lives in the Red Sea. Cthulhu's unsettling octopus-like form is not out of the question for djinn, who can shapeshift into any form, especially a disturbing one.

According to Lovecraft, the Old Ones are worshipped by a depraved cult with origins dating back to the first human beings. The cult, wrote Lovecraft in his story:

… had always existed and always would exist, hidden in distant wastes and dark places all over the world until the time when the great priest Cthulhu, from his dark house in the mighty city of R'lyeh under the waters, should rise and bring the earth again beneath his sway. Some day he would call, when the stars were ready, and the secret cult would always be waiting to liberate him.[19]

Similarly, the djinn reside in wasteland-type places and desolate areas, biding their time.

The theme of liberating the Old Ones to let them back into the world appears again in the story "The Dunwich Horror" (1929). The protagonist, Wilbur Whateley, the son of a deformed albino woman and Yog-Sothoth, a type of god, searches for a Latin edition

---

17 *Sahih Muslim*, 39.6754.

18 In some modern views, Iblis' throne is located in the Bermuda Triangle, and all the disappearing ships are sacrifices to him.

19 H. P. Lovecraft, *The Call of Cthulhu*, 1926. Published online at http://dagonbytes .com/thelibrary/lovecraft/thecallofcthulhu.htm. Accessed November 2010.

of the *Necronomicon* so he may open the gates for the return of the Old Ones. Whateley is unfortunately killed trying to steal the book, and his twin brother terrorizes the town of Dunwich as an invisible monster.

The *Necronomicon* appears elsewhere in Lovecraft's works. "The Book" (1934) does not mention it by name, but revolves around a "worm-riddled book" of rituals obtained by the narrator, who uses it to access what appears to be a parallel dimension. After chanting a "monstrous litany" from within five concentric circles, he acquires a permanent shadow entity and is swept away by a black wind into an unknown abyss. When he manages to return, his perception of the world is permanently changed, and the shadow is permanently attached to him. The shadow is interesting—could it be similar to the shadow people phenomenon described earlier?

Did Lovecraft possess secret occult knowledge of the djinn, or did his fertile imagination access their realm without his realizing it? Many science fiction, fantasy, and horror authors are visionaries of genuine realities, and they bring awareness of those realities into our dimension via their work. Perhaps Lovecraft had experiences he never acknowledged that seeded his inspiration. Carl L. Johnson, Lovecraft scholar and founder of the H. P. Lovecraft Commemorative Activities Committee notes:

> One may further postulate that he was capable of receiving such knowledge from an ethereal repository outside himself...in his words, 'the Mind which is held by no head.' Time may reveal if Lovecraft was merely a weaver of convincing tales, or something of a prophet in his own right. Cultists still do devise and perform rituals intended to open chasms to the Dread Dimension and unleash denizens of the nether world(s), with rites based largely on the fantasy of Lovecraft.[20]

---

20 Carl L. Johnson, "Providence's Master Spirit," revised November 2009, in correspondence to the authors.

Anton Szandor LaVey (1930–1997), who founded the Church of Satan in 1966, was inspired by Lovecraft in creating rituals for his church. LaVey, whose real name was Howard Stanton Levey, believed Lovecraft was influenced by real occult sources. Wrote LaVey:

> Whether his sources of inspiration were consciously recognized and admitted or a remarkable psychic absorption, one can only speculate. There is no doubt that Lovecraft was aware of rites not quite "nameless," as the allusions in his stories are often identical to actual ceremonial procedures and nomenclature, especially to those practiced and advanced around the turn of the 19th–20th centuries![21]

Djinn and the Golden Dawn

LaVey's comments move us into the Hermetic Order of the Golden Dawn, the greatest Western esoteric order, founded in England in 1888 by individuals steeped in occultism, including the Kabbalah, Freemasonry, Theosophy, Rosicrucianism, and Western esoteric and magical lore.

The Golden Dawn began as an esoteric order and evolved along magical lines, using as primary sources the *Key of Solomon*, *The Book of Sacred Magic of Abra-Melin the Mage*, and Enochian magic—all of which have djinn roots.

The Book of Sacred Magic of Abra-Melin the Mage is heavily derivative of the *Key*. It is attributed to Abra-Melin (also spelled Abramelin), a Jewish Kabbalistic mage of Wurzburg, Germany, who supposedly wrote the grimoire for his son in 1458. Though the manuscript claims to be a translation of Abra-Melin's original

---

21 LaVey, *op. cit.*

Hebrew manuscript, it was written in French in the eighteenth century, probably by an anonymous source. According to the story presented in the manuscript, Abra-Melin learned his Kabbalah-based magical knowledge from angels, who told him how to conjure demons and tame them into personal servants and workers—similar to King Solomon—and how to raise storms. He said that all things in the world are created by demons, who work under the direction of angels. Each person has an angel and a demon as familiar spirits, similar to the daimones and the qarin. Abramelin magic is based on sacred names and on magical squares of numbers, for purposes such as conjuring spirits, invisibility, levitation and flight, commanding spirits, necromancy, shapeshifting, and other feats, all within the abilities and powers of the djinn.

Enochian magic evolved from the sixteenth-century occult work done by John Dee, the royal astronomer to Queen Elizabeth I, and his assistant, Edward Kelly, who claimed to have psychic ability. Dee and Kelly used scrying and Kelly's mediumship to communicate with beings they identified as angels. Dee and Kelly developed an alphabet and genuine language—Enochian—for constructing "calls" for contacting angels and spirits, and for projecting consciousness into levels of awareness called "aethyrs." Enochian has a melodic sound similar to Sanskrit, Greek, or Arabic. Kelly—who had a reputation for fraud—may have invented the language himself, telling Dee that it was spoken by angels in the Garden of Eden. Dee and Kelly developed nineteen calls of ascending magnitude. The nineteenth call included thirty aethyrs that were never precisely defined, but which the Golden Dawn believed represented new levels of consciousness. The only member of the Golden Dawn during its short original life ever known to work actively with the aethyrs was Aleister Crowley.

Aleister Crowley, "The Beast of the Apocalypse"

Aleister Crowley (1875–1947) was arguably the most colorful figure to ever emerge in Western magical history. Precocious and dark in temperament from an early age, he seemed to possess an innate rapport with the spirit world, as well as a natural ability to tap into its power. Though his mother referred to him as "the Beast" and he later called himself "the Beast of the Apocalypse," he was not a Satanist. He envisioned ushering in a new religion and spiritual age, the Aeon of Horus, based on his system of Thelemic magic inspired by his experiences with entities. In 1898, he joined the Golden Dawn, but clashed violently in personality and power issues with Samuel Liddell MacGregor Mathers, one of the original founders. Within a couple of years, Crowley was kicked out and went off on his own.

Crowley had numerous entity contacts and was adept at conjuring, or evoking, them in magical rituals. In addition to his own inspirations, he used Abramelin and Enochian magic. Three entities are of interest to us for their possible djinn connections.

In 1903, Crowley married Rose Kelly, the first of two wives, who had mediumistic ability. They spent their honeymoon in Cairo in 1904, where Rose spontaneously made contact with an entity named Aiwass (originally spelled Aiwaz). Aiwass said he was a messenger for the Egyptian trinity of deities Isis, Osiris, and Horus. Crowley had a vision of him, seeing Aiwass as a man dressed in old Assyrian or Persian clothing and having what he described as:

> ...a body of "fine matter" or astral matter, transparent as a veil of gauze or a cloud of incense-smoke. He seemed to be a tall, dark man in his thirties, well-knit, active and strong, with the face of a savage king, and eyes veiled lest their gaze should destroy what they saw.[22]

---

22 Guiley, *The Encyclopedia of Demons & Demonology, op. cit.*, p. 46.

Aiwass ordered Crowley to take dictation. For three hours between April 8 and 10, 1904, the entity spoke in a voice that emanated directly out of the air, while Crowley wrote in longhand. The result was the *The Book of the Law*, the seminal work of Thelemic magic, which contains the axiom "Do what thou wilt shall be the whole of the law." In other words, do what you must to surrender to total alignment with cosmic law.

For years, Crowley remained in awe of Aiwass, and admitted he never fully understood exactly who or what the entity was. He alternately described him as a god, demon, devil, preterhuman intelligence, minister or messenger of other gods, and his own guardian angel. For a time, he considered Aiwass part of his own subconscious, but then rejected the idea, favoring at last the explanation that the entity was his holy guardian angel, or an aspect of his higher self. Crowley also said he was occasionally allowed to see Aiwass in a physical appearance, inhabiting a human body like a normal human being.

Over the years, opinions on Aiwass have run the gamut from benign to evil. It cannot be determined whether or not Aiwass was a djinni, of course, but his smoke-like dark appearance, Middle Eastern garb, and ability to take on human form evoke djinn associations. Was Crowley in contact with a djinn representative who wished to channel certain ideas into the mortal world?

In 1909, Crowley made contact with Choronzon, an entity known by Dee (who spelled the name "Coronzon" and referred to it as 333). Dee never considered Choronzon a demon, but Crowley called it "the Demon of Dispersion" and "the Demon of the Abyss." He also said Choronzon was the "first and deadliest of all the powers of evil," and a being comprised of "complete negation."[23] Could Choronzon be Iblis, or one of his high-ranking djinn?

---

23 *Ibid.*, p. 40.

In December of 1909, Crowley and his assistant, Victor Neuberg, went into the desert outside Algiers to conduct rituals for the purpose of accessing the high-level aethyrs in the nineteenth call of Enochian magic. Crowley had a number of breakthroughs in consciousness as a result, including the instruction that he would have to confront Choronzon and cross the Abyss.

In an evocation, a magician stays within the protection of a magical circle and evokes an entity into a separate magical triangle. Crowley intended to break that rule and sit within the triangle, go into trance, and offer his own body for possession—a dangerous magical act.

According to Crowley's account, Neuberg, standing within the protected magical circle, got the brunt of the entity's force. First Choronzon manifested in the form of a seductive female prostitute, and then turned into an old man, and then into a snake. Choronzon told Neuberg he spat upon the name of the Most High. He was Master of the Triangle who had no fear of the pentagram. He said he would give Neuberg words that seemed like great secrets of magic but would be worthless, as a joke.

Choronzon breached the protection of the magical circle around Neuberg, and the two wrestled physically. Although some observers have opined that Neuberg wrestled with a demon-entranced Crowley, Neuberg insisted he fought the entity itself. It had froth-covered fangs and attempted to tear out his throat. After a considerable struggle, Neuberg forced Choronzon back into the triangle, and repaired his magical circle. The two hurled insults and threats at each other, and Choronzon vanished.

Crowley and Neuberg felt they had bested the demon, and Crowley considered himself to have achieved great magical status as a result. Some critics of Crowley's work believe that Choronzon left a permanent mental and psychic scar upon him.

We cannot prove Choronzon's true identity, but like Aiwass, djinn presence is strongly suggested. The snake is a favored form of djinn, and the Trickster-like taunting is telling as well. A hostile djinni summoned from the depths of its realm in another dimension might easily attack in such an aggressive manner, boasting that the magical "rules" of mortals had no effect upon him.

In 1918, Crowley made contact with a powerful entity named Lam, who was to help him fulfill the work Aiwass had began. The contact was made through a sex magic ritual in which he opened a portal "in the spaces between stars" (a parallel dimension), enabling Lam to enter the physical universe. Crowley believed Lam to be the soul of a dead Tibetan lama from Leng, between China and Tibet. *Lam* is Tibetan for "Way" or "Path," which Crowley said had the numerical value of 71, or "No Thing," a gateway to the Void and a link between the star systems of Sirius and Andromeda.

Since that time, some followers of Crowley's work have come to believe that the portal he opened continues to widen, enabling other entities to enter our world that are behind our experiences with UFOs and extraterrestrials. As we have noted, we found a significant connection between djinn and UFOs/ETs. Crowley drew an image of Lam, and it is believed by some that meditating on or contemplating this image enables contact with Lam and access to the portal. The entry of entities through a portal to a parallel realm is yet another interesting correlation with the history and activities of djinn.

The idea that the djinn may be behind major forces of Western occult thought will undoubtedly be controversial to some, and be outright rejected by others. We believe the evidence is there, and has been hiding in plain sight for centuries, just like the djinn themselves. If factions of the djinn are intent on regaining their hold on the physical world, they would infiltrate as many streams of human thought and action as possible. Certainly we should expand our perspective beyond the entities familiar to us in the West, an act that could help us gain valuable insight into the nature of all our extraordinary experiences.

Real-Time EVP of Djinn

There is yet another way we might be in contact with djinn, one that is quite popular with modern paranormal researchers and investigators: electronic voice phenomena, or EVP. Ever since the development of the telegraph, tape recording, the telephone, the radio, and high-tech communications, people have been hearing and recording mysterious voices of unknown origin. In the 1970s, these voices came to be called electronic voice phenomena. Most of the voices are thought to be of the dead, and some from extraterrestrial or ultraterrestrial realms.

In traditional EVP (developed since the early twentieth century), a recorder is turned on, questions are asked, time is allowed to elapse for an answer, and the recording is played back. Answers to the questions—EVP—may appear in the gaps. Newer techniques involve real-time answers, that is, hearing the voices live rather than passively after they are recorded. Real-time EVP is one of the cutting-edge technologies of paranormal research.

We have been experimenting with a range of equipment for real-time EVP, taking it to different paranormal hot spots to see if we can contact the dead or beings in other dimensions. The devices used for this employ radio sweep. They are popularly known as "ghost boxes" and "Frank's boxes," the latter name referring to one of the developers in the field, Frank Sumption. The boxes rapidly scan the AM band of radio (some also scan FM) to create a jumbled noise matrix composed of broadcast fragments. This matrix of sound seems to facilitate the manifestation of mystery voices. Their answers do not come from the fragments of radio broadcast, but are superimposed on top of the jumbled sound. We acknowledge that the use of real-time EVP boxes is controversial and unpredictable—you never know what you are going to get, and it is often impossible to validate the identities of communicators, because the communications are brief. Like passive EVP, answers to questions usually are just one to several words. Getting a communicator to "stay on the line," so to speak, is difficult, probably because of our limited technology.

How Real-Time Radio Sweep EVP Works

Because of his scientific background, Phil has been trained to question extraordinary claims; he was very skeptical when he first heard about the "ghost box." However, after working with it a number of times with Rosemary, he became convinced that it was picking up voices that were beyond this realm of reality. Phil felt there was no other explanation—according to our current understanding of modern physics, the voices should not be there. What is most remarkable about the "ghost box" is that who- or whatever is on the other end responds to questions the operator(s) ask.

The "ghost box" operates by scanning through an entire band with the EVP being received over a number of adjacent frequencies in the AM, FM, and upper and lower sidebands. This means the EVP is not on any particular channel, but is a signal with a very wide bandwidth that our research shows is spread over 100 kHz or greater. In our opinion, this is what makes it so unusual. In order for the device to work and pick up a "spirit voice" you must have a strong standard signal, so the more crowded the band with radio stations, the better chance you have of getting EVP. It seems the EVP part of the signal is so weak that it needs a stronger standard AM signal on which to "piggyback" in order to be heard. The piggyback effect is simple to understand: one weaker radio signal on the same frequency rides on another stronger one to reach the receiver. This is what seems to be happening with the mystery voices on the ghost box—they are riding (or piggyback-ing) on standard AM radio station transmissions to the receiver. Due to the sweeping effect, the commercial AM transmission is garbled, but the EVP comes through clearly with a different sound and with fully formed words.

Light and radio signals follow the curvature of space, so theoret-ically, these messages should not be able to reach our reality from another dimension unless tiny holes, perhaps the size of atoms, are somehow created in the space-time continuum. Such holes could create a bridge or tunnel to connect our world with the dimension of the djinn. What makes matters so puzzling is that the opera-tor uses no transmitting equipment at all! It seems that the voice of the operator and the questions asked are heard by the entity directly on the "other side." Or, it may be possible that the voice of the operator is being transmitted through the circuits in the ra-dio. It is interesting to note that sometimes, despite optimal con-ditions, the ghost box does not work at all. The person operating the device seems to play an important part in its success—some people never get results, while others frequently do. We believe that the psychic makeup and attitude of the individual operating the ghost box is an important component in its success though we also must consider that the intelligence on "the other side" may want to communicate only with certain people. There is a consid-erable amount of research and analysis to be done in this area, but the one conclusion we have reached is that the ghost box, although limited in its performance, does work.

Djinn Communication Using the MiniBox

One of our favorite real-time EVP devices is the MiniBox, developed by Ron Ricketts of Carrollton, Texas.[24] The MiniBox features multiple scan methods, programmable memory, printed circuit boards, a long-lasting rechargeable gel battery, and a controllable rate of scan. We have taken the MiniBox to some of the stone chambers in upstate New York that Phil researched in connection with his UFO investigations. The chambers have been associated with apparitions, poltergeist activity, mysterious lights, visions, appearances of shadow people and hooded beings, and other phenomena. We believe the chambers sit on energized sites that serve as interdimensional portals. At one, we got quite a surprise when the communicators identified themselves as djinn!

On a hot summer day in 2009, we took the MiniBox to one of the most famous stone chambers (we prefer not to disclose the exact location in order to protect the site's integrity) and set it up at the entrance.

In a typical session, it takes five to ten minutes to synchronize with whoever is communicating. There is an initial warm-up period, after which intense communication usually begins. After about thirty to forty-five minutes of peak intensity, the links start breaking up and communication declines. We can only speculate that the energy can hold for just a certain amount of time. During the peak, various communicators come and go. We believe it is possible to get only a fraction of what is being issued from their side—and perhaps they only hear a fraction of what we say in return.

The session at this particular chamber was exceptionally long, about seventy minutes. The communicators accurately told us our first names as recognition. We asked, "Who built this chamber?"

---

24 The story of the development of the MiniBox is featured in *Talking with the Dead* (Tor, 2011), co-authored by Rosemary and George Noory, the host of *Coast to Coast AM*.

and heard back, "*God did... weapon... Satan.*" Was the chamber a portal or tool of some sort in the perpetual struggle between good and evil, we wondered. It was not the answer we expected.

"Who are you?" we asked the unseen speakers. "*Djinn,*" was the immediate answer. They also told us they liked our box device for communication, and that the chamber was a portal. "Do you come through the chamber?" we asked. "*Through,*" they said. "Where are you?" we asked. "*In the park*" and "*in the chamber*" they said (the chamber is located in a state park, deep in the woods). It seemed as though the communicators had come through an interdimensional portal and manifested in the space around us.

We usually repeat questions to see if we get consistent responses. "Are you human?" we asked.

"*Negative... demon.*"

"Are you djinn?"

"*Unh-huh... surprises.*"

"Who is here besides demons?"

"*Satan... demons... monster.*" (After this reply, we heard strange-sounding laughter.)

"Tell us who you are," we repeated.

"*Djinn.*"

"Is anyone here besides djinn?"

"*No.*"

"Give us more information."

"*No.*" This was followed by more weird laughter.

We could not get past this Trickster-like exchange for the remainder of the session.

During the peak intensity, we both felt enveloped by a strange energy or atmosphere, as though the air around us was being electromagnetically charged. Neither of us had expected djinn to show up and identify themselves—in fact, in all the years that both of us have been experimenting with EVP of varying types, neither of us had ever heard directly from djinn in a manner such as this. We have heard communicators identify themselves as the dead, entities in other realms, and as extraterrestrials. Perhaps the djinn decided to reveal themselves because they knew about the research we were conducting for this book!

Our results made us wonder just how many other EVP communications are a summoning of djinn who masquerade as the dead, aliens, angels, and other entities. Given the present limits of technology, we have little way of knowing for certain who is at the other end of the connection. At the very best, we might be the victims of a Trickster. At worst, we could be already led astray in accordance with the djinn agenda.

Future EVP Experimentation

The success of picking up complex EVP on the standard AM band has produced limited success, but it has proved to us that communication can be established with another reality using standard electromagnetic radiation. One of the problems with the commercial AM band is that it is simply too noisy! If the djinn exist in another nearby dimension, it seems the only way for them to get clear reception of possible EVP signals is to punch "holes" in the earth's magnetosphere and dimensional rift. As stated earlier, occurence of these "holes" may be natural and dependent on the amount of solar radiation reaching earth.

Theoretically, one might have more success in obtaining clear EVP by eavesdropping on a frequency that is able to pick up signals from beyond the ionosphere (a portion of earth's upper atmosphere). The section of the radio band best suited for this is the Very Low Frequency (VLF) area of the electromagnetic spectrum. VLF receivers are simple but relatively uncommon. Consisting only of an antenna and an audio amplifier, they are sensitive to radio waves with frequencies between a few hundred hertz and several hundred kHz. For comparison, AM broadcast band radios—like the ones in the ghost boxes and most automobiles—span the much higher frequency range 540 kHz to 1.6 mHz.

A signal on this frequency possesses a very long wavelength and would be able to reach us from the magnetic field that encompasses our planet. This band is very quiet with few man-made transmissions. For many years, scientists, researchers, and radio enthusiasts have picked up strange signals from this region that have not been fully understood.

If the human body had radio antennas instead of ears, people would hear a remarkable symphony of strange noises coming from the space that surrounds our planet. Scientists call them "tweeks," "whistlers," and "snap, crackle, and pop." At times, these sounds picked up in the VLF band are so strange they seem suited for the background noise of a science fiction film. These remarkable radio emissions are real and although scientists don't fully understand how they are produced, they are around us all the time.

The source of most VLF emissions on earth is lightning. Lightning bolts emit a broadband pulse of radio waves, just as they unleash a visible flash of light. VLF signals from nearby lightning, heard through the loudspeaker of a radio, sound like bacon frying in a pan or the crackling and popping of a campfire. Even if there is no lighting in your area, depending on the size and efficiency of your antenna and the sensitivity of the receiver, you can still hear VLF lightning crackles from storms thousands of kilometers away. Sometimes the ionosphere leaks lightning pulses into space. These pulses exit the atmosphere entirely and follow earth's magnetic field lines that guide them more than 13,000 kilometers above the surface, and back into our planet's magnetosphere. It is this phenomenon that scientists think are responsible for the "whistlers" because they sound like slowly descending tones. Whistlers are dispersed because they travel great distances through magnetized plasmas, which coincidently enough are strongly dispersive media for VLF signals.

It is theorized by scientists at the NASA Marshall Space Center that some of these returning flashes of lightning produce plasma that could create holes in the magnetic field of our planet. This theory intrigued us since this is what might be needed to connect the world of the djinn with our own.

In 2009, Rosemary was able to purchase a Panasonic RF-4900 radio receiver, a model the company no longer manufactures. This receiver was one of the great radios from an earlier period before the days of satellite transmissions. It is amazing that she was able to find one, as the few that are left are owned by die-hard, old-time ham radio operators and SWLs who see them as a collector's item.[25] Although the receiver has the potential to become a super EVP box, it lacks one feature—it does not receive in the VLF area. Rosemary was able to find a converter, and with Phil's know-how (being an old ham radio operator himself), we were able to connect the receiver and get the converter working properly. However, at that low frequency, the wavelength is very long and one needs an antenna several hundred feet long to even hope of picking up signals from the upper atmosphere and beyond.

As a temporary fix, we hooked up twenty feet of 20-gauge insulated copper wire to act as an antenna. On our first attempt, at a frequency of 100 kHz, we picked up a strange series of faint tones that sounded like navigation signals. The sounds lasted for about five minutes, then grew fainter, and eventually vanished. The tones sounded artificial in nature and definitely should not have been there. It seemed odd to us that we turned on the receiver at the exact time and frequency to pick up this transient signal. Perhaps some other intelligence was involved and wanted us to hear some-

---

25 Short Wave Listeners.

thing on our first attempt. Was the signal coming from another dimension or a parallel reality? We might never know for sure, but two things are certain: the signals should not have been there, and we never picked them up again.

Over the next several weeks of listening in the wee hours of the morning, Phil was able to pick up sounds that sounded like popping and crackling, which he was able to identify as electrical bursts in the upper atmosphere. However, on more than one occasion, he picked up unusual sounds that were almost musical in nature. After considerable research, we found out that NASA, in addition to a number of independent researchers around the globe, had also been receiving the sounds for years—no one can fully explain them. The sounds have been attributed to natural discharges of plasma energy in the magnetosphere. Again, the word *plasma* caught our attention, as it relates to djinn physiology. It is possible they might discharge energy in the same way as other celestial bodies, resulting in some of it spreading across the VLF spectrum. Of course, this is pure speculation, but speculation often leads to discovery!

A Bold Experiment

We intend to do more research with both the MiniBox and the Panasonic, and to use the VLF band and fully document these signals. We plan to find a large field where we can set up a series of very long dipole antennas, which will greatly expand our capabilities in receiving the mysterious signals on the low-frequency radio band. As EVP is rather weak, we are also in the process of designing a low-power transmitter that will produce a signal with a "dead carrier," which will allow the EVP to piggyback on it.

Besides the many technical difficulties that await us, the biggest problem still lies ahead: communication is a two-way street and if the other side is not interested in conversation, there will not be any results. Perhaps the djinn like using the crowded radio bands to communicate with us, since most of the messages are partial and almost cryptic in nature. Perhaps the communication is a game that green djinn play with humans. We cannot tell you what the chances of success are, but one thing is for sure: if we do not try, our results definitely *will* be zero. In the months that follow the publication of this book, we will publish any successful results. Our readers are invited to get in touch with us at the emails and website listed in the "About the Authors" section.

DEALING WITH THE DJINN

How can humanity counter the influences of beings as powerful as the djinn? They seem to have many advantages over us—but we are not without recourse. Since ancient times, people have developed ways of warding off and repelling all sorts of negative entities and their effects. Some remedies against demons can be applied to troublesome djinn but others do not work. Here we discuss some of the ways humans have successfully dealt with djinn.

Exorcizing Djinn

Islamic belief holds that djinn possess people for a variety of reasons. They attack those whose faith is weak or nonexistent and those who are not religiously inclined. Sudden emotional and physical shocks, bouts of depression, and fear and anxiety make a person vulnerable to possession by ripping tears in his or her barrier of spiritual protection (the aura). The djinn, having no defined form, can slip through these tears and cracks quite easily. It is believed that a person should never go to bed crying or with feelings of fear and worry, as this invites the djinn to attack during sleep. A fall in the bathroom—considered a polluted place—is especially dangerous, and can result in djinn possession. People who willfully or accidentally injure djinn can become ill or possessed as well. And as explained earlier, people with whom the djinn have become infatuated may become possessed. Whatever the causes of djinn possession, exorcism is usually required.[1]

Exorcism is not only rightful, but obligatory, part of one's duty to aid the oppressed, fight evil, and promote righteousness. Muhammad said that those who aid others will be rewarded on the Day of Resurrection. The duty to alleviate suffering extends to both humans and djinn. Some modern scholars dispute the reality of djinn possession, but traditionalists point to the Qur'an, hadith literature, and the anecdotal record as evidence that possessions have indeed occurred throughout history and continue to plague people in modern times. It is not permissible to abandon or decline to treat a person who is possessed if someone has the ability and time to do so. Exorcism, said the Qur'anic scholar Ibn Tameeyah, "is the most noble of deeds. It is among the deeds performed by the prophets and the righteous who have continually repelled the devils from mankind using what has been commanded by Allah and His Messenger."[2] Aid should be rendered in only the same way that Muhammad and his companions acted. Whatever actions are allowed concerning humans are allowed concerning djinn.

Djinn have been ordered to worship Allah, according to Islamic law.[3] Possession without the consent of the human is a grave of-

1 As noted earlier concerning *zar* cases, cajoling, reconciliation, and bribery are sometimes used to appease possessing djinn who cause domestic problems.

2 Abu Ameenah Bilal Philips, *Ibn Taymeeyah's Essay on the Jinn (Demons)* (New Delhi: Islamic Books Service, 2002), p. 81.

3 Umar Sulaiman al-Ashqar, *The World of the Jinn and Devils* (Boulder, CO: Al Basheer Co., 1998), p. 205.

fense against God and is forbidden—but djinn do it anyway. They must be informed that they do not have the right to occupy a human body—or home, for that matter—without consent. If a djinni has possessed a person out of lust, it must be so informed that it has committed a forbidden act. If it possesses a person who has accidentally harmed a djinni, it must be told that the person acted out of ignorance and with no intent to harm.

If the djinn do not cease after being warned, it is permissible to punish them. A person can summon one djinni to banish or kill another who is causing possession—but whether or not they obey such commands is questionable.

Taking Refuge in the Qur'an

The most reliable and permissible ways of exorcizing or repelling djinn involve reciting certain verses from the Qur'an. All of the verses of the Qur'an are considered the will of Allah, and create a structure and order to daily life. The words are powerful, and if recited with deep faith, have a great positive effect. In relation to djinn, certain verses will chase them away and purify any environment. Angels listen to the words as well, and can be called upon for help.

Qur'anic verses considered especially effective against the djinn and their whisperings in the ear are the Al-Mu'awwidhatayn and the Al-Kursi. The Al-Mu'awwidhatayn are the last two chapters of the Qur'an, Al-Falaq (The Dawn) and An-Nas (Mankind), 113 and 114, respectively:

Al-Falaq (The Dawn)
Say: I seek refuge in the Lord of the Dawn,
From the evil which He has created,
From the evil of the night when it falls,
From the evil of sorceresses who blow on knots,
And from the evil of the envier when he is envious.

An-Naas (Mankind)
Say: I seek refuge in the Lord of mankind,
The King of mankind, the God of mankind,
From the evil of the slinking whisperer,
Who whispers in the hearts of men,
From among the Jinn and mankind.

The Al-Kursi (The Footstool or The Throne) is verse 255 from the second surah of the Qur'an, Al-Baqarah (The Cow). It is considered to be highly effective in warding off djinn and countering their evil spells, as well as exorcizing them from the possessed. It also nullifies illusions caused by the djinn, devil-aided supernatural feats, and the erroneous thinking and acts of musicians, tyrants and the lecherous and lustful:

In the name of Allah, the Beneficent, the Merciful.
Allah! There is no God but He,
The Living, the Self-subsisting, the Eternal.
No slumber can seize Him, nor sleep.
All things in heaven and earth are His.
Who could intercede in His presence without His permission?
He knows what appears in front of and behind His creatures.
Nor can they encompass any knowledge of Him except what he
   wills.
His throne extends over the heavens and the earth,
and He feels no fatigue in guarding and preserving them,
for He is the Highest and Most Exalted.
Allah, the Most High, speaks the truth.

According to hadith literature, the Al-Kursi recommendation came from a djinni. The *Sahih al-Bukhari* tells a story of a man whom Muhammad put in charge of the food collected for charity at the end of Ramadan. One night, the man caught a stranger rummaging through the food. The stranger said he was in great need because he was poor and had a family. The man let the stranger go. When informed, Muhammad said the stranger was a liar and would return. Sure enough, he did, and once again begged off on claims of poverty, promising he would not return. The man let him go. Muhammad repeated that the stranger was a liar and would return. On the next night, the stranger came back and the man grabbed him. This time, the stranger said that in exchange for letting him go, he would give him some words that would prevent Satan from approaching during sleep at night. It was the Al-Kursi. Muhammad told the man that the stranger told the truth, but revealed his identity as an "evil djinni."[4]

Reading the entire chapter of Al-Baqarah at night is good for keeping evil djinn away and for banishing a troublesome qarin. Muhammad said, "Everything has a hump and the Qur'an's hump is *surah al-Baqarah*. Satan will not enter the house of whoever reads it at night for three days."[5]

Another accepted practice is to read just the last two verses (285 and 286) of Al-Baqarah for three consecutive nights:

> The Messenger believes in what has been sent down to him from his Lord, and (so do) the believers. Each one believes in Allah, His Angels, His Books, and His Messengers. They say, "We make no distinction between one another of His Messengers"—and they say, "We hear, and we obey. (We seek) Your Forgiveness, our Lord, and to You is the return (of all)."
>
> Allah burdens not a person beyond his scope. He gets reward for that (good) which he has earned, and he is punished for that (evil) which he has earned. "Our Lord! Punish us not if we forget or fall into error, our Lord! Lay not on us a burden like that

4 *Sahih al-Bukhari*, vol. 6, p. 491, no. 530.

5 *Ibn Taymeeyah's Essay on the Jinn (Demons), op. cit.*, p. 76.

which You did lay on those before us (Jews and Christians); our Lord! Put not on us a burden greater than we have strength to bear. Pardon us and grant us Forgiveness. Have mercy on us. You are our Matron (Protector) and give us victory over the disbelieving people."

Invoking the name of Allah and cursing is another tactic. Muhammad repelled Iblis once when the djinni attempted to interfere with his prayer. Iblis thrust a fiery torch in his face, and Muhammad said three times, "I seek refuge in Allah from you" and then three times, "I curse you by Allah's perfect curse."[6] But Iblis did not back off, so Muhammad grabbed hold of him and choked him, and could feel the coldness of the djinni's spittle on his hands. Had it not been for Solomon's prayer, Muhammad said, he would have tied Iblis to a post as a public spectacle.[7] Allah forced the djinni away. This incident established the precedent for evoking Allah's curse against offending djinn.

"I seek refuge in Allah from the accursed Satan" is recited prior to reading the Qur'an and serves as a general protection from the influences of evil. There are ninety-nine "beautiful names" of Allah that can be invoked. Each name has an angel servant. Some believe there are both a djinni and an angel who attend each name. Repeating a name with enough faith can make its servant appear. If a person is pure, the angel comes; if not, the djinni comes.[8]

Possessing djinn should be urged to convert to Islam. As we noted earlier, djinn who say they will convert or have converted often lie, and repeatedly possess people. In 1987, a possession case of a

---

6 *Sahih Muslim*, vol.1, pp. 273–274, no. 1106.

7 According to *Saad 38:35*, Solomon's prayer was "My Lord forgive me and grant me sovereignty not allowed to anyone after me."

8 Barbara Drieskens, *Living with Djinns: Understanding and Dealing with the Invisible in Cairo* (London: SAQI, 2008), p. 90.

Muslim woman in Riyadh made international news. The offending djinni had supposedly already converted to Islam, but possessed the woman anyway. The exorcist reminded the djinni that it was committing a sin, and it replied (through the female victim but in a male voice) that it was a Buddhist djinni from India. The exorcist cajoled and shamed the djinni into converting to Islam, and to agreeing to preach conversion to its own people. It departed the woman, who remained free of possession for at least two months, at the last report. Whether or not the deceitful djinni possessed anyone else, or fulfilled its promise to proselytize to other djinn, is not known.[9]

Beating the Djinn Out of a Body

If Qur'anic recitations, orders, cajoling, and cursing have no effect on djinn, tradition holds that it is permissible to threaten them with beating and strike them by actually beating the victim. It is believed that only the djinni, and not the victim, feels any pain from the blows. If the victim screams, it is really the djinni screaming in agony. Hundreds of blows may be necessary to drive a djinni from a person's body—which supposedly will show no signs of the beating.[10]

Muhammad used beatings to exorcize djinn. He struck one possessed boy with great force, and then wiped his face with water and said a prayer over him. The exorcism was successful.

The Power of Breath

In esoteric lore, breath has supernatural or mystical power, either for good or for bad. Breath transmits power—and can also deplete the life force.

---

9 *Ibn Tameeyah's Essay on the Jinn (Demons) op. cit.,* pp. 107–108.

10 http://www.inter-islam.org/faith/jinn2.html#Exorcism. Accessed October 2010.

Muhammad once used the sacred power of his breath to expel djinn. He blew three times into the mouth of a possessed boy and said, "In the name of Allah, I am a slave of Allah, be driven away, oh enemy of Allah." The boy was healed.[11]

Popular Exorcisms

In addition to the official religious ways of dealing with djinn, there are myriads of folk remedies. Books offering help to counter djinn oppression and possession, witchcraft, and the evil eye are popular in marketplaces. The books' rituals are often complicated, and readers mix them with folklore they have learned from their own families, usually their mothers. It is usually advised to keep these books hidden away.

Some of the lore in these books is undoubtedly derived from Solomonic tradition. Flavius Josephus said Solomon left behind exorcism techniques that others successfully used. He himself witnessed such an exorcist, named Eleazar, who expelled a demon in a demonstration to the Roman Emperor Vespasian, his sons, military captains, and troops:

> He put a ring that had a foot of one of those sorts mentioned by Solomon to the nostrils of the demoniac, after which he drew out the demon through his nostrils; and when the man fell down immediately, he abjured him to return into him no more, making still mention of Solomon, and reciting the incantations which he composed. And when Eleazar would persuade and demonstrate to the spectators that he had such a power, he set a little way off a cup or basin full of water, and commanded the demon, as he went out of the man, to overturn it, and thereby to let the spectators know that he had left the man; and when this was done, the skill and wisdom of Solomon was shown very

---

11 Ahmad Ibn Hanbal, *Hadith Musnad*, vol. 4, p. 170.

manifestly: for which reason it is, that all men may know the vastness of Solomon's abilities, and how he was beloved of God, and that the extraordinary virtues of every kind with which this king was endowed may not be unknown to any people under the sun.[12]

An example of a folk remedy for possession comes from folk tales such as found in *The Book of 1001 Nights:*

Take seven hairs out of the tail of a cat that is all black except for a white spot on the end of its tail. Burn the hairs in a small closed room with the possessed victim, filling their nose with the scent. This releases them from the spell of the djinn.[13]

The simplest djinn repellent, also acceptable from a religious perspective, is to say the word *bismillah* (sometimes spelled *basmala*, "in the name of Allah" or "In the name of God the Compassionate and Merciful"). For example, one should not say that Satan must be degraded, for it will have the opposite effect of enabling him to become as big as a house. Instead one should say *bismillah*, which will reduce him to the size of a fly.[14]

In the 1950s, a surveyor for an oil company in Saudi Arabia was in a remote part of the desert. He drove a surveying stake into the sand and accidentally hit a djinni who lived underground. That night after he went to bed in his tent, invisible djinn attacked him. They bound his hands with invisible ties. He felt an intense burning in his wrists and was unable to move his arms. He was unable

---

12 Flavius Josephus, *The Antiquities of the Jews*, pp. 250–251.

13 In Jewish lore from the book of Tobit, the archangel Raphael teaches the young man Tobias how to exorcize demons—especially the dreaded Asmodeus—with the smoke of burning fish gall.

14 *Ibn Taymeeyah's Essay on the Jinn (Demons), op. cit.,* p. 77.

to speak. Others in camp heard a strange voice shout, "You have attacked us, you must be punished!" but they could not see anyone.

The surveyor was flown to a hospital. Doctors were able to stop the burning pain, but they could not restore his ability to speak. They sent him home. His wife cared for him, but his condition did not improve. Finally, she took him to see a *mutawwa* (religious man) who was famous for his djinn exorcisms. The *mutawwa* determined that the surveyor was possessed by several djinn, who told him how one of their kind must have been injured by the surveyor's stake. The *mutawwa* read the Qur'an over the man, and the djinn agreed to depart. When they did, the pain left the man and he could speak again. Prevailing wisdom held that his possession could have been avoided if he had said the *bismillah* before he drove the stake into the ground.[15]

Another case in which the *bismillah* could have prevented djinn malice concerned a falconer who was visited by an acquaintance. The guest picked up a small lizard on the ground and fed it to the falcon, which killed it by spearing it in its right eye. The falcon ate the lizard. Soon after that, the guest felt a searing pain in his right eye, which then popped out of his head. The man fell over dead. He had killed a djinni in the form of the lizard, and other djinn exacted swift revenge. According to prevailing wisdom, if the man had said the *bismillah* before giving the lizard to the falcon, the djinni would have disappeared and become a meal for the bird.[16]

Many people with djinn and black magic problems consult a sheikh for help, to exorcize, cast, or break spells. Sheikhs vary in their exorcism and magical skills and must be confident and know what to do at all moments, for the djinn will try to paralyze their tongue and prevent the right words from being said, ensuring things will go wrong. For example, a woman in Cairo was con-

---

15 Robert Lebling, Jinn Discussion Group, www.yahoogroups.com, Nov. 6, 2009.
16 *Ibid.*

vinced that a spirit was in love with her, and came to her at night to make passionate love. She consulted a sheikh to chase it away. It departed, but came back as a dog, and then in the form of her husband.[17]

Some sheikhs perform exorcisms with special amulets, talismans and incantations from magical texts, but these are considered *shirk*, a neglect of one's duty, or in some cases, unforgivable sin. Making animal sacrifices to djinn is strictly forbidden.

Like mediums everywhere, some sheikhs are not above fraud. Ibn Taymeeyah related an account of a sheikh who fraudulently caused possessions, and then performed exorcisms for fees. He would send djinn in his service to possess someone, and then be hired to exorcize the djinn. In addition, his servant djinn stole food and valuables from those they possessed, and delivered them to the sheikh.[18]

A favored respectable remedy is Zamzam water, a miracle water that a sheikh may decide to administer to a possessed person. Zamzam is a famous well in al-Masjid al-Haraam (the Sacred Mosque in Mecca), near the Ka'bah. The well is only five feet deep and is self-replenishing. Its water plays an important role in Islamic faith. Allah quenched the thirst of the infant Isma'el, son of Ibrahim, when he was an infant. His mother, Haajra, searched for water in vain. She climbed to the tops of Mount al-Safaa and Mount al-Marwah, praying to Allah for help. Allah sent the archangel Jibril, who struck the earth; water appeared.[19] When Muhammad was a child, two angels appeared and washed his heart in Zamzam water, to strengthen and purify it, and enable him to see the kingdoms of earth and heaven. Muhammad also drank from the well. According to hadith literature, the water of Zamzam is

---

17 *Ibn Taymeeyah's Essay on the Jinn (Demons), op. cit.,* p. 59.

18 *Ibid.,* p. 52.

19 Similarly, in Christian lore holy wells and springs were created by saints striking the ground with their staffs.

for whatever purpose it is drunk for: "It is a blessing and it is food that satisfies."[20] Zamzam water is used for magical, exorcism, and healing purposes.

Applying the words of the Qur'an directly to the possessed body is considered an effective and popular way to ward off or expel possessing djinn. Verses from the Qur'an are written in certain kinds of approved ink on paper, which is dipped in water. The treated water is used for bathing or drinking by the afflicted and sick. Verses are carved onto bread, which is baked and eaten. Verses are put into alphabet soup and eaten. When the Qur'an is recited before sleep, one should first blow into one's hands and wipe them over the body.

Adults who experience sudden shocks and upsets should immediately spit on their chests. This practice has pre-Islamic roots in ancient and universal folklore that holds that spittle is a protective agent against evil entities and forces, especially the evil eye. Spittle represents the soul, and to spit it out—on the body or on the ground—is an offering to the gods for luck and protection. According to widespread custom, spitting should be done immediately when one senses supernatural danger. Practices in early Roman times include spitting in the right shoe every morning, spitting into the toilet after urination, spitting on the breast or on the ground three times, and spitting while passing any place where danger might exist.[21]

---

20 *Sahih Muslim*, 4:1922.

21 Rosemary Ellen Guiley, *The Encyclopedia of Magic & Alchemy* (New York: Facts On File, 2007), p. 299.

Protection Using Science

We do not claim that the methods above are successful when dealing with the djinn. Many rituals of exorcism are so ancient that they come from a time when fear of the supernatural ruled everyone's mind. These older rituals might work if you encounter a djinni who believes in the old ways or is afraid it will be held accountable by God at the end of time. Some older djinn believe in the existence of angels, and might be fearful that one might intervene. Having free will, djinn think like people do: some are religious and can be controlled by saying the name of God, others are atheists and cannot be controlled in this manner. If a djinni does not believe in God or angels, reciting passages from the Bible and Qur'an will have no effect. In some of the cases that we have investigated or researched, the entity seemed to show increased anger and aggression when a Bible or other religious book is used as a weapon to try to drive it away. In some instances, the entity played along and seemed amused at the attempts of the exorcist.

Westerners may not have access to Muslim experts, sheikhs, Zamzam water, or be able to recite the Qur'an in its native Arabic. Are there other ways to counter the djinn?

Electromagnetic Disruptions

We must regard djinn as another form of intelligent beings in the universe and not as supernatural creatures. Although when compared to humans they are capable of incredible feats and have a very long life span, they are still beings with limited abilities. It is our belief that the djinn are composed of plasma; this is their strength but also a weakness. Plasma can be affected by electromagnetic pulses and other types of magnetic fields. Plasma can also be disrupted by a high-voltage burst of electricity. We have many cases in our files of people being tormented by some unseen force in their own homes. In such cases, the victims found that when they turned on their lights, radio, television, and computer, the disturbances decreased in severity or stopped completely. However, if everything was shut off, the disturbances would start again within a short time. Alternating current and the electrical items listed above create magnetic fields. The djinn are not permanently harmed by them, but they suffer pain or other discomfort. It's important to note that this electrical method may only work on the less powerful green djinn; it may have little or no effect on a djinni of greater power belonging to a higher order.

The Tesla coil

A Tesla coil is a resonant transformer that will produce high voltage and current. It was invented by Nikola Tesla in 1891.[22] The Tesla coil works by generating an electrical field in the air. Depending on the coil's size, it can light fluorescent lights, neon tubes, cathode ray tubes, and other gases without a physical connection. The Tesla coil produces an electromagnetic wave that can interfere with radio and television reception and cause digital watches to malfunction. Small coils can be purchased from a number of scientific distributors and although they tend to be somewhat pricey, are interesting to use in experiments. We have two small coils at our disposal, but have not used them in the field, since we are waiting for the right case to try them. The small coil may not drive the djinn away, but theoretically it could be used to keep the disturbances at a minimum. The range of these small Tesla coils is limited to a small room. Operating one may not banish a djinni, however—it may only retreat to another part of the house in frustration and anger, and then cause even greater disturbances there.

---

22 Nikola Tesla (1856–1943) was an inventor and electrical engineer. He was one of the most important contributors to the birth of commercial electricity and is best known for his many revolutionary developments in the field of electromagnetism.

Their Energy Level Is Sporadic

Djinn consume energy as a main source of sustenance. Like humans, they get tired when they are very active and then they require rest. In many homes that are experiencing paranormal phenomena the activity is sporadic and sometimes cyclic in nature. If a djinni is responsible, then during times of inactivity it may be resting. Djinn have longer life spans than humans. When we rest, some of us may sleep for eight hours. When a djinni sleeps, it could remain dormant for decades. The length of time a djinni "sleeps" depends on its age, its level of power, its health, and how much energy it has used. While at rest, a djinni is at its most vulnerable, perhaps presenting the best oppportunity to remove it.

Final Words

Djinn are composed of plasma, and like all plasma, are greatly affected by magnetic fields. If you are having paranormal disturbances in your home such as shadow people, poltergeists, strange lights, and other signs of a "haunting," try keeping lights and electrical appliances turned on. Unless you are an engineer, we don't recommend buying devices that generate electromagnetic fields like the Tesla coil, as they consume a considerable amount of power and could be dangerous if used improperly. We are constantly seeking information to learn more about the djinn and their purpose in this world. If you are having experiences similar to the ones we've discussed, please contact us. We respond to all letters and in some cases may want to visit your home and do an on-site investigation.

One final word to all paranormal investigators: please consider the djinn as part of the paranormal world. We believe that once you become acquainted with the djinn race, many of the more perplexing cases you investigate might make more sense. Also, consider that you are dealing with very old entities, and even the youngest of these beings are much older than most of human history. We hope the publication of this book will help inform people in Western countries, about this ancient race of neighbors who live next door, but who we rarely see.

APPENDIX I

DJINN SOCIAL STRUCTURE

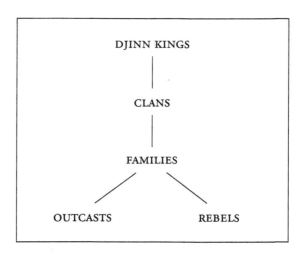

Kings

Powerful black djinn. It is not known if all djinn are ruled by one
king or many.

Clans

No one really knows how many clans exist. They are ruled by blue or yellow djinn and obey a djinn king.

Families

A yellow djinn or older green djinn may head a djinn family. A family usually consists of djinn who are related, but this may not always be the case.

Outcasts

Djinn who have no living family or those who have been exiled from a family or clan are considered outcasts. Most are not necessarily evil, but may be dangerous to other djinn and humans.

Rebels

Djinn that have broke away from the order of a king, clan or family. They are called red djinn and are considered evil and very dangerous to humans. Red djinn may be the "demons" of religious writings. They follow Iblis instead of God.

APPENDIX II

DJINN ORDER OF POWER

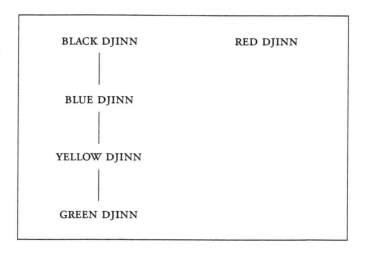

BLACK DJINN   RED DJINN

|

BLUE DJINN

|

YELLOW DJINN

|

GREEN DJINN

Black Djinn

The most powerful of all djinn, little is known about them. The only reference we have is from ancient Persia, where they were called *shamir*.

Blue Djinn

The elders and clan leaders of the djinn order. They have little interaction with humans, but have been known to participate in important moments of history. They are known as Marid, Nekratael, and Afreet.

Yellow Djinn

Middle-aged djinn with considerable power. Most are family leaders. They have little if no interest in the human race and the physical world. They are known as Juzam and the nastier ones are called Efreeti.

Green Djinn

Youngest and least powerful of the djinn. They are curious and like to interact with the human race in the physical world. Many young ones like to play pranks on humans. They are known as Erhnam, Kookus, Aamar, Arwaah, Jann, and Amir.

Red Djinn

Very old and powerful djinn. Most were once blue djinn. They worship Iblis and their goal is to destroy all humans. They are served by other djinn, and in rare cases, humans. Some serve willingly, some by force. They are known as ghouls, shaitan or shayteen, and ifrit.

BIBLIOGRAPHY

Ahmad, Salim. *An Invisible World: Revealing the Mystery Behind the World of Jinn.* Privately published, www.booksurge.com, 2008.

Al-Ashqar, Umar Sulaiman. *The World of the Jinn and Devils.* Boulder, CO: Al Basheer Co., 1998.

Boddy, Janice. *Wombs and Alien Spirits: Women, Men and the Zar Cult in Northern Sudan.* Madison, WI: University of Wisconsin Press, 1989.

Briggs, Katharine. *The Vanishing People.* New York: Pantheon Books, 1978.

Carmichael, Alexander. *Carmina Gadelica.* Edinburgh: T. & A. Constable, 1900.

Drieskens, Barbara. *Living with Djinns: Understanding and Dealing with the Invisible in Cairo.* London: SAQI, 2008.

E. J. Brill's First Encyclopedia of Islam 1913–1936. Leiden, the Netherlands: Brill Academic Publishers, 1993.

El-Zein, Amira. *Islam, Arabs, and the Intelligent World of the Jinn.* Syracuse, NY: Syracuse University Press, 2009.

Evans-Wentz, W. Y. *The Fairy Faith in Celtic Countries.* New York: Carroll Publishing Group, 1990. First published 1911.

Guiley, Rosemary Ellen. *The Encyclopedia of Angels.* 2nd ed. New York: Facts On File, 2004.

———. *The Encyclopedia of Demons & Demonology.* New York: Facts On File, 2009.

———. *The Encyclopedia of Ghosts & Spirits.* 3rd ed. New York: Facts On File, 2007.

———. *The Encyclopedia of Magic & Alchemy.* New York: Facts On File, 2006.

———. *The Encyclopedia of Witches, Witchcraft & Wicca.* 3rd ed. New York: Facts On File, 2008.

Hynek, J. Allen and Philip J. Imbrogno and Bob Pratt. *Night Siege: The Hudson Valley UFO Sightings.* New York: Ballantine Books, 1988.

Ibn Ibraaheem Ameen, Abu'l-Mundir Khaleel. *The Jinn & Human Sickness: Remedies in the Light of the Qur'aan & Sunnah.* London: Darussalam, 2005.

Ibn Taymeeyah's Essay on the Jinn (Demons). Abridged annotated and translated by Dr. Abu Ammenah Bilal Philips. New Delhi: Islamic Books Service, 2002.

Imbrogno, Philip J. *Files from the Edge: A Paranormal Investigator's Explorations into High Strangeness.* Woodbury, MN: Llewellyn Worldwide, 2010.

———. *Interdimensional Universe: The New Science of UFOs, Paranormal Phenomena and Otherdimensional Beings.* Woodbury, MN: Llewellyn Worldwide, 2008.

Imbrogno, Philip J. and Marianne Horrigan. *Celtic Mysteries in New England: Windows to Another Dimension in America's Northeast.* New York: Cosimo Publishing, 2005.

Jawaid, Mahmood. *Secrets of Angels, Demons, Satan and Jinns: Decoding Their Nature through Quran and Science.* Self-published, 2006.

Kelleher, Colm A. and George Knapp. *Hunt for the Skinwalker.* New York: Paraview/Pocket Books, 2005.

Krull, Kathleen. *A Pot O' Gold: A Treasury of Irish Stories, Poetry, Folklore, and (of Course) Blarney.* New York: Hyperion Books for Children, 2004.

Lady Wilde. *Ancient Legends, Mystic Charms, and Superstitions of Ireland.* Boston: Ticknor & Co., 1887.

Lane, Edward William. *The Manners and Customs of the Modern Egyptians.* London: J. M. Dent & Sons, 1908.

LaVey, Anton Szandor. *The Satanic Rituals.* New York: Avon Books, 1972.

McManus, D. A. *The Middle Kingdom: The Faerie World of Ireland.* London: Max Parrish, 1959.

O'Brien, Christopher. *Stalking the Tricksters: Shapeshifters, Skinwalkers, Dark Adepts and 2012.* Kempton, IL: Adventures Unlimited Press, 2009.

————. *Secrets of the Mysterious Valley.* Kempton, IL: Adventures Unlimited Press, 2007.

Radin, Paul. *The Trickster: A Study in American Indian Mythology.* New York: Shocken Books, 1972.

Seymour, John D. *Tales of King Solomon.* London: Oxford University Press, 1924.

Vallee, Jacques. *Passport to Magonia.* Chicago: Henry Regnery Co., 1969.

Yeats, William Butler. *The Celtic Twilight: Men and Women, Ghouls and Faeries.* London: Lawrence & Bullen, 1893.

INDEX

FILES FROM THE EDGE
A Paranormal Investigator's Explorations into High Strangeness
PHILIP J. IMBROGNO

Ghost lights, otherworldly creatures, visits from another dimension. The most bizarre and amazing case studies from a renowned paranormal investigator are presented here.

In this thirty-year career, Philip J. Imbrogno has researched a vast array of fascinating supernatural phenomena—the perpetually haunted mines of Putnam County, New York; encounters with strange entities at sacred megalithic stones; Bigfoot, yeti, and other human-oids; sea creatures; psychic phenomena; the dangerous Jinn; and a vast array of life forms from other worlds. The author's objective, scientific analysis—combined with credible witness testimonials and Imbrogno's own thrilling experiences—provides eye-opening, convincing evidence of our multidimensional universe.

978-0-7387-1881-1
336 pp., 5³⁄₁₆ x 8 $17.95

ULTRATERRESTRIAL CONTACT
A Paranormal Investigator's Explorations into the Hidden Abduction Epidemic
PHILIP J. IMBROGNO

This book investigates the most extreme and bizarre UFO reports—cases that most UFO investigators are afraid to tackle—and presents a radical new quantum approach to understanding the contact phenomenon.

When Philip Imbrogno collaborated with famed UFO researcher Dr. J. Allen Hynek on *Night Siege*, Dr. Hynek requested that the more sensational cases of "high strangeness"—claims of contact with not only alien intelligence, but also angels, demons, and otherdimensional beings—remain unpublished. Hynek thought the reports would detract from the credibility of the entire ET investigation field. *Ultraterrestrial Contact* reveals the details of these controversial reports for the first time and presents Imbrogno's startling scientific conclusions from thirty years of research into the alien contact phenomenon.

978-0-7387-1959-7
336 pp., 5³⁄₁₆ x 8 $17.95

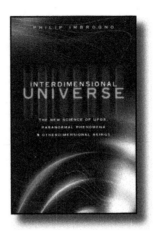

INTERDIMENSIONAL UNIVERSE
The New Science of UFOs, Paranormal Phenomena & Otherdimensional Beings
PHILIP IMBROGNO

Over the course of his thirty years of investigation into UFOs, including his own field research, photographic evidence, and meticulously compiled case studies, Philip Imbrogno has provided fascinating new insight into paranormal phenomena. In this book, he reveals for the first time the detailed experiences of prominent paranormal experts as well as his own firsthand experiences. Using the latest quantum theories, Imbrogno sheds new light on classic UFO cases, government cover-ups, and the hidden connections between UFOs and other unexplained phenomena—from crop circles and animal mutilations to angels and jinns (or genies).

Imbrogno's intimate knowledge spans the very early UFO activities to present-day sightings. He personally investigated four of the best-known UFO flaps of the modern era—Hudson Valley, Phoenix lights, the Belgium sightings, and the Gulf Breeze Florida sightings—and shares information never released before, including photographic evidence that something very unusual is taking place on planet Earth.

978-0-7387-1347-2
312 pp., 5³⁄₁₆ x 8 $17.95

Encounters with Flying Humanoids
Mothman, Manbirds, Gargoyles & Other Winged Beasts
Ken Gerhard

A strange creature with gigantic, blood-red embers for eyes crept out of the dark in West Virginia. Dozens of witnesses reported seeing the winged beast—later identified as the Mothman—take flight, chasing cars at speeds exceeding 100 miles per hour.

Cryptozoologist Ken Gerhard has traveled the world collecting evidence on the Mothman, the Owlman, the Van Meter Creature, the Valkyrie of Voltana, the Houston Batman, and other strange "bird people" that have been sighted throughout history. Packed with famous historical cases and dozens of chilling first-person accounts, this is the first book to focus exclusively on flying humanoids—a wide array of airborne entities that seem to "feed off our fear like psychic vampires."

978-0-7387-3720-1
240 pp., 5¼ x 8 $15.99

TO ORDER, CALL 1-877-NEW-WRLD
Prices subject to change without notice
Order at Llewellyn.com 24 hours a day, 7 days a week!

To Write to the Authors

If you wish to contact the authors or would like more information about this book, please write to the authors in care of Llewellyn Worldwide and we will forward your request. Both the authors and publisher appreciate hearing from you and learning of your enjoyment of this book and how it has helped you. Llewellyn Worldwide cannot guarantee that every letter written to the authors can be answered, but all will be forwarded. Please write to:

Rosemary Ellen Guiley & Philip J. Imbrogno
c/o Llewellyn Worldwide
2143 Wooddale Drive
Woodbury, MN 55125-2989

Please enclose a self-addressed stamped envelope for reply,
or $1.00 to cover costs. If outside the U.S.A., enclose
an international postal reply coupon.

Many of Llewellyn's authors have websites with additional information and resources. For more information, please visit our website at:

www.llewellyn.com